INTERNATIONAL LAW AND THE CONSTRUCTION OF THE LIBERAL PEACE

This book argues that since the end of the Cold War an international community of liberal states has crystallised within the broader international society of sovereign states. Significantly, this international community has demonstrated a tendency to deny non-liberal states their previously held sovereign right to non-intervention. Instead, the international community considers only those states that demonstrate respect for liberal democratic standards to be sovereign equals. Indeed the international community, motivated by the theory that international peace and security can only be achieved in a world composed exclusively of liberal states, has engaged in a sustained campaign to promote its liberal values to non-liberal states. This campaign has had (and continues to have) a profound impact upon the structure and content of international law.

In light of this, this book deploys the concepts of the international society and the international community in order to construct an explanatory framework that can enable us to better understand recent changes to the political and legal structure of the world order and why violations of international peace and security occur.

Volume 47 in the series Studies in International Law

Studies in International Law

Recent titles in this series

The Militarisation of Peacekeeping in the Twenty-First Century
James Sloan

Accounting for Hunger: The Right to Food in the Era of Globalisation
Edited by Olivier De Schutter and Kaitlin Y Cordes

Promises of States under International Law
Christian Eckart

Multilevel Regulation of Military and Security Contractors: The Interplay between International, European and Domestic Norms
Edited by Christine Bakker and Mirko Sossai

Europe and Extraterritorial Asylum
Maarten den Heijer

The Practice of International and National Courts and the (De) Fragmentation of International Law
Edited by Ole Kristian Fauchald and André Nollkaemper

The Politics of International Criminal Justice: A Spotlight on Germany
Ronen Steinke

Fighting Corruption in Public Procurement: A Comparative Analysis of Disqualification or Debarment Measures
Sope Williams-Elegbe

The Interception of Vessels on the High Seas: Contemporary Challenges to the Legal Order of the Oceans
Efthymios Papastavridis

Integration at the Border: The Dutch Act on Integration Abroad and International Immigration Law
Karin de Vries

An Equitable Framework for Humanitarian Intervention
Ciarán Burke

Democratic Statehood in International Law: The Emergence of New States in Post-Cold War Practice
Jure Vidmar

For the complete list of titles in this series, see 'Studies in International Law' link at www.hartpub.co.uk/books/series.asp

International Law and the Construction of the Liberal Peace

Russell Buchan

• HART •
PUBLISHING
OXFORD AND PORTLAND, OREGON
2013

Published in the United Kingdom by Hart Publishing Ltd
16C Worcester Place, Oxford, OX1 2JW
Telephone: +44 (0)1865 517530
Fax: +44 (0)1865 510710
E-mail: mail@hartpub.co.uk
Website: http://www.hartpub.co.uk

Published in North America (US and Canada) by
Hart Publishing
c/o International Specialized Book Services
920 NE 58th Avenue, Suite 300
Portland, OR 97213-3786
USA
Tel: +1 503 287 3093 or toll-free: (1) 800 944 6190
Fax: +1 503 280 8832
E-mail: orders@isbs.com
Website: http://www.isbs.com

British Library Cataloguing in Publication Data
Data Available

ISBN: 978-1-84946-244-0

Typeset by Hope Services, Abingdon
Printed and bound in Great Britain by
Lightning Source UK Ltd

Acknowledgements

This book is broadly based upon my PhD, which was successfully defended at the University of Bristol in January 2010. As with any project of this size and nature, many people and organisations need to be thanked, for without their support and encouragement neither the PhD nor this book would have been possible. In particular, I would like to thank my colleagues at the University of Bristol Law School and the University of Sheffield School of Law for their patience and assistance. Special mention, however, is extended to the supervisors of my PhD, who are respected colleagues and, more importantly, close friends: Patrick Capps and Nicholas Tsagourias. They have both provided huge amounts of advice and guidance over the years and I owe a great debt to them both. In addition, I would like to especially identify Matthew Bacon for his intellectual and emotional support during the completion of this project.

Several chapters of this book have been published in alternative forms elsewhere: chapter 1 builds upon an article published in the *International Community Law Review* in 2008 (R Buchan, 'A Clash of Normativities: International Society and International Community' (2008) 10 *International Community Law Review* 3); chapter 3 is a revised version of an article that appears in the *International Community Law Review* in 2010 (R Buchan, 'Explaining Liberal Aggression: The International Community and Threat Perception' (2010) 12 *International Community Law Review* 413) and chapter 7 develops ideas that appear in the *Journal of Conflict and Security Law* in 2007 (R Buchan, 'The International Community and the Occupation of Iraq' (2007) 12 *Journal of Conflict and Security Law* 37).

Finally, I would like to extend my sincere gratitude to my parents, Andy and Carol Buchan, for all that they have done and sacrificed over the years in order to provide me with the opportunities that I have before me today. For this reason, this book is dedicated to them.

Russell Buchan, January 2013

Table of Contents

Introduction

THE OBJECTIVE OF this book is to construct an explanatory framework that can enable us to better account for recent changes to the political and legal structure of the world order and allow us to better understand why violations of international peace and security occur.[1]

Scholars of international relations and international law have generated various theories in order to explain why violations of international peace and security occur and, where it is achieved, why international peace and security is maintained. According to Slaughter, '[t]he dominant approach in international relations theory for virtually the past two millennia, from Thucydides to Machiavelli to Morgenthau, has been Realism, also known as Political Realism'.[2] Although there are different strands of realist theory, certain core assumptions can nevertheless be distilled.[3] For realists, the defining feature of the world order is its anarchic structure. This means that the world order does not possess an overarching world government that is capable of guaranteeing the security of each state. In the absence of a world government, each state becomes responsible for protecting its own security and preserving its own existence. To this end, each state must necessarily develop military capabilities in order to deter and, where necessary, repel potential aggressors and aggrandisers. When the fact that all states of the world order will possess some form of military power is combined with the belief that no state is able to genuinely predict the intentions or likely conduct of another state, states must assume the worst, prepare for conflict and be ready to defend their sovereignty. To do otherwise would be to put the very survival of the state at risk. Consequently, ensuring their survival becomes the overriding objective of all states. If a state is itself incapable of developing sufficient military power it may ally

[1] In this sense, the objective of this book is to construct a theory that 'enlightens'. 'Theories enlighten. A theory is a set of related propositions that will explain why events occur the way they do. A theory is an abstract, conjectural or speculative representation of reality. Thus, one does not ask of a theory whether it is true or false, rather one asks whether it is enlightening. To theorize is to speculate with an intention to understand or explain': TL Knutsen, *A History of International Relations Theory* (Manchester, Manchester University Press, 1997) 1. See further M Hollis and S Smith, *Understanding and Explaining International Relations* (Oxford, Clarendon Press, 1991).

[2] A-M Slaughter, 'International Law in a World of Liberal States' (1995) 6 *European Journal of International Law* 503, 507.

[3] Seminal proponents of realist theory include EH Carr, *The Twenty Years' Crisis, 1919–1939: An Introduction to the Study of International Relations* (London, Papermac, 1995); HJ Morgenthau, *Politics among Nations: The Struggle for Power and Peace* (New York, McGraw-Hill, 1985); and K Waltz, *Theory of International Politics* (London, McGraw-Hill, 1979).

with another state(s) in order to bolster its physical presence. Thus, the theory runs, international peace and security will be achieved within this anarchic world when no state possesses military dominance over another. To put the same idea another way, the maintenance of international peace and security hinges upon the existence of a balance of material power between all states within the world order. Where this balance is disturbed the maintenance of international peace and security becomes vulnerable to violation. Consequently, where violations of state sovereignty occur it can be attributed to the imbalance of material power within a world order that possesses no central government.

Certainly since the end of the Second World War and the creation of the United Nations system (UN), the main theoretical competitor to realism has been institutionalism.[4] According to this theory, states are considered to be rational actors that are capable of discerning the interests and desires of other states. Moreover, states are considered capable of recognising interests that they hold in common and are prepared to cooperate in order to formulate rules and institutions that will enable these common interests to be regulated and achieved. In the context of international peace and security, institutionalists argue that states are able to recognise that they possess a common interest in maintaining their political independence and territorial integrity. In order to achieve this common interest states have constructed legal rules that prohibit intervention in the internal affairs of all states, regardless of their military power. Indeed, more generally '[w]hatever inequality may exist between states as regards their size, power, degree of civilization, wealth and other qualities, they are nevertheless equals as international persons'.[5] For institutionalists, therefore, state sovereignty is protected by legal rules rather than military strength. An effective legal framework (buttressed through effective institutions) can protect state sovereignty and thus enable international peace and security to be maintained.

Realists, of course, dispute the explanatory strength of institutionalism. Realists contend that although states have developed legal rules in order to protect their sovereignty (most notably Article 2(4) of the UN Charter), these legal rules do not in fact significantly impact upon the conduct of states. In the context of international peace and security, realists point to the numerous violations of Article 2(4) as illustrative of the importance of military power (and the futility of legal rules) in protecting state sovereignty.[6] In

[4] See generally the work of the English School theorists, such as H Bull, *The Anarchical Society: A Study of Order in World Politics* (Basingstoke, Palgrave, 2002) and M Wight, *Systems of States* (Leicester, Leicester University Press, 2002).

[5] L Oppenheim, *International Law: A Treatise, Volume I*, 3rd edn (London, Longmans Green & Co, 1920–21) 15.

[6] Although I am not suggesting that Thomas Franck was a realist, nevertheless see his important empirical studies which document the seemingly continual violation of the requirement upon states to refrain from the threat or use of force in their international relations:

essence, legal rules have not replaced military power as the bulwark against external intervention. Institutionalists respond by contending that although these legal rules are violated, these violations are often condemned by the majority of other states as an infringement of international law, thus illustrating the influence and importance of law. Moreover, institutionalists argue that although Article 2(4) has been repeatedly violated, this does not tell us anything about how instrumental it has been in preventing conflicts between states that, but for Article 2(4), would have sought to resolve their international disputes by using force. As Henkin famously explained, '[a]lmost all nations observe almost all principles of international law and almost all their obligations almost all of the time'.[7]

Realism and institutionalism are theories that compete to *explain* why violations of international peace and security occur. Historically, in its international setting liberalism has been characterised as a largely normative theory. Thus, liberalism developed as a prescriptive theory that was intended to instruct liberal states as to *how* they should conduct their foreign policies and the advantages this would yield for international peace and security. At the heart of liberalism is the recognition that states are not black boxes; they are not opaque billiard balls whose intentions and likely conduct cannot be predicted. Liberals therefore caution against anthropomorphising the state. Instead, liberal theorists recognise that states are represented by political actors: namely, their governments (or, more specifically, the individuals that comprise the government). Liberals thus argue that liberal states should scrutinise the political preference of the government of each state and determine whether or not it is liberal. For liberals, this is crucial because of the positive implications that liberal states yield for international peace and security; in particular, the belief that liberal states are able to achieve a liberal peace where the use of force as a mechanism for resolving disputes is averted. This is achieved not because of legal rules or military power. Peace is achieved because liberalism demands the peaceful resolution of disputes. In this sense, protection of state sovereignty derives from adherence to particular values and norms rather than legal rules or military strength. For this reason, liberals argue that liberal states should act in concert on the international stage, seeking to promote their liberal values to non-liberal states in order to defend and expand their zone of liberal peace. This objective should be pursued until all states within the world are liberal. According to theory, where this is achieved the liberal peace becomes a perpetual peace where the fear of conflict is permanently surmounted.

T Franck, 'Who Killed Article 2(4)?' (1970) 64 *American Journal of International Law* 809 and, more recently, T Franck, 'What Happens Now? The United Nations after Iraq' (2003) 97 *American Journal of International Law* 607.

[7] L Henkin, *How Nations Behave* (Cambridge, Polity Press, 1979) 47.

With the end of the Cold War, however, liberalism has increasingly been presented as a positivist (and by this I mean explanatory) theory of international relations and international law. In particular, Andrew Moravcsik and Anne-Marie Slaughter have both dedicated much academic energy to presenting liberalism as empirical, scientific and non-normative. Their argument is that liberalism has made the transition from a normative theory which makes recommendations about how liberal states *should* interact with other states in the world order to an explanatory theory that is able to accurately account for how liberal states *do* interact with other states.[8]

In light of the practice of liberal states since the end of the Cold War, in this book I subscribe to this liberal theory of international relations and international law and seek to enhance its presence within academic literature as an explanatory (rather than normative) theory. My argument contributes to existing literature in two main ways.

First, especially in the period 1990–2000, liberalism as a positivist theory gained considerable traction within both international relations and international legal literature. Significantly, however, with the turn of the new millennium and the rise of American exceptionalism in the wake of 9/11,[9] liberalism has come under considerable attack. Indeed, some have lamented its 'death' as a positivist theory of international law.[10] In essence, the argument runs that contemporary practice demonstrates that liberal states no longer elide with other liberal states as a solidaristic community that is determined to promote liberal democracy to non-liberal states. Consider the following quotation by Jean d'Aspremont in 2011, who had previously been a key proponent of liberalism as a positivist theory of international relations and international law:[11] 'Contemporary practice shows signs of a return to realist and non-ideological foreign policies, threatening the centrality of democracy promotion in the foreign policies of most democratic states'.[12]

In this book I challenge this claim and provide evidence to support the argument that, notwithstanding considerable changes to the political and

[8] A Moravcsik, 'Taking Preferences Seriously: A Liberal Theory of International Politics' (1997) 51 *International Organization* 513; A-M Burley (now A-M Slaughter), 'Toward and Age of Liberal Nations' (1992) 33 *Harvard International Law Journal* 393; A-M Slaughter, 'International Law and International Relations Theory: A Dual Agenda' (1993) 87 *American Journal of International Law* 205.

[9] H Koh, 'On American Exceptionalism' (2002–03) 55 *Stanford Law Review* 1479.

[10] C Reus-Smit, 'The Strange Death of Liberal International Theory' (2001) 12 *European Journal of International Law* 573.

[11] J d'Aspremont, 'Legitimacy in the Age of Democracy' (2006) 38 *NYU Journal of International Law and Politics* 877 and J d'Aspremont, *L'État Non Démocratique en Droit International. Étude Critique du Droit International Positif et de Law Pratique Contemporaine* (Paris, Pedone, 2008).

[12] J d'Aspremont, 'The Rise and Fall of Democracy Governance in International Law: A Reply to Susan Marks' (2011) 22 *European Journal of International Law* 549, 551.

legal structure of the world order since 9/11, liberalism *remains* a convincing theory to explain the way in which liberal and non-liberal states interact in the contemporary world order. In this context the reaction of liberal states to the 'Arab Spring' is extremely important.

Secondly, although liberalism has received much academic attention since the end of the Cold War, liberal scholars have generally failed to locate liberalism within an adequate conceptual framework. This lack of conceptualisation has seriously undermined the explanatory strength of liberalism as a positivist theory of international law and international relations. For this reason, in this book I deploy the concepts of the international society and the international community in order to construct a theoretical apparatus so that liberalism can be better conceptualised and thus presented as a more convincing explanatory framework.

The concepts just mentioned of the international society and the international community are central to the argument that I develop. I use the concept of the international society as a descriptive tool in order to capture an association of states that formed in the years following the end of the Second World War. When confronted with the massive destruction wrought by the Second World War those states existing within the world order recognised their common interest in formulating a comprehensive international regulatory framework that enabled them to coexist without fear of obliteration. The product was an international society that eventually became universal in scope and that is constituted by the legal norm that casts all states *qua* states as sovereign equals which are entitled to determine their internal affairs without external intervention.

This legal framework represented by the international society can be largely accounted for by the institutional theory that I outlined above: states formulating legal rules and developing institutions in order to secure common interests. However, I argue that the political and legal structure of the contemporary world order cannot be accurately captured by the language of the international society alone. Rather, I argue that in the post-Cold War era an international community of liberal states has formed within the wider, politically pluralist international society.

Importantly, the doctrine of the international community was employed by former British Prime Minister Tony Blair to articulate and explain Britain's participation in NATO's bombing campaign in order to protect ethnic Albanians in Kosovo in 1999.[13] Indeed, Blair then developed this doctrine in three further speeches, all of which provide important insights

[13] T Blair, *'Doctrine of International Community', Speech to the Economic Club of Chicago* (22 April 1999), available at: webarchive.nationalarchives.gov.uk/20040308042406/http://pm.gov.uk:80/output/Page1297.asp.

into the political structure of the world order and the international legal framework that this engenders.[14]

The essence of the international community, I argue, is that those liberal states that comprise it make normative judgements about the political quality of other states.[15] To put the matter simply, this international community has demonstrated a tendency to regard only those states that embrace liberal democracy as legitimate. More importantly, where the international community determines that a state is non-liberal it is not only excluded from the international community and considered illegitimate but is also susceptible to being denied its previously held sovereign rights.[16] Motivated by the theory that international peace can be only achieved between liberal states, the international community has frequently intervened in the domestic affairs of non-liberal states with a view to steering them towards respect for liberal values. Indeed, although a grandiose aspiration, I suggest that ultimately the *telos* of the international community is to construct a world composed exclusively of liberal states and thus dissolve the distinction between itself and the international society. When cast in this light, it becomes quite clear that the interface between the international society and the international community yields profound implications for the international realm (both political and legal) and for international peace and security in particular.

Before I move on to set out the structure of this book two broad caveats are necessary. First, I must reiterate that the objective of this book is to propose an *explanatory* framework that can provide a better understanding of the political and legal structure of the contemporary world order and why violations of international peace and security occur. Significantly, I do not make any normative judgements about the desirability of the

[14] T Blair, *Prime Minister's Speech to the US Congress* (18 July 2003), available at: webarchive.nationalarchives.gov.uk/20040105034004/http://number10.gov.uk/output/Page4220.asp; T Blair, *Speech on the Threat of Global Terrorism* (5 March 2004), available at: webarchive.nationalarchives.gov.uk/20040308042406/http://pm.gov.uk:80/output/Page5470.asp; T Blair, *Clash of Civilizations* (21 March 2006), available at: www.guardian.co.uk/politics/2006/mar/21/iraq.iraq1.

[15] Or, as d'Aspremont explains, the international community looks to their 'legitimacy of exercise' ie the way in which the government exercises its power: see d'Aspremont, 'Legitimacy in the Age of Democracy' (n 11).

[16] It should be noted here that Simpson uses the concepts of liberal pluralism and liberal anti-pluralism in order to describe the regulatory frameworks that I term the international society and the international community: G Simpson, 'Two Liberalisms' (2001) 12 *European Journal of International Law* 537. However, I prefer to use the concepts of the international society and the international community, as these concepts feature most prominently in the normative vocabulary of states and international organisations. As I have indicated above, former British Prime Minister Tony Blair has in particular adopted the vocabulary of the international community. For this reason, I believe that by utilising the concepts of the international society and the international community a more accurate explanatory model can be constructed.

conduct of states or international organisations.[17] For example, I do not attempt to make any normative judgements about whether or not the liberal peace thesis represents the most secure foundation upon which to build international peace and security and thus whether the international community is justified in pursuing liberal reforms in non-liberal states. That is a discussion for another time. Instead, by utilising the concepts of the international society and the international community, my intention is to construct a model that can explain why states act in the way that they do and the implications that their conduct has for international peace and security. Appreciating this objective is therefore crucial to understanding the discussion that follows and to preventing misunderstandings.

Secondly, I recognise that there are those that will contest the explanatory strength of the framework offered here. For example, some may suggest that this theory is not sufficiently sensitive to historical realities. For instance, international legal historians focusing intensively upon the international legal framework applicable during the Cold War may identify evidence to support the claim that states did in fact turn their attention towards the protection and promotion of fundamental human rights and that this was reflected and represented in developments in international law. Thus, the argument would be that to describe the Cold War as being dominated by an international society that constructed international legal rules to protect state sovereignty at the expense of human rights is not sensitive to the complexities of the international legal reality during this period. However, such a criticism somewhat misses the objective of this book. Rather than conducting an intricate analysis of international legal instruments during any particular period, the objective is to take a step back and examine the overarching trajectory of the political and legal structure of the international order since the end of the Second World War.

In a similar vein, there will be those that argue that the concept of the international community in particular is an overly reductivist abstraction. Indeed, Sean Murphy has been a notable critic, asserting that liberal states do not determine the legitimacy of other states solely on the basis of whether or not they respect liberal democracy. Murphy submits that liberal states have close relationships with non-liberal states. His argument is not that liberal states merely interact with non-liberal states. In the era of globalisation this is of course inevitable. The pressures of globalisation

[17] Although I do to a certain extent accept Mégret's point in his review of several books that subscribe to liberal international relations theory in order to explain the proliferation of international criminal tribunals in the post-Cold War era: F Mégret, 'The Politics of International Criminal Justice' (2002) 13 *European Journal of International Law* 1261, 1271 ('And although Bass [the author whose book is under review] invokes the usual warning that he is not interested in normativizing, a theory that says that only liberal states are likely to create rule-of-law war crimes trials is not exactly norm-free either').

demand that all states within the world order engage in a minimum degree of political, commercial and financial cooperation. Rather, the argument is that during such interaction liberal states have made acts or gestures towards non-liberal states which illustrate that they are respectful of the political ideology adopted by non-liberal states and that they therefore continue to recognise non-liberal states as legitimate in a broader sense:[18] 'the international community does not refuse to recognise governments simply by virtue of their being non-democratic' and that '[t]he continuing recognition of non-democratic governments by democratic governments cannot be explained as vestiges of history anomalously "grandfathered in" amid contemporary pro-democratic practice'.[19] In particular, Murphy cites the 'transfer of governance of the democratically governed Hong Kong from the democratic United Kingdom to non-democratic China on 1 July 1997',[20] the UK being fully aware that China would extend legislation to Hong Kong that violated the most basic civil and political rights. Sanger makes a similar argument, criticising former US President Bill Clinton's repeated renewal of China's 'most favoured nation trade' status despite significant concerns over its human rights record.[21] 'Thus, the international community has in recent years affirmatively recognised the non-democratic government in Beijing as the legitimate government of China'.[22] The essence of the argument is that the national interests of liberal states prevent them from transforming their grand political rhetoric, which hails liberal democracy as the only legitimate form of governance, into practice. Such examples (and in particular the frequency of such examples), Murphy submits, have a pernicious impact upon the thesis of the international community. In response, I argue that the social realities of the institution of recognition within the international community are complex and can take on different meanings within a particular context. So the point is that factors other than a state's political constitution may also influence the way that it is perceived by a

[18] This has been denied by the former US Under-Secretary of State for Global Affairs. She labeled it as 'incorrect' that the Bush administration cooperated with authoritarian regimes and turned a blind eye to the non-liberal practices carried out by its ostensible allies: cited in P Dobriansky, 'The Core of US Foreign Policy' (2003) 82 *Foreign Affairs* 141, 141–43 ('this administration, whenever it encounters evidence of serious human rights violations or antidemocratic practices in specific countries, has raised a voice of opposition to such violations and sought to address this problem . . . In general we do this irrespective of the offender . . . Ironically, many of the world's countries, including some of our allies, often chide us not for failing to do enough in the democracy arena, but for trying to do too much, for elevating democratic imperatives above those of trade and diplomatic politesse').

[19] S Murphy, 'Democratic Legitimacy and the Recognition of States and Governments' (1999) 48 *ICLQ* 545, 571.

[20] ibid at 571–72.

[21] D Sanger, 'Support Shrinks for China's Trade Status', *New York Times* (4 June 1999) A19, available at: www.nytimes.com/1999/06/04/world/support-shrinks-for-china-s-trade-status.html.

[22] Murphy, *Democratic Legitimacy and the Recognition of States and Governments* (n 19) at 571.

liberal state, such as the desire to preserve beneficial economic arrangements[23] or to maintain cooperative relationships in order to combat international terrorism.[24] In this sense, classic realist concerns relating to the protection of national interests still impact upon the conduct of liberal states when operating on the international plane. However, the purpose of this book is not to construct an explanatory framework that accounts for every micro-aspect of international social reality. Instead, the objective is to propose a *general explanatory account* that utilises an abstraction like the international community to explain generic transformations to the structural and normative configuration of the world order.[25] To recapitulate, my objective is to develop an explanatory framework that is able to highlight important *consistent trends* within the world order and allow them to be captured and better understood. In the context of recognising the legitimacy of governments during the Cold War years and in the post-Cold War era, I argue that this can be adequately achieved by the concepts of the international society and the international community.

With these caveats noted, it is now necessary to provide a brief overview of the structure of the book. This book is organised into two separate parts. The first four chapters, which comprise Part I, set out the character of the international society and the international community and assess the consequences that their interactions yield for international relations in general and for international peace and security in particular.

In chapter one the concepts of the international society and the international community are introduced and their value as explanatory tools is defended. In brief, I argue that the international society represents an association of states that subscribes to the legal norm that all political entities that qualify as states under international law are sovereign equals irrespective of their political preferences. With the end of the Cold War, however, I suggest that an international community has gained significance within this international society and only considers liberal states to be legitimate and therefore sovereign equals. In particular, the practice of liberal states (and their liberal regional organisations) is examined in

[23] A recent example would be the UK's close relationship with Saudi Arabia. More generally see 'UK Spends Millions Training Security Forces from Oppressive Regimes', *The Guardian* (25 September 2012), available at: www.guardian.co.uk/politics/2012/sep/25/uk-millions-training-oppressive-regimes.

[24] Although complex and often under strain, the US's relationship with Pakistan since 9/11comes to mind.

[25] Liberalism is thus not a 'theory of everything'. But this is not a criticism. Indeed, it is well accepted by international lawyers and political scientists that no theory can be totally comprehensive and any attempt to construct such a theory would be a futile task. As Müllerson explains, 'no approach can explain the reality of international law and politics both comprehensively and profoundly . . . That is why international law needs different theoretical approaches, which not only compete with but also complement each other': R Müllerson, *Ordering Anarchy: International Law in International Society* (The Hague, Martinus Nijhoff, 2000) 3.

order to illustrate that liberal states are now prepared to hold non-liberal states illegitimate because of their failings against standards associated with liberal democracies.

Chapter two examines the impact of the international society and the international community upon international law. I submit that in order to protect the internal affairs of states from external intervention the international society developed international legal principles such as sovereign equality, non-intervention and the prohibition against the threat or use of force. Since the end of the Cold War it can be seen that existing legal principles have been adapted by the international community so as to allow for the protection of fundamental human rights, democracy and the rule of law. This is illustrated through a discussion of the changing nature of the principles of non-intervention and the prohibition on the threat or use of force since the end of the Cold War. In addition, I argue that the international community has created (or at least sought to create) new legal rules in order to facilitate the protection and promotion of liberal values. The emerging right to democratic governance in customary international law and the responsibility to protect doctrine are two examples I use to illustrate my claims.

In chapter three I uncover the ideological motivation for the international community's determination to promote liberal democracy to non-liberal states. I suggest that the international community subscribes to the liberal peace thesis, which submits that liberal states are able to forge a zone of peace wherein any disputes that emerge between them are resolved peacefully through dialogue and mediation. Non-liberal states are considered to exist as a threat to this peace. According to existing academic literature, the suggestion is that liberal states perceive non-liberal states to be a threat to this peace because they do not embrace liberal norms. Liberal states find it difficult to discern the peaceful intentions of non-liberal states and so must assume the worst and prepare for conflict. In this sense, the relationship between liberal and non-liberal states is accounted for by classic realist theory. I argue, however, that the international community relies upon a stronger justification for non-liberal states being perceived to be a threat to their liberal peace and therefore requiring liberal reformation. I argue that the international community considers non-liberal states to be a threat on the basis that non-liberal states are perceived to be in a state of aggression with their own people. I suggest that this is because the international community perceives liberal democracy to represent a universally desired system of governance. Thus, where the government of a state does not adopt liberal democratic standards, liberal states tend to consider it to be in an hostile and aggressive relationship with its population because it is denying the realisation of a rightful or just political system. Significantly, this domestic aggressive behaviour is considered to be an important indicator that the non-liberal state is likely to be aggressive internationally. Non-liberal governments are therefore considered to be probable (as opposed to potential) threats to the peace. Furthermore, I suggest that the more aggressive a non-liberal state is towards its own people (in essence, the greater the denial of recognised human rights protection), the more likely it is that the international community will consider it to be a particularly aggressive actor internationally. This, in turn, increases the likelihood that the international community will prioritise that non-liberal state for liberal reformative action.

Chapter four assesses the relationship between the international community and the Security Council. The Security Council has the unique power to issue mandatory resolutions under the UN Charter when international peace and security is threatened. Thus, Security Council authorisation is essential for the international community to pursue its aims. However, this jars with the formulation of the Security Council as an organisation of the international society which was always intended to promote the principles of sovereign quality and non-intervention in domestic affairs. Indeed, I illustrate that during the Cold War this is how the Security Council interpreted Chapter VII. In those instances where the Security Council engaged Chapter VII it did so in order to defend state sovereignty and the right to non-intervention. By examining the practice of the Security Council in the post-Cold War era my intention is to illustrate that the Security Council is more prepared to utilise its powers under Chapter VII in order to promote respect for liberal values. Thus, I illustrate that the Security Council is increasingly demonstrating that it now accepts only liberal democracy as the legitimate form of political governance and that this transformation in normative commitment is attributable to the influence of the international community within the world order.

In the second part of this book I illustrate the claims in Part I by focusing upon recent peacebuilding operations. My suggestion is that peacebuilding is a mechanism employed by the international community so as to promote liberal democracy to non-liberal states. Consequently, I argue that peacebuilding is being used by the international community as a method of conflict resolution not only in the domestic setting but also at the *international* level.

In chapter five I look to the establishment of peacekeeping operations and their deployment during the Cold War. Clearly, at this time the UN created peacekeeping in order to prevent states from resolving their disputes through the use of force. By placing UN personnel between warring states the intention was to protect state sovereignty and thus maintain international peace and security. When cast in this light, peacekeeping can be seen as an expression of the international society and an attempt to protect its most fundamental norms ie state sovereignty, non-intervention. I further suggest that such was the utility of peacekeeping in protecting state sovereignty that the UN began deploying peacekeeping forces within states that were experiencing *internal* violence. By focusing upon deployments of peacekeepers in the Congo and Cyprus I show that UN peacekeeping forces deployed *within* (rather than *between*) states were not intended to impose externally defined solutions to internal political problems. Instead, the intention of these peacekeeping forces was to eliminate violence and create an environment where the parties could resolve their dispute through reconciliation and mediation rather than intimidation and violence. By eliminating violence the legal edifice of statehood could be preserved. In turn, this would enable the state to retain its sovereign status, retain membership of the international society and thus contribute more widely to the maintenance of international peace and security. To this end, although deployed in response to intra-state disputes, I argue that the objective of these peacekeeping forces remained constant and can be perceived as an expression of the international society.

In chapter six it is argued that in the post-Cold War era there has been a fundamental shift in the nature and objectives of peacekeeping operations. In particular, that the UN is now deploying peacekeeping forces with the explicit mandate to reconstruct post-conflict societies upon a liberal basis. The UN is now authorising the deployment of peacekeeping missions within states not just to eliminate violence and create a political environment where dialogue and mediation can take place but also to establish national and local democratic institutions and to create a legislative and judicial framework that allows for the effective protection of human rights. Adopting UN terminology, I call this new form of peacekeeping *peacebuilding*. I illustrate this shift from peacekeeping to peacebuilding by examining the UN's activities in post-conflict Kosovo and East Timor. In addition, I also examine the UN's role in post-conflict Afghanistan. Although some might question my interpretation of the Afghanistan reconstruction given that the UN adopted a 'light footprint' approach towards it, my claim is that this represented a change in *strategy* rather than *normative* commitment. By revealing the liberal nature of reforms undertaken in Afghanistan I suggest that the international community has remained equally committed to promoting liberal democracy in Afghanistan as it was in Kosovo and East Timor. Thus, notwithstanding the absence of a comprehensive territorial administration in Afghanistan, the reconstruction efforts can nevertheless be perceived as a manifestation of the international community's desire to defend and expand its zone of liberal peace.

In chapter seven I focus upon the reconstruction of Iraq after the invasion in 2003. Like in Kosovo, East Timor and Afghanistan, the reconstruction of Iraq demonstrated an unambiguous liberal bias. Significantly, however, unlike in Kosovo and East Timor, the UN did not authorise this liberal reconstruction under Chapter VII of the UN Charter. Rather, the members of the international community conducting the liberal reconstruction (principally the United States of America and the United Kingdom) were occupying powers and so subject to the international law of belligerent occupation. I argue that the law of occupation was developed by the international society in order to protect state sovereignty; specifically, by preventing an occupying power from intervening in the domestic affairs of the occupied territory. Evidently, the law of occupation would clearly render unlawful many of the substantial and sweeping liberal reforms implemented by the occupying powers in Iraq. This notwithstanding, I argue that because of the close relationship between liberal democracy and international peace (the liberal peace thesis), for the occupying powers it was the promotion of liberal democratic standards that was considered necessary rather than strict adherence to what were considered anachronistic principles of international law that prioritised the protection of state sovereignty over the protection of fundamental human rights.

Part 1

1

The International Society and the International Community

'The vision of a single social space of "the international" has been replaced by a fragmented or kaleidoscopic understanding of the world where the new configurations of time and space have completely mixed up what is particular and what is universal'.[1]

1. INTRODUCTION

IN THIS CHAPTER I argue that when confronted with the destruction wrought by the Second World War those states existing within the world order expressed a common interest in constructing a regulatory framework that would enable them to coexist peacefully.[2] As Dupuy argues, with the end of the Second World War states sought to establish a 'law of coexistence' that compelled them to 'choose the path of compromise and negotiated settlement'.[3] In order to achieve this peaceful coexistence, states subscribed to a common legal standard. This was a standard that regarded all states *qua* states as legal equals regardless of their internal condition. As sovereign equals, all states were conferred absolute legal protection against external intervention in their domestic affairs. In this chapter I employ the concept of the international society to describe this international legal framework.[4] As this was an international society of

[1] M Koskenniemi, *The Gentle Civilizer of Nations: The Rise and Fall of International Law* (Cambridge, Cambridge University Press, 2002) 515.

[2] W Friedmann, *The Changing Structure of International Law* (London, Stevens & Sons, 1964).

[3] P-M Dupuy, 'The Place and Role of Unilateralism in International Law' (2004) 11 *European Journal of International Law* 19, 22–25.

[4] It is important here to distinguish my definition of the international society from the definition accorded to the concept of 'international society' by English School theorists. The English School employs the concept of international society to describe 'a group of states (or, more generally, a group of independent political communities) which not merely form a system, in the sense that the behaviour of each is a necessary factor in the calculations of the others, but also have established by dialogue and consent common rules and institutions for the conduct of their relations, and recognise their common interest in maintaining these arrangements': H Bull and A Watson, 'Introduction' in H Bull and A Watson (eds), *Expansion of International Society* (Oxford, Clarendon Press, 1989) 1. English School theorists therefore

which all states were members and where all members advocated the society's key norm of sovereign equality, at least until the end of the Cold War this association was universal in scope and created what Koskenniemi characterised as 'a single social space of the international'.

However, in the years following the end of the Cold War a profound structural and legal transformation of the world order took place. I suggest that within this international society of states an *international community* of liberal states has emerged that makes normative judgements about the political quality of states.[5] In particular, I contend that this international community has demonstrated an increased preparedness to regard only liberal states as legitimate.[6] I argue that the international community consistently dismisses non-liberal states as illegitimate, which therefore remain members of the international society only. Liberal states also retain membership of the international society as membership is granted de jure to all states. Technically, therefore, the international society remains a universal association. In reality, however, liberal states possess only nominal membership of the international society, as they now possess overriding membership of (and so overriding commitments to) the international community. The consequence is that liberal states now largely reject the legal standards endorsed by the international society and instead subscribe to the legal framework advocated by the international community; whereas the international society considers all states to be sovereign equals, members of the international community consider only liberal states to be sovereign equals as only liberal states are legitimate equals. Being cast as illegitimate, non-liberal states become susceptible to being denied their previously held sovereign rights and the protection that this status confers against external intervention. Indeed, motivated by the theory that international peace and security can be only achieved in a world composed exclusively of liberal states,[7] the international community has engaged in a sustained campaign to promulgate its liberal values to non-liberal states.

use the concept of international society generally to describe instances where two or more states have created legal rules in order to secure a common interest. Importantly, in this chapter I use the concept of *the international society* to describe a specific regulatory framework that emerged in the years following the end of the Second World War in order to secure the common objective of maintaining international peace and security.

[5] My distinction between a (international) society and (international) community largely corresponds to Tönnies's understanding of these terms, whereby a community (*gemeinschaft*) represents a grouping of individuals (here states) within the wider pluralistic society (*gesellschaft*) on the basis of shared values/ideology: F Tönnies, *Community and Association* (East Lansing MI, Michigan State University Press 1957).

[6] As Bodansky explains, in the post-Cold War era liberal democracy has become 'the touchstone of legitimacy' for states: D Bodansky, 'The Legitimacy of International Governance: A Coming Challenge for International Environmental Law?' (1999) 93 *American Journal of International Law* 596, 599.

[7] For discussion of the liberal peace thesis see chapter 3 of this volume.

The emergence of the international community has therefore destroyed any conception of 'a single social space of the international'. In the post-Cold War era, then, the social, political and legal structure of the world order has become fragmented and is now of 'mixed character and uneven depth'.[8] Broadly speaking, the world order now comprises two forms of state association: the international society (which although technically extending membership to all states, in practical reality contains only non-liberal states); and the international community (which contains only liberal states). Significantly, the interface between these associations and their competing conceptions of sovereign statehood yields important implications for our understanding of international relations and for international peace and security in particular.[9] 'Two world views collide'.[10] To this end, the objective of this chapter is to elaborate upon the theoretical identities of the international society and the international community. Specifically, my intention is to engage in a detailed evaluation of how these associations define sovereign statehood, ie what political qualities a state must exhibit in order to be regarded as sovereign, and to assess how their understanding of sovereign statehood relates to the maintenance of international peace and security.

2. THE INTERNATIONAL SOCIETY

According to international law a political community will be recognised as a state where it exhibits the following features: a defined territory, a population and an effective government.[11] It is important to realise that this is a highly practical test and not dependent upon any normative assessment of the political quality of a state.[12] For example, the requirement that a government has to be 'effective' refers to its ability to command effective physical control over the population, rather than the

[8] R Jackson, *The Global Covenant: Human Conduct in a World of States* (Oxford, Oxford University Press, 2000) 128.

[9] R Buchan, 'A Clash of Normativities: International Society and International Community' (2008) 10 *International Community Law Review* 3.

[10] P Kooijmans, *Internationaal Publiekrecht in Vogelvucht* (trans M Brus) (Deventer, Kluwer, 2000) 359; see M Brus, 'Bridging the Gap between State Sovereignty and International Governance: The Authority of Law' in G Kreijin (ed), *State, Sovereignty and International Governance* (Oxford, Oxford University Press, 2002) 3).

[11] These criteria can be found in Article I of the Montevideo Convention on the Rights and Duties of States (signed 26 December 1933, in force 26 December 1934). See generally J Crawford, *The Creation of States in International Law* (Oxford, Clarendon Press, 2006).

[12] In arguing against a request for an Advisory Opinion of the International Court of Justice on the status of Palestine in 1948, the Israeli Foreign Minister explained that 'the existence of a State is a question of fact and not of law. The criterion of statehood is not legitimacy but effectiveness': A Eban, SCOR 340th Meeting (27 July 1948) 29–30.

quality of the relationship between the government and the population.[13] The controversial issue, however, is when a state can be regarded as sovereign. This is so important because where a state is sovereign it enjoys the absolute legal entitlement to determine its domestic affairs without external intervention;[14] the right to non-intervention is therefore the 'corollary' of sovereignty.[15]

Sovereignty is therefore an extremely important quality for a state to possess. This necessarily poses the question, however, of what features a state must exhibit in order to qualify as sovereign.[16] The concept of sovereignty is generally regarded as having been established by the Peace of Westphalia 1648. This peace settlement sought to end the violent conflict between the Catholic and Protestant communities within the Holy Roman Empire and allow peace to be enjoyed in the region. The settlement sought to achieve this objective by dividing the Empire up into a series of horizontally aligned states that were no longer under the authority of the Holy Roman Empire. However, although the parties to the peace settlement agreed to terminate the centralised authority of the Empire, they nevertheless remained committed to Christianity. Thus, all states had to endorse Christianity, be it Protestant or Catholic in denomination. Importantly, these states would only enjoy sovereignty if they endorsed Christianity. Although statehood was formally granted to all the political communities existing within the Empire, only those states that endorsed Christianity were conferred the status of sovereignty and thus entitled to regulate their internal affairs without external intervention.[17] The Peace of

[13] As the UN General Assembly has explained, a government will possess effective control 'if that government exercises effective control and authority over all or nearly all of the national territory, and has the obedience of the bulk of the population of that territory in such a way that this control, authority, and obedience appears to be of a permanent character': UN Doc A/AC.38/L.21 (1950).

[14] As Henkin explains, 'sovereignty means "leave us alone"': L Henkin, 'That "S" Word: Sovereignty, and Globalization, and Human Rights, Et Cetera' (1999) 68 *Fordham Law Review* 1, 5. The exact scope of the non-intervention principle will be discussed in detail in chapter 2 of this volume.

[15] 'Each state, according to international law, has a duty of non-intervention into the affairs of other states . . . At the basis of this duty lies the concept of state sovereignty, of which in fact the duty of non-intervention is considered a "corollary"': D Luban, 'Just War and Human Rights' (1980) 9 *Philosophy and Public Affairs* 160, 164.

[16] The discussion that follows intends to trace the development of the legal principle of sovereignty from its creation (which I will identify as the Peace of Westphalia (1648)) through to the end of the Second World War (1945), and assess the different features that a state has had to exhibit historically in order to be regarded as sovereign. It is important to note that my approach is an episodic account which only takes into account the *major normative changes* in the understanding of sovereignty that have occurred between 1648 and 1945. I accept that between these dates other understandings of what characteristics a state has had to exhibit in order to qualify as sovereign may have existed. However, space precludes a more comprehensive historical analysis. For such an analysis see J Donnelly, 'Human Rights: a New Standard of Civilization?' (1998) 74 *International Affairs* 1.

[17] As Simpson explains, '[a]t first, Christianity was the test for "good breeding"': G Simpson, 'Two Liberalisms' (2001) 12 *European Journal of International Law* 537, 545.

Westphalia thus engendered a society of Christian (and by implication European) states that was constituted by their sovereign equality,[18] the objective of which was to devise a regulatory framework that allowed these former enemies to coexist peacefully. Significantly, however, states that did not adhere to Christianity were dismissed as illegitimate and consequently proscribed entry to this international society, being denied the sovereign rights conferred on Christian states (specifically the right to non-intervention).[19] As a result, intervention in non-Christian states became legally permissible.[20]

However, as this European international society began to have more interaction with the previously unencountered states of the New World,[21] members of this international society became quickly aware of 'how problematic a preoccupation with Christendom could be'.[22] The consequence of denying sovereignty to states that did not adhere to Christianity was that they would not recognise the sovereignty of members of the international society. Members of the international society thus became vulnerable to intervention. The international society therefore recognised the 'disadvantages of permanent chaos if interstate relations remain wholly unregulated'.[23] From the perspective of their individual security it was thus considered beneficial to allow previously excluded states entry to the international society (and thereby confer on them sovereignty) so as to lock them within its regulatory framework. In other words, by granting sovereignty to previously excluded states, members of the international society were conferred greater personal security. To this end, during the mid-nineteenth century the international society removed the requirement of

[18] For Bobbit, Westphalia inaugurated 'a new society of states characterized by their sovereign equality': P Bobbit, *The Shield of Achilles: War, Peace and the Course of History* (London, Allen Lane, 2002) 508. Although the Treaty of Westphalia did not explicitly refer to these newly created states as sovereign (indeed the concept of sovereignty does not appear at all within this treaty), the substance of its provisions nevertheless had the practical effect of conferring this status: see generally I Clark, *Legitimacy in International Society* (Oxford, Oxford University Press, 2005).

[19] 'In a number of respects, non-Christian states lived for many years on the margin of the international [society], in the sense that they did not take a very active part, nor did they play any major role, in it': A Cassese, *International Law in a Divided World* (Oxford, Clarendon Press, 1986) 39.

[20] 'In short, it can be argued that this body of law greatly facilitated the task of European powers, offering them, as it did, a large number of legal instruments designed to render conquest smooth and easy. First of all, international law authorized States to acquire sovereignty over those territories, both by downgrading the latter to *terrae nullius*, namely, territories belonging to no one, and by depriving the local communities or rulers [of] any international standing': ibid at 42.

[21] As Buzan notes, 'the projection of European power brought previously isolated peoples and political communities into regular contact with each other': B Buzan, 'From International System to International Society; Structural Realism and Regime Theory meet the English School' (1993) 47 *International Organization* 327, 331.

[22] Clark, *Legitimacy in International Society* (n 18) at 45.

[23] Buzan, 'From International System to International Society' (n 21) at 334.

Christianity from its admission test and, consequently, from the test for sovereignty. However, although this international society was prepared to be more inclusive it still refused to confer membership (and thus sovereignty) on all states. In particular, this society continued to exclude states that did not attain 'the standard of civilisation'. 'What we then witness is the emergence of a notion of civilization, initially as an adjunct of Christendom, but finally as a displacement of the latter as the operative basis of international society'.[24] The international society considered itself unable to tolerate such 'barbarous nations'.[25] Gong suggests that the international society would only recognise a state as civilised where that state demonstrated respect for the rights of foreigners to life, personal dignity, property, freedom of travel, commerce, and religion. In addition, civilised states were also expected to prohibit heinous, uncivilised practices such as slavery, piracy, polygamy, infanticide and barbaric penal practices.[26] Failure to demonstrate such respect resulted in a state being classified as uncivilised and placed outside the legitimate boundaries of the international society. Non-civilised states were therefore denied sovereignty and the protection this status conferred against external intervention. As Westlake put it, 'of uncivilised natives international law takes no account', leaving their treatment 'to the conscience to which the sovereignty is awarded'.[27] Indeed, members of the international society embarked upon civilising missions (known as the *mission civilisatrice* of colonisation), intervening in the affairs of states that were considered to have failed to attain the standard of civilisation, 'instructing the natives and bringing home to them the blessings of civilization'.[28] Importantly, over time the international society's definition of the standard of civilisation altered. By the beginning of the twentieth century the international society regarded a state as civilised and thus a legitimate member of the international society where it did not just respect the human rights of foreigners but where it also accorded this same protection to its own citizens.[29] This dividing line between inclusion

[24] Clark (n 18) at 45.

[25] J Lorimer, *Institutes of International Law: A Treatise of the Jural Relations of Separate Political Communities* (Edinburgh/London, W Blackwood & Sons, 1883) 101.

[26] G Gong, *The Standard of 'Civilization' in International Society* (Oxford, Clarendon Press, 1984) 14–15.

[27] L Oppenheim (ed), *The Collected Papers of John Westlake on Public International Law* (Cambridge, Cambridge University Press, 1914) 138, 145. See further J Westlake, *Chapters on the Principles of International Law*, L Oppenheim (ed) (Cambridge, Cambridge University Press, 1894) 141–43.

[28] Article VI of the General Act of the Conference of Berlin (1885). Also see Lorimer, who advocated the forcible domination of uncivilised ('barbarous') states: 'Colonisation, and the reclamation of barbarians and savages, if possible in point of fact, are duties morally and jurally inevitable; and where circumstances demand the application of physical force, they fall within necessary objects of war. On this ground, the wars against China and Japan, to compel these countries to open their ports, may be defended': Lorimer, *Institutes of International Law* (n 25) at 28.

[29] Simpson, 'Two Liberalisms' (n 17) at 546.

and exclusion again demarcated those states that were entitled to claim sovereignty and those that were not.

Despite this modification in the test for sovereignty, the international society was still not universal in coverage, as its member states still felt unable to confer membership on those states that did not meet the standard of civilisation. However, this remaining exclusion is something that would undergo fundamental revision as the international society endured 'the most violent century in human history'.[30]

The first attempt to alter the legitimate boundaries of the international society and make admission available to all states came at the end of the First World War. This is reflected in the creation of the League of Nations, which in essence formed part of the First World War peace settlement. This was an organisation that required that its members pledge 'to respect and preserve as against external aggression the territorial integrity and existing political independence of all Members of the League'.[31] In this sense, although membership of the League did not formally grant state sovereignty, membership of the League did buttress state sovereignty, providing its members with legal (treaty-based) protection against external aggression.[32]

When the Covenant was being drafted there was considerable debate as to which states could become members. As is well known, US President Woodrow Wilson publicly stated that attainment of 'the principle[s] of peace and justice' demanded an organisation that was only available to democratic states[33] that accorded racial, religious and national minorities the same degree of protection as the majority of society.[34]

However, and in a move that is often identified as a contributing factor to the US Congress's decision not to ratify the Covenant and thus why the US did not become a member of the League, the Commission responsible for drafting the Covenant refused to make membership contingent upon respect for democracy and the protection of human rights. Instead, Article 1 of the Covenant explained that membership of the League was available to any 'fully self-governing State, Dominion or Colony'. Given the absence of any reference to a state's internal political quality, Schwarzenberger therefore explains that Article 1 indicates that the members 'intended to create a League of Nations based on the principle of universality'.[35] At least on the

[30] W Goulding, cited in E Hobsbawm, *Age of Extremes: The History of the Short Twentieth Century 1914-1991* (London, Abacus, 1995) I.

[31] Article 10 Covenant of the League of Nations (Paris, 28 June 1919).

[32] A Duxbury, *The Participation of States in International Organisations: The Role of Human Rights and Democracy* (Cambridge, Cambridge University Press, 2011) 64.

[33] President Woodrow Wilson, 'Address to a Joint Session of Congress Calling for a Declaration of War' (2 April 1917).

[34] The British representative also lobbied the Commission for membership to be based on respect for democratic principles: see Duxbury, *The Participation of States* (n 32) at 69

[35] G Schwarzenberger, *The League of Nations and World Order* (London, Constable & Co, 1936) 44.

face of it, membership of the League was not dependent upon adherence to democracy or, indeed, any other particular political or religious affiliation.

This being said, in its admission practice the League seemed reluctant to fully embrace the principle of universality.[36] In particular, in determining new applications for membership the admission committee continued to place emphasis upon adherence to human rights protection. For example, in their membership applications the Baltic and Caucasian states were required to give assurances to the Second Assembly that they would ensure the adequate protection of minority rights within their territories.[37] Furthermore, in relation to Abyssinia's application for membership, the Assembly expressed concern about Abyssinia's apparent endorsement of slave labour. In response, Abyssinia agreed to sign the 1919 Convention of St Germain-en-Laye, which prohibited the slave trade, and was subsequently permitted admission to the League. Upon membership Abyssinia declared

> herself ready now and hereafter to furnish the Council with any information which it may require, and to take into consideration any recommendations which the Council may make with regard to the fulfilment of these obligations, in which she recognises that the League of Nations is concerned.[38]

In this way, despite its 'goal'[39] to be a universal organisation, in practice the League nevertheless continued to require states to exhibit minimal standards of human rights protection in order to become members of the League.[40] As the Assembly stated itself, admission criteria exhibited during membership applications illustrated that the League was premised upon 'different degrees of civilisation'.[41] Thus, during the interwar years adherence to human rights standards continued to provide the yardstick to test which states could be regarded as legitimate equals and who could rely upon international legal rules to protect them from external intervention.

[36] And this is conceded by Schwarzenberger: 'the practice of the League tended away from the principle of homogenous university . . . as it was envisaged by the authors of the Covenant, towards that of heterogeneous universality': ibid at 94.

[37] Second Assembly, Plenary Meetings (Geneva, 1921), League of Nations Records, 317–20.

[38] Fourth Assembly, Seventeenth Plenary Meeting (Geneva, 1923), League of Nations Records, 4.

[39] Duxbury (n 32) at 83.

[40] Although distinguish the claims of the Canadian representative: 'While believing firmly in the long run, [that] the League can succeed only by the application in the international sphere of these ideals of liberty and democracy, we recognise that, for the present we must agree to differ and that we cannot require other States to conform to such principles, or reject their collaboration in the league, so long as they share in the one indispensable condition of readiness to work together for the peace of the world': Records of the Fifteenth Assembly, Sixth Committee (Geneva, 1934) League of Nations Official Journal, Supplement 130, 25.

[41] Records of the Fourth Assembly, Meetings of the Committees, Minutes of the Sixth Committee (Geneva, 1923) League of Nations Official Journal, Supplement 19, 15.

In genuinely realising a universal international society, the end of the Second World War proved to be a pivotal moment in history. When world leaders were faced with the devastation apparent at the end of the Second World War (a World War that was considered unimaginable after the First World War) members of the international society were provided with sufficient impetus to reassess the existing apparatus for maintaining international peace and security. The massive inter-state violence inflicted by the Second World War revealed the failings of a security system that was exclusionary. In order for this system to be effective its application needed to be universal in scope; the covenant on non-intervention needed to be operative globally. This is because the sovereign-state security apparatus is based upon an 'institutional grip'[42] that seeks to 'ensnare'[43] its members within a legal framework premised upon the mutual abstention from intervention in other states' domestic affairs. As Bull observes,

> from the perspective of any particular state what it chiefly hopes to gain from participation in the society of states is recognition of its independence of outside authority, and in particular of its supreme jurisdiction over its subject and territory. The chief price it has to pay for this is recognition of like rights to independence and sovereignty on the part of other states.[44]

The argument runs that if a state is excluded from this arrangement, being denied sovereign status and thus the right to non-intervention, it will not recognise the sovereignty of those states inside the international society and accord them the legal right to non-intervention.[45] As history has revealed, excluded states are not within the grip of this security system and so for them waging war remains an unrestricted prerogative. Evidently, in a world where all states are constantly interacting, the refusal to confer sovereignty on a state because of some perceived normative inferiority, and thus their exclusion from participating within this regulatory framework, would severely diminish its effectiveness in maintaining international peace and security. As Jackson identifies, historically the failure of the international society to recognise the sovereign equality of all states has proved a 'recipe for chaos'.[46] Thus, the

[42] B Simma, *The Charter of the United Nations: a Commentary* (Oxford, Oxford University Press, 2002) 208.

[43] Jackson, *Global Covenant* (n 8) at 120.

[44] H Bull, *The Anarchical Society: A Study of Order in World Politics* (Basingstoke, Palgrave, 2002) 16–17. In a similar vein, Wight explains that 'it would be impossible to have a society of sovereign states unless each state, while claiming sovereignty for itself, recognised that every other state had the right to claim and enjoy its own sovereignty as well': M Wight, *Systems of States* (Leicester, Leicester University Press, 1977) 135.

[45] As Duxbury notes, 'it was better to admit a state to the 'peace-club', whatever its internal policies, than leave it on the outside, free to engage in war-like activities': Duxbury (n 32) at 83.

[46] Jackson (n 8) at 15.

perception became that the recognition of all states as sovereign equals was the key to maintaining international peace and security.[47]

To this end, in the ashes of the Second World War the political qualities that a state had to display in order to be regarded as sovereign (and thus a member of the international society) underwent profound redefinition. Importantly, since the Second World War sovereignty has been conferred immediately and automatically on all states *qua* states. Although as we shall see this position has been significantly challenged by the emergence of the international community since the end of the Cold War, providing a state exhibits the physical features of statehood required by international law (these being territory, population and effective government), the international society grants sovereignty de jure. Statehood and sovereignty therefore arise contemporaneously. As I already explained, this test for statehood is ideologically neutral and does not require assessment of the state's political or religious quality. As members of this society, all states are conferred the exclusive right to determine their domestic affairs without external intervention irrespective of their political constitution.[48] Thus, from the perspective of the international society 'the integrity of a fascist dictatorship is entitled to as much respect as the government of a social democracy'.[49] To this end, in the years following the end of the Second World War the international society became an inclusive association, being universal in scope.[50] The intention was to achieve 'peace though universality'.[51]

With the intention of strengthening its norms, this universal international society sought to formally institutionalise its association by creating the United Nations (UN).[52] In this sense, the UN is the 'legitimate

[47] According to the ICJ, the institution of sovereign equality has proved to be 'an instrument for effective co-operation . . . enabling States, irrespective of their differing constitutional and social systems, to achieve mutual understanding': *United States Diplomatic and Consular Staff in Tehran* (1979) ICJ Rep 7, 19 (Order of 15 December).

[48] 'Every State has an inalienable right to choose its political, economic, social and cultural systems, without interference in any form by another State': GA Res 2625 (24 October 1970).

[49] A Fellmeth, 'Feminism and International Law: Theory, Methodology and Substantive Reform' (2000) 2 *Human Rights Quarterly* 658, 703.

[50] Although I identify the end of the Second War as the moment when sovereignty was redefined and conferred to all states *qua* states (and thus the international society became universal in scope), I recognise that this transformation was not instantaneous. It took many years for all states to be finally regarded as sovereign. Indeed, the international society would not be universal in scope until the end of the process of decolonisation. I therefore use the end of the Second World War for heuristic purposes, representing a point in time when the legal structure of the world order started to undergo profound change. Thus, it is at the end of the Second World War that I suggest the notion of all states being sovereign equals was born.

[51] Duxbury (n 32) at 82.

[52] As McCorquodale notes, with the creation of the UN by the international society '[t]he dominant legal doctrine became institutionalized': R McCorquodale, 'International Community and State Sovereignty: An Uneasy Symbiotic Relationship' in C Warbrick and S Tierney (eds), *Towards an International Legal Community?* (London, British Institute of International and Comparative Law, 2006) 242.

representative' of the international society.[53] Thus, the UN is a universal organisation that is open to all entities that qualify as a state under international law. Although Article 4(1) requires that a state must also be 'peace-loving' importantly this qualification of peace-loving refers to the state's (pacific) international conduct rather than its internal politics.[54] Upon membership, all states are regarded as sovereign equals irrespective of their internal condition.[55] In particular, Article 2(4) specifically outlaws the threat or use of force against the territorial integrity or political independence of member states. Although the UN Charter does not explicitly confer on all member states the right to non-intervention, the International Court of Justice (ICJ) has explained that such a prohibition should be read as the 'corollary' of Article 2(1).[56] Thus, even though the UN Charter does not explicitly confer the right to non-intervention, members of the international society have, by way of customary international law, developed a wider a prohibition against intervention in the sovereign affairs of another state.[57] As the ICJ has noted, this would certainly confer upon states the right to choose their own political, social, economic and cultural systems:

> [h]owever the regime in Nicaragua be defined, adherence by a State to any particular doctrine does not constitute a violation of customary international law; to hold otherwise would make nonsense of the fundamental principle of State

[53] '[T]he UN has been called upon to play the role of implementation mechanism . . . the UN ultimately acts in the interest and on behalf of the whole world community, of which it is the legitimate representative': Cassese, *International Law in a Divided World* (n 19) at 159.

[54] Thus, the Rapporteur of the Committee responsible for dealing with the matter of rightful membership of the UN explained '[t]he Committee did not feel that it should recommend the enumeration of the elements which were to be taken into consideration. It considered the difficulties which would arise in evaluating the political institutions of States and feared that the mention in the Charter of a study of such nature would be a breach of the principle of non-intervention or, if preferred, non-interference': UNCIO, Report of the Rapporteur of the Committee 1/2 on Chapter III (Membership), Doc 1178.1/2/76(2), 3, Docs VII, 326. See generally T Grant, *Admission to the United Nations: Charter Article 4 and the Rise of Universal Organization* (Leiden, Martinus Nijhoff, 2009). Although do note that, especially since the end of the Cold War, the UN Credentials Committee has on several occasions refused to accept the credentials of a government on the basis that it has achieved power through undemocratic means and/or has committed serious violations of human rights against its people. See generally M Griffin, 'Accrediting Democracies: Does the Credentials Committee of the United Nations Promote Democracy through its Accreditation Process and Should It?' (1999) 32 *NYU Journal of International Law and Politics* 725.

[55] Article 2(1) UN Charter. As Simpson explains, by constructing the UN the international society thus formally expressed its intention to abolish the standard of civilisation: G Simpson, *Great Powers and Outlaw States: Unequal Sovereigns in the International Legal Order* (Cambridge, Cambridge University Press, 2004) 4–7.

[56] The ICJ explained that although the prohibition against intervention is 'not, as such, spelt out in the Charter', it is 'a corollary of the principle of the sovereign equality of states' contained in Article 2(1): *Military and Paramilitary Activities in and against Nicaragua (Nicaragua v United States of America)* (1986) ICJ Rep at para 202.

[57] For a more detailed discussion of the scope of the non-intervention principle see chapter 2 of this volume.

> sovereignty, on which the whole of international law rests, and the freedom of the political, social, economic and cultural system of a State.[58]

In realising that the prohibition against external intervention was unlikely to always attract total conformity, the members of the UN established a collective security system which could be employed in order to respond to situations where a member state violates the UN's constitutive norms. Under Chapter VII of the UN Charter the Security Council is authorised to take mandatory enforcement action against a state where it determines that there is 'a threat to international peace and security'.[59] As I illustrate in chapter four, when the UN Charter was created this concept of 'a threat to international peace and security' was always intended to mean the violation of state sovereignty: a threat to international peace and security would emerge (and the jurisdiction of the Security Council would therefore be engaged) where one state intervened in the domestic affairs of another state. Thus, Chapter VII of the UN Charter represents an attempt by the member states to construct a centralised collective security system that protects and defends state sovereignty from external intervention and thereby enables the maintenance of international peace and security.

In the event that a member state 'has persistently violated the Principles contained in the present Charter'[60] Article 6 of the UN Charter enables the UN to expel the member state. The UN, however, has never exercised this provision. This is certainly not because member states have not violated the principles of the Charter. On the contrary, many examples present themselves where member states have acted extremely aggressively towards fellow members, in clear violation of their obligations under the Charter.[61] Perhaps the most obvious example is Iraq's invasion of Kuwait in 1990 and its unlawful annexation of part of Kuwait's territory, committing the most flagrant violation of the UN's core principles. Despite the unequivocal condemnation of Iraq's conduct by the UN Security Council,[62] Iraq continued to enjoy membership of the UN. Indeed, the question of expelling Iraq from the UN was never discussed.

The UN's failure to expel a member can be explained, however, on the basis of the international society's determination to maintain international peace and security.[63] As I suggested, the international society's turbulent

[58] *Nicaragua v United States of America* (1986) ICJ Rep at para 263.

[59] Article 39 UN Charter. Under Article 25 UN Charter all member states are required to 'carry out decisions of the Security Council'.

[60] Article 6 UN Charter. The full provision reads '[a] Member of the United Nations which has persistently violated the Principles contained in the present Charter may be expelled from the Organization by the General Assembly upon the recommendation of the Security Council'.

[61] T Franck, 'Who Killed Article 2(4)?' (1970) 64 *American Journal of International Law* 809.

[62] SC Res 660 (2 August 1990).

[63] That the UN has never expelled a member state in the event that it has seriously violated its constitutive norms is important in the context of the international community. As

history of exclusion vividly illustrates that the international society must remain inclusive (indeed universal) if its regulatory system is to be effective. Expelling a state would therefore be counterproductive.[64] Indeed, for similar reasons political communities continue to possess membership of the UN even though they no longer exhibit the physical features of statehood. The UN is reluctant to expel them from its grip because the effectiveness of its security system necessitates inclusiveness. The situation in Somalia in 1992 provides a good example of the UN providing formal title (and so continued membership) despite the fact that any organised political system that had previously existed had been destroyed by fierce civil war. The UN was prepared to accept this fiction because maintaining the features of statehood (and thus sovereignty) was considered indispensable to achieving the wider objective of maintaining international peace and security.[65]

3. THE INTERNATIONAL COMMUNITY

3.1 Liberalism and Legitimate Statehood

As the formal institutionalisation of the international society the UN is agnostic as to the political quality of its member states. This being said, a series of international treaties have been created under the auspices of the UN that appear to change the focus of the UN away from the state and protecting its right to determine its internal affairs without external intervention and towards the individual and protecting individual liberty. Notably, the UN adopted the Universal Declaration of Human Rights 1948 (UDHR), the International Covenant on Civil and Political Rights 1966 (ICCPR) and the International Covenant on Social, Economic and Cultural Rights 1966 (ICSECR). In particular, the latter two treaties impose binding obligations upon parties to protect the stipulated human rights.

I reveal in the next section, in the post-Cold War era liberal states frequently violate the sovereignty of non-liberal states in order to promote liberal reform in non-liberal states. Notwithstanding these violations, however, the UN has failed to expel these liberal states. This is important because it means that liberal states retain their membership of the UN. As I discuss in chapter 4 of this volume, liberal states are now exploiting their continued membership of the UN and using the organs of this organisation (ie the Security Council, the General Assembly) to promote respect for the values of the international community (democracy, human rights and the rule of law) rather than the values of the international society (sovereign equality, non-intervention).

[64] L Sohn, 'Expulsion and Forced Withdrawal from an International Organisation' (1964) 77 *Harvard Law Review* 1381.

[65] It is therefore unsurprising that 'the death rate of sovereign states has been remarkably low . . . [where] the rate of disappearances has declined to almost zero after 1945': B Kingsbury, 'Sovereignty and Inequality' (1998) 9 *European Journal of International Law* 599, 618.

Ostensibly, in developing these obligations the members of the UN no longer considered the relationship between the state and the people as immune from international scrutiny. This necessarily poses the question of whether the UN sought to (re)introduce the notion of legitimate statehood into international vocabulary, being prepared to regard only those states that protect human rights as legitimate, thereby redefining the legitimate boundaries of the international society. I suggest that although the UN produced these international human rights instruments, these nevertheless remained pious aspiration. Although they represent legal obligations, certainly during the Cold War the UN did not demonstrate any concerted or consistent effort to enforce these obligations against non-compliant member states.[66] Instead, the UN remained loyal to its founding principles of sovereignty and non-intervention: 'the traditional notion of state sovereignty trumped human rights . . . How states treated their own citizens was considered a domestic matter'.[67] Notwithstanding the creation of these human rights instruments, the international society retained its integrity. As Simpson explains, '[t]he failure to expel, or even to sanction seriously, the likes of Kampuchea, Idi Amin's Uganda or Guatemala spoke volumes for the continuing commitment to inter-state pluralism'.[68]

The end of the Cold War, however, represents another significant turning point in the evolution of the structure of the world order. With the ideological 'triumph'[69] of liberal democracy over communism an international community of liberal states has emerged *within* this international society that is dedicated to the protection of human rights and has thus (re)introduced the notion of legitimate statehood into the world order.[70] In essence, this international community of liberal states only considers fellow liberal states to be legitimate.[71] 'Since the end of the Cold War, rightful

[66] J Watson, *Theory and Reality in the International Protection of Human Rights* (Ardsley NY, Transnational Publishers, 1999).

[67] B Frederking, *The United States and the Security Council: Collective Security since the Cold War* (London/New York, Routledge, 2007) 131.

[68] Simpson, 'Two Liberalisms' (n 17) at 557.

[69] C Brown, '"Really Existing Liberalism", Peaceful Democracies and International Order' in R Fawn and J Larkins (eds), *International Society after the Cold War: Anarchy and Order Reconsidered* (1996) 30 ('it does make some sense to talk of the triumph of Western liberalism'). See generally F Fukuyama, 'The End of History' (1989) 16 *National Interest* 3.

[70] Although I suggest that the international community emerged at the end of the Cold War it is important to appreciate that I use this date for largely heuristic purposes. I recognise that even before the end of the Cold War liberal states had started placing the protection of human rights above state sovereignty in terms of normative priority. However, it was not until the end of the Cold War that this international community of liberal states crystallised and gained coherence.

[71] '[L]iberalism, within the international realm . . . is of growing importance because of its dominance as a value system against which state forms are legitimized': F Robinson, 'Globalising Liberalism? Morality and Legitimacy in a Liberal Global Order' in M Shaw (ed), *Politics and Globalization: Knowledge, Ethics and Agency* (London, Routledge, 1999) 143.

membership has been expressed, not simply about states, but about certain types of state'.[72]

It is necessary to be absolutely clear in identifying the features that a state must display in order for the international community to regard it as liberal and therefore legitimate. For the international community, I argue, the essence of a liberal state is its dedication to protecting individual liberty, which necessitates the protection of certain human rights. I submit that the human rights that must be protected in order for individual liberty to be enjoyed include all those civil, political, economic, social and cultural rights that are stipulated in the two international covenants.[73] As the World Conference on Human Rights explains, the human rights contained in the two covenants are 'interdependent, indivisible and interrelated'.[74] If individual liberty is to be protected, all rights must be protected by the state. *Ergo*, if a state is to be regarded as liberal all these rights must be protected. Sure, from the practice of liberal states it is apparent that when assessing whether a state is liberal or not greater emphasis is placed upon the protection of civil and political rights.[75] In scrutinising a prospective (and indeed current) member state for conformity with liberal values it is apparent that members of the international community will focus more intently upon the protection the state accords to civil and political rights. However, this does not mean that economic, social and cultural rights are ignored. Rather, the international community requires that economic, social and cultural rights are given a minimum degree of protection. In this sense, the international community does not accord economic, social and cultural rights a truly objective definition. Indeed, this is consistent with the approach adopted by the ICSECR, which explains that each party to the treaty

> undertakes to take steps . . . to the maximum of its available resources, with a view to achieving progressively the full realization of the rights recognised in the present Covenant by all appropriate means, including particularly the adoption of legislative measures.[76]

As Brownlie observes, social, economic and cultural rights are thus 'programmatic' and 'promotional', whereas civil and political rights are far more specific in the obligations they impose.[77] I suggest that this

[72] Clark (n 18) at 173.

[73] In its definition of liberal democracy at the Warsaw Declaration the Community of Democracies explained that 'all human rights – civil, cultural, economic, political and social – be promoted and protected as set forth in the Universal Declaration of Human Rights and other relevant human rights instruments': Community of Democracies, Warsaw Declaration (June 2000), available at: www.ccd21.org/articles/warsaw_declaration.htm.

[74] World Conference on Human Rights (Vienna, 14–25 June 1993). For the full report see UN Doc A/CONF.157/24 (Part I) (1993).

[75] See the practice of the EU in its scrutiny of prospective members, discussed below.

[76] Article 2(1) ICSECR, signed 16 December 1966, in force 3 January 1976.

[77] I Brownlie, *Principles of Public International Law*, 7th edn (Oxford, Oxford University Press, 2008) 566.

relative approach to the protection of economic, social and cultural rights encouraged by the ICSECR is reflected in the admission criteria of the international community.

Of the human rights protected by the international community the right to democracy is particularly important,[78] not least because the protection of all other rights is generally considered dependent upon the existence of democracy.[79] The key issue here is that in the determination and implementation of policy the government of the state is accountable to the people through free, fair, regular and competitive elections. Sure, democracy can take many different procedural forms.[80] For the international community, however, all forms are legitimate to the extent that they afford the population the opportunity to hold the government accountable for its actions through free, fair and regular elections.[81]

Finally, the international community places much emphasis upon the rule of law. Although historically the concept of the rule of law has been narrowly defined as the existence of an independent and impartial judicial system that is capable of protecting human rights and rendering them effective against governmental abuse, the international community accords this concept a far more substantive definition. I argue that for the international community the

> rule of law refers to a principle of governance in which all persons, institutions and entities, public and private, including the State itself, are accountable to laws that are publicly promulgated, equally enforced and independently adjudicated, and which are consistent with international human rights norms and standards. It requires, as well, measures to ensure adherence to the principles of supremacy of law, equality before the law, accountability to the law, fairness in

[78] See Article 25 ICCPR (every citizen has the right '(a) To take part in public affairs, directly or through freely chosen representatives; (b) To vote and to be elected at genuine periodic elections which shall be by universal and equal suffrage and shall be held by secret ballot, guaranteeing the free expression of the will of electors'). See also Article 21 of the Universal Declaration of Human Rights (Paris, 10 December 1948), which explains that '[t]he will of the people shall be the basis of the authority of government'.

[79] The General Assembly has explained that 'periodic and genuine elections are a necessary and indispensable element of sustained efforts to protect the rights and interests of the governed and that . . . the right of everyone to take part in the government of his or her country is a crucial factor in the effective enjoyment of all of a wide range of other human rights and fundamental freedoms, embracing political, economic, social and cultural rights': GA Res 45/150 (18 December 1990). Additionally, UN Secretary-General Boutros-Ghali explained that 'democracy . . . [is] regarded as essential to progress on a wide range of human concerns and to the protection of human rights': UN Secretary-General Boutros Boutros-Ghali, *An Agenda for Democratization*, UN Doc A/51/761 (20 December 1996) at 1.

[80] D Held, *Models of Democracy* (Cambridge, Polity Press, 2006).

[81] As the UN Secretary-General explained, 'it is not for the United Nations to offer a model of democratization or democracy or to promote democracy in a specific case . . . [because there is] . . . no one model of democratization or democracy suitable to all societies': UN Secretary-General Boutros-Ghali, *An Agenda for Democratization* at 1–2. For the Secretary-General's report on the implementation of the Agenda for Democratization see GA Res A/52/513 (21 October 1997).

> the application of the law, separation of powers, participation in decision making, legal certainty, avoidance of arbitrariness and procedural and legal transparency.[82]

Consequently, a state will be regarded as liberal and therefore considered a legitimate member of the international community where it possesses some form of representative government, constitutional guarantees of civil, political, economic, social and cultural rights, and a functioning system dedicated to the rule of law.[83] For analytical convenience, I condense this definition into three requirements: a liberal state is a state that demonstrates respect for democracy, human rights and the rule of law.[84] A state that does not demonstrate respect for all of these requirements will be regarded as a non-liberal state, thus being refused admission to the international community and considered illegitimate.[85] It is particularly important to stress here that just because a state is democratic does not mean that it is a member of the international community.[86] The international community is mindful of what Zakaria has termed 'illiberal

[82] UN Secretary-General Kofi Annan, *The Rule of Law and Transitional Justice in Conflict and Post-Conflict Societies*, UN Doc S/2004/616 (23 August 2004) para 6. The OSCE defined the rule of law in a similar way: 'the rule of law does not mean merely a formal legality which assures regularity and consistency in the achievement and enforcement of democratic order, but justice based on recognition and full acceptance of the supreme value of the human personality and guaranteed by institutions providing a framework for its fullest expression': Document of the Copenhagen Meeting of the Conference on the Human Dimension of the CSCE (29 June 1990) para 2. See generally S Golub, 'Make Justice the Organizing Principle of the Rule of Law Field' (2009) 1 *Hague Journal on the Rule of Law* 61.

[83] The UN Secretary-General defined liberal democracy as requiring 'the functioning of effective representative institutions. It means upholding fundamental principles – particularly the rule of law and respect for human rights. The rule of law – and its pre-eminent condition, equality before the law – is the platform upon which the edifice of democracy rests. Respect for human rights is vital for the democratic edifice to stand': Press Release, *Rule of Law and Human Rights are Vital for Democracy, Especially in Arab World*, SG/SM/9110/L/3045 (13 January 2004). See generally G Fox, *Humanitarian Occupation* (Cambridge, Cambridge University Press, 2008) ch 5 ('Constructing the Liberal State').

[84] See generally J d'Aspremont, 'Legitimacy of Governments in the Age of Democracy' (2006) 38 *NYU Journal of International Law and Politics* 877.

[85] Consider, for example, former British Prime Minister Gordon Brown's response to Zimbabwe's presidential election, which was widely regarded to be a sham: 'I believe we [the G8] have got to say they are an illegitimate regime [in Zimbabwe] because of the way they are holding power without an election that is seen as free and fair to anyone'. It is important to reflect upon the language employed by Brown. Significantly, Brown considered that the members of the G8 'have got to' dismiss the regime as illegitimate on the basis that its mandate to rule was not conferred via elections that could be regarded as free and fair: 'G8 Agrees to Zimbabwe Sanctions after Brown's Shock Tactics', *The Guardian* (8 July 2008), available at: www.guardian.co.uk/world/2008/jul/08/g8.zimbabwe.

[86] British Prime Minister David Cameron explains that 'democracy is not – and never has been – just about simply holding an election. It is not one person, one vote, once. It's about establishing the building blocks of democracy, the independence of the judiciary and the rule of law, with the majority prepared to defend the rights of the minority, the freedom of the media, a proper place for the army in society and the development of effective state institutions, political parties and wider civil society': D Cameron, Statement to 67th Session of the UN General Assembly (26 September 2012), available at: www.fco.gov.uk/en/news/latest-news/?view=PressS&id=816006082.

democracies'.[87] A state can be democratic, but nevertheless non-liberal. In order to be regarded as liberal a democratic state must in addition demonstrate respect for human rights and provide an independent and impartial judicial system so that these rights can be enforced.

A good illustration of members of the international community dismissing a state as illegitimate on the basis that it did not demonstrate respect for liberal democratic standards is in relation to the situation that unfolded in Libya in 2011. Inspired by the Arab Spring (as it has become known), citizens across Libya engaged in large-scale protests in favour of democratic reform. The then Head of State, Colonel Muammar Gaddafi, refused to stand down and fiercely resisted democratic change, engaging in a prolonged and bloody campaign against those that were considered hostile to the government. As the violence intensified (and with war crimes and crimes against humanity being reported),[88] members of the international community dismissed Gaddafi's regime as illegitimate and instead recognised the Transitional National Council (TNC) as the legitimate authority (government) in Libya. In the words of US Secretary of State Hilary Clinton, '[t]he United States views the Qaddafi regime as no longer having any legitimate authority in Libya'. Accordingly, she explained, 'I am announcing today that, until an interim authority is in place, the United States will recognize the TNC as the legitimate governing authority for Libya, and we will deal with it on that basis'.[89] Indeed, many other states adopted a similar position, dismissing the Gaddafi government as illegitimate and instead recognising the authority of the TNC.[90]

Significantly, whilst the international society is represented formally through the UN where its core principles are codified in the UN Charter, the international community exists informally and in abstraction because its members have not produced a formal institution or constitutive document that clearly differentiates between liberal (legitimate) states and non-liberal (illegitimate) states.[91] This does not mean, however, that the

[87] F Zakaria, 'The Rise of Illiberal Democracies' (1997) 76 *Foreign Affairs* 22.

[88] 'Libya Conflict: UN Accuses both sides of War Crimes', *BBC News* (1 June 2011), available at: www.bbc.co.uk/news/world-africa-13622965.

[89] Reported in *The National* (15 July 2011) available at: www.thenational.ae/news/world/africa/world-powers-including-us-declare-qaddafi-government-illegitimate.

[90] See the statement by the Chair of the Libya Contact Group, a committee of 30 states concerned at the increasing violence in Libya at: www.mfa.gov.tr/fourth-meeting-of-the-libya-contact-group-chair_s-statement_-15-july-2011_-istanbul.en.mfa ('The Contact Group reaffirmed that the Qaddafi regime no longer has any legitimate authority in Libya and that Qaddafi and certain members of his family must go. Henceforth and until an interim authority is in place, participants agreed to deal with the National Transitional Council (NTC) as the legitimate governing authority in Libya').

[91] 'While on the formal diplomatic sense no change has been made in the conditions for international recognition, informally there now operates a set of principles that justify a more restrictive concept of international society': Clark (n 18) at 159.

international community is a falsity or fabrication.[92] In particular, that liberal states are prepared to thoroughly examine the political quality of other states and distinguish between liberal and non-liberal standards is particularly evident from the practice of regional international organisations. In this sense, these regional organisations have become the formal institutionalisation of the international community at the regional level. The European Union (EU) provides a paradigmatic example of an international organisation that articulates a liberal standard of legitimate statehood within its region. Historically, a state could gain admission to the EU (or the European Economic Council, as it then was) on the basis of geographical location. Any European state could become a member.[93] However, with the end of the Cold War the admission criteria underwent considerable change. In 1992 the Treaty on European Union declared that the EU was an association for members 'whose systems of government are founded on the principles of democracy'[94] and demonstrated respect for fundamental freedoms.[95] In Copenhagen in 1993 the European Council, in relation to membership applications from countries in Central and Eastern Europe, outlined in more detail the characteristics that a prospective state must exhibit in order to gain entry to the EU. The Council required that any prospective Member State demonstrate that it had established stable institutions guaranteeing democracy, the rule of law, human rights and the respect for and protection of minority rights. In addition, an applicant state needed to possess a functioning market economy that could cope with competitive pressures and market forces within the Union.[96] Importantly, these criteria are now contained in the Treaty on European Union (TEU), as amended by the Treaty of Lisbon 2007. Article 6 TEU now provides that

> the Union is founded on the values of respect for human dignity, freedom, democracy, quality, the rule of law and respect for human rights, including the rights of persons belonging to minorities. These values are common to the Member States in a society in which pluralism, non-discrimination, tolerance, justice, solidarity and equality between women and men prevail.

[92] As the UN Secretary-General explained, 'some people say the international community is a fiction. Others say it is too elastic a concept to have any real meaning . . . I believe these sceptics are wrong. The international community does exist. It has an address. It has achievements to its credit': UN Secretary-General Kofi Annan, *Meaning of International Community*, Address to DPI/NGO Conference, Press Release SG/SM/7133, PI/1176 (15 September 1999).

[93] Article 237 Treaty of Rome 1957.

[94] Article F1 Treaty on European Union 1992.

[95] ibid, Article F2.

[96] To access the admission criteria outlined by the European Council visit: europa.eu/rapid/pressReleasesAction.do?reference=DOC/93/3&format=HTML&aged=1&language=EN&guiLanguage=en.

Article 49 TEU provides that '[a]ny European State which respects the values set out in Article 6(1) may apply to become a member of the Union'. Before they can be admitted to the EU, candidate states are subjected to considerable examination to ensure compliance with these standards.[97]

Importantly, the EU allows for suspension of the rights enjoyed by Member States if their adherence to liberal democracy wanes. In particular, Article 7 TEU provides a controlling mechanism in case a Member State violates the principles contained within Article 6(1). Article 7(2) and 7(3) provides that the Council of Ministers, after finding that a Member State has committed a serious and persistent breach of the rules relating to the EU (such as Article 6(1)), can suspend membership rights of Member States.[98] Significantly, the powers of the EU to suspend Member States that deviate from its liberal values came into focus in 2000 when the right-wing Freedom Party formed part of a coalition government in Austria. In particular, the leader of the Party, Jorg Haidar, caused particular concern.

> Haidar ha[d] been closely linked with the Nazi past and ha[d] publicly spoken of his approval of a number of aspects related to the Nazi regime. He ha[d] also taken a blatantly racist anti-foreigner stance in many of his policy statements as the governor of Carinthia.[99]

This included referring to Nazi concentration camps as 'punishment centres', praising Hitler's 'orderly employment policies' and declaring Waffen SS veterans as 'decent men of character'.[100] In response, both European and non-European liberal states quickly condemned Austria's deviation from liberal standards, downgrading or terminating their relations with the right-wing coalition government. Such actions clearly illustrate that these states (members of the international community) regarded Austria as placing itself outside the legitimate boundaries of the international community.[101]

Interestingly, the EU did not invoke Article 7 TEU and suspend Austria from the EU. However, this can be explained on the basis that EU considered that suspending Austria would not be effective because it 'simply removes the recalcitrant member from the very pressures of general opinion which . . . are perhaps the best means of securing a return to fulfilment

[97] See for example the considerable scrutiny that Romania and Bulgaria were subjected to before they were permitted admission to the EU: ec.europa.eu/enlargement/pdf/key_documents/2006/sept/report_bg_ro_2006_en.pdf.

[98] Article 7 TEU, as amended by the Treaty of Lisbon 2007.

[99] R Burchill, 'The Promotion and Protection of Democracy by Regional Organization in Europe: The Case of Austria' (2001) 7 *European Public Law* 79, 80.

[100] Quoted in M Happold, 'Fourteen Against One: The EU member States' Response to the Freedom Party Participation in the Austrian Government' (2000) 49 *ICLQ* 953, 955.

[101] For the international condemnation of this right-wing coalition see *Keesing's Record of World Events* 43223, 43373.

of obligations'.[102] Although the EU did not formally suspend Austria from the organisation, the EU organs were nevertheless unequivocal in their condemnation of Austria, informing Austria that it had violated the liberal principles upon which the EU was premised and had thus de facto placed itself outside of the legitimate boundaries of the organisation.[103] The European Parliament, for example, declared its 'concern to defend common European values' and called upon the Commission and the Council to monitor developments in Austria and be prepared to use their powers to suspend Austria in the event that the government took action that resulted in a serious breach of the principles of freedom, democracy and respect for human rights.[104] Indeed, the External Affairs Commissioner of the Commission stated that the 'EU is an organisation of rules and treaties, and we in the Commission act as the guardian . . . of that legal framework'.[105]

The EU is not the only example of a regional organisation that is now prepared to restrict its membership to liberal states only. The Council of Europe also provides a good example of a regional organisation imposing a strict admission test that requires prospective (and current) member states to demonstrate respect for human rights, democracy and the rule of law.[106] Indeed, like the EU the Council of Europe also possesses the power to suspend members from its association where they violate liberal democratic standards.[107] NATO provides yet another example of a regional organisation whose membership criteria are dominated by the requirement to demonstrate respect for liberal democracy. At its creation in 1949, NATO did not refer to any political standards in order for a member to be admitted.[108] However, in the 1995 Study on NATO Enlargement and the 1999 Membership Action Plan NATO unambiguously stated that all its members (both future and current) must dedicate themselves to protecting individual liberty, which requires respect for human rights, the rule of

[102] P Sands and P Klein (eds), *Bowett's Law of International Institutions*, 5th edn (London, Sweet & Maxwell, 2001) 551.

[103] Independently of the EU, the EU's 14 Member States did however impose their own sanctions against Austria. See generally Happold, 'Fourteen Against One' (n 100).

[104] See 'Austria – Haider's Views Condemned', *European Parliament, Daily Notebook* (3 February 2000)

[105] Quoted in Happold (n 100) at 957.

[106] See Article 3 of the Statute of the Council of Europe, which provides that '[e]very member of the Council of Europe must accept the principles of the rule of law and of the enjoyment by all persons within its jurisdiction of human rights and fundamental freedoms'. In 1993 the Heads of Government at Vienna expanded Article 3 by requiring that members adhere to 'democracy, the rule of law and respect for human rights'.

[107] Article 8 Statute of the Council of Europe.

[108] Under Article 10 of the North Atlantic Treaty 'any other European State in a position to further the principles of this Treaty and [who can] contribute to the security of the North Atlantic area can accede to this Treaty'.

law and democracy.[109] In addition, the Commonwealth provides yet another example of an international organisation that is only prepared to accept liberal states into its association. The Commonwealth is also an example of a transnational organisation open to those states that are former colonies of the British Empire or at least have a direct constitutional link to the British Empire. However, in the post-Cold War era this organisation has asserted that, in addition to being a former colony or exhibiting a direct constitutional link to the British Empire, only those states that demonstrate a commitment to human rights, the rule of law and democracy can be members. In 1991 the member states signed the Harare Declaration which stated that:

> [h]aving reaffirmed the principles to which the Commonwealth is committed, and reviewed the problems and challenges which the world, and the Commonwealth as part of it, face, we pledge the Commonwealth and our countries to work with renewed vigour, concentrating especially in the following areas:
>
> the protection and promotion of the fundamental political values of the Commonwealth:
>
> democracy, democratic processes and institutions which reflect national circumstances, the rule of law and the independence of the judiciary, just and honest government;
>
> fundamental human rights, including equal rights and opportunities for all citizens regardless of race, colour, creed or political belief.

On numerous occasions since, the Commonwealth has reaffirmed that it is an organisation predicated upon respect for liberal values.[110] Indeed, that this is a Commonwealth committed to upholding liberal democracy is clearly revealed by the Commonwealth's decision to suspend several states from the association on the basis of their failure to adhere to liberal standards. In 1995 Nigeria was suspended because of the use of lethal force against environmental supporters. Fiji was suspended in 1987 and in

[109] See generally R Müllerson, 'NATO Enlargement and the NATO-Russian Founding Act: The Interplay of Law and Politics' (1998) 47 *ICLQ* 174. It is important to note that Turkey is a member of both NATO and the Council of Europe. Historically, however, it has been denied entry to the EU, ostensibly on the grounds that it has failed to meet the requirements of Article 6 TEU. This appears strange considering the admission standards of the EU approximate largely to those of NATO and the Council of Europe. There are, as I see it, two possible explanations for this incongruity. First, the EU requires its members to satisfy economic criteria that NATO and the Council of Europe do not. Economic criteria, however, do not feature in Article 6 TEU (although they did in the earlier Copenhagen criteria). The second possible explanation is that EU states such as France and Germany block Turkey's membership irrespective of whether it exhibits a liberal identity because of discrete national interest concerns, such as the fear that EU law would pave the way for mass migration from Turkey.

[110] See for example The Commonwealth, Commonwealth Heads of Government Meeting: Final Communiqué (25 November 2007) para 4 and The Commonwealth, Affirmation of Commonwealth Values and Principles (29 November 2009).

2000 following military coups that overthrew elected governments. In 2009 Fiji was suspended again on the basis that the military government refused to hold democratic elections. Pakistan was suspended in 1999 after a military coup, with the Commonwealth declaring that 'no legitimacy shall be accorded to the military regime'.[111] In 2002 Zimbabwe was suspended following a report by election observers that the election could not be regarded as free and fair.[112]

Significantly, there are other non-Western international organisations that are also increasingly presenting liberal democracy as the only acceptable form of political governance. Consider, for example, the Organisation of American States (OAS) and the African Union (AU).[113] Article 3(g) of the Constitutive Act of the AU explains that the Union is founded upon 'respect for democratic principles, human rights, the rule of law and good governance'.[114] Similarly, the Charter for the OAS explains that it is an organisation that is based upon the principles of representative democracy and the protection of fundamental rights and freedoms.[115]

These declarations notwithstanding, it is nevertheless important to note that neither of these organisations formally stipulates that admission is dependent upon respect for liberal democracy. Any African state may become a member of the AU.[116] Similarly, any independent American state may become a member of the OAS.[117] This being said, both organisations do provide for the suspension of members. In this sense, suspension can act as a de facto admission test.

In this context it is important to note that in June 1991 the OAS Assembly passed Resolution 1080, which provided that in the case of 'sudden or irregular interruption of the democratic political institutional process or of the legitimate exercise of power by the democratically elected government in any of the Organization's member states' an emergency meeting of OAS organs could be convened.[118] In short, under Resolution 1080 the Permanent Council may call a meeting of the Ministers of Foreign Affairs which can then take decisions in relation to the matter in question, but do not have the power to impose sanctions. For example, Resolution 1080 was engaged in response to the overthrow of the democratic regime in Haiti in 1991. The Ministers for Foreign Affairs called upon OAS members

[111] Durban Communiqué, 1999 Commonwealth Heads of Government Meeting (12–15 November 1999).

[112] In 2003 Zimbabwe withdrew from the Commonwealth.

[113] The Association for South East Asian States (ASEAN) and the Organisation of Islamic Conference (OIC) would also fall into this category.

[114] Article 4(m) Constitutive Act of the AU (signed 11 July 2000, Lome, Togo).

[115] Charter of the OAS (signed Bogota, 1948), Article 3, sections d) (representative democracy) and l) (human rights).

[116] Article 29 Constitutive Act of the AU.

[117] Chapter III Charter of the OAS.

[118] OAS Doc AG/RES.1080 (XXI-0/91). Although note that this resolution only permits the calling of an emergency meeting, and does not prescribe any particular course of action.

to suspend diplomatic relations with the military government, sever their economic, financial and commercial ties with Haiti and to recognise the representatives of the democratically elected President Aristide.[119] However, under Resolution 1080 there was no power for the OAS to suspend Haiti from membership. Significantly, this position was changed in 1992 with the signing of the Washington Protocol. This Protocol amended Article 9 of the OAS Charter to provide that '[a] Member of the Organization whose democratically constituted government has been overthrown by force may be suspended from the exercise of the right to participate in the sessions of the Assembly'. Moreover, in 2001 the OAS adopted the Inter-American Democratic Charter, with Article 1 declaring that '[t]he peoples of the Americas have a right to democracy and their governments have an obligation to promote and defend it'. Importantly, Article 20 of this Charter explains that where there is 'an unconstitutional alteration of the constitutional regime that seriously impairs the democratic order' of a member state, the 'Secretary General may request the immediate convocation of the Permanent Council to undertake a collective assessment of the situation and to take such decisions as it deems appropriate'. If decisions by the Permanent Council under Article 20 prove ineffective, Article 21 then provides the General Assembly with the power to suspend the state. Article 21 has only been formally engaged on one occasion by the OAS, which was in relation to the overthrow of the democratic regime in the Republic of Honduras in 2009, resulting in Honduras being suspended from the OAS.[120]

However, despite the OAS's willingness to both implement and engage these various procedures, it is notable that they have only been used in response to severe interruptions to pre-existing democratic procedures. The OAS has not employed these procedures in response to existing members that are constituted upon a non-democratic basis or where human rights abuses have been committed.[121] As one study explains, the OAS 'has tended to use these instruments only for the most extreme cases of democratic interruption, such as coups and *autogolpes*, and never directly in relation to violations of electoral or constitutional procedures'.[122]

In relation to the AU, Article 30 of the Constitutive Act does allow for a state to be suspended where the government has come to power via

[119] Support to the Democratic Government of Haiti, MRE Resolution 1/91, OAS Permanent Council, PEA/SER.F/V.1, OAS Doc MRE/RES 1/91 (1991). Resolution 1080 has since been invoked in order to respond to interruptions to democratic procedures in Peru (1992), Guatemala (1993) and Paraguay (1996).

[120] See www.oas.org/en/media_center/press_release.asp?sCodigo=E-219/09.

[121] See generally J Leininger, 'Democracy and UN Peace-keeping – Conflict Resolution through State-Building and Democracy Promotion in Haiti' (2006) 10 *Max Planck UNYB* 465, 483 ff.

[122] T Legler, S Lean and D Doniface (eds), *Promoting Democracy in the Americas* (Baltimore MD, The Johns Hopkins University Press, 2007) 58. See Duxbury (n 32) at 177 ff.

unconstitutional means. Although 'unconstitutional means' is not defined in the Constitutive Act, a Declaration adopted on the same day as the Constitutive Act indicates that 'unconstitutional means' refers (and is limited to) a coup against a democratic state.[123] There is no indication that this suspension procedure relates to *currently* undemocratic states or in instances where human rights are being systematically violated.[124]

The creation of the Community of Democracies in June 2000 is also important in the context of the current discussion.[125] This is an association that is open to all those states within the world order that demonstrate respect for liberal democracy.[126] Failure to adhere to these standards will result in the state not being invited to the next meeting. Ostensibly, therefore, this Community appears to be the formal institutionalisation of the international community. However, notwithstanding the importance of the emergence of an international association of liberal states that clearly articulates liberal democracy as the only form of acceptable governance, this Community must be approached with caution. In practice, this Community has been prepared to admit members that quite obviously do not meet the liberal standards required in its various declarations.[127] To put the matter bluntly, the Community has failed to transform its political rhetoric into actual practice. 'The Community of Democracies launched in Warsaw in 2000 has far more relaxed admission criteria [than the international community], which is why its membership has included such countries as Afghanistan, Bahrain and Jordan'.[128] Similarly, Daalder and Lindsay suggest that

> [t]he great weakness of the Community of Democracies, an effort launched in Warsaw in 2000 to bring together countries 'committed' to democracy, is that it cast its net far too wide. Among the initial invitees were countries like Egypt,

[123] Declaration on the Framework for an OAU Response to Unconstitutional Changes of Government, AHG/Decl.5 (XXXVI) (1–12 July 2000). And this has indeed been confirmed by subsequent practice of the AU, which has only engaged Article 30 and suspended members where there has been a coup against a democratically elected regime.

[124] Article 4(h), however, provides the AU with the power to forcibly intervene in a member state where necessary to prevent the commission of war crimes.

[125] www.community-democracies.org/. See generally T Grant, 'A League of their Own: The Rationale for an International Alliance of Democracies' (2009) 41 *George Washington International Law Review* 243.

[126] The Warsaw Declaration stresses that this is a Community founded upon respect of all human rights (political, civil, economic, social and cultural), genuine accountability of the government through free and fair elections and the existence of independent and effective judicial systems: n 73. These principles have been restated on numerous occasions. See for example the 'Seoul Plan of Action' (12 November 2002) the 'Santiago Ministerial Commitment' (30 April 2005) and most recently the 'Vilnius Declaration' (1 July 2011).

[127] For example, Jordan, Algeria, Tunisia and Bangladesh were permitted to participate in the 2000 Warsaw summit and subsequently signed the resulting Warsaw Declaration.

[128] J Lindsay, 'The Case for a Concert of Democracies' (2009) 23 *Ethics and International Affairs* 5.

Qatar and Azerbaijan – where even a commitment to genuine democracy, let alone its practice, is lacking.[129]

All in all, although we have seen that the OAS, the AU and the Community of Democracies do not impose admission standards that require strict adherence to liberal democracy in the same way that the EU does, for example, the existence and practice of these organisations are still extremely important because they illustrate that greater emphasis (especially regionally but also more broadly) is now being placed upon the protection of liberal values and, to this end, that legitimate statehood is being increasingly equated with liberal statehood.

3.2 Illegitimacy and the Denial of Sovereignty

According to the explanatory framework that I have constructed, the international community represents an association of liberal states that has become increasingly prepared to recognise only liberal states as legitimate; non-liberal states are proscribed admission to the international community and dismissed as illegitimate.[130]

Perhaps more importantly, however, non-liberal states also become vulnerable to being 'stripped of their internationally recognized rights'.[131] For the international community, entitlement to full sovereign rights is conditional upon a state's liberal identity. Thus, 'societies that do not honour Western liberal practices regarding governance and rights are legitimate targets of reformative international action'.[132] Indeed, I suggest that the international community has engaged in a campaign for liberal development, seeking to promulgate its liberal values to non-liberal states, encouraging them to adopt liberal democratic standards of governance.[133] What is therefore happening is that

[129] I Daalder and J Lindsay, 'Democracies of the World, Unite' (March/April 2007) 2 *The American Interest* 5.

[130] 'Non-liberal states thus represent "the other" and are the dividing line between membership of the international community and exclusion; a "community" does not only possess an inside aspect, but also presupposes an outside, an environment against which it defines and delineates its identity': B Simma and A Paulus, 'The "International Community": Facing the Challenge of Globalization' (1998) 9 *European Journal of International Law* 266, 268.

[131] B Barber, *Fear's Empire: War, Terrorism and Democracy* (New York, WW Norton & Company, 2003) 106.

[132] S MacFarlane, *Intervention in Contemporary World Politics* (Oxford, Oxford University Press, 2002) 79.

[133] In 1993 the US National Security Advisor Anthony Lake explained that within US national strategy the policy of containment had been replaced by 'a strategy of enlargement . . . of the world's free community of market democracies': A Lake, *From Containment to Enlargement* (21 September 1993), available at: www.mtholyoke.edu/acad/intrel/lakedoc.html.

> a core of like-minded, democratic, free-market-orientated nations is building norms and rules to govern their own behaviour as well as imposing those rules on, and trying to bring into their own number, the still developing or still-unfree 'peripheral' states'. Pursuant to this campaign, the core dispenses with sovereignty when it 'is enforcing one of its rules on the periphery.[134]

As this book progresses I will discuss, inter alia, the international community's intervention in Somalia, Haiti, Bosnia, Kosovo, East Timor, Sierra Leone, Afghanistan, Iraq and Libya, and submit these as examples of the international community's intervention in a state's internal affairs in order to promote respect for democracy, human rights and the rule of law. The *telos* of the international community is thus to construct a world that comprises exclusively liberal states.[135] In chapter three I discuss the reasons why the international community has redefined sovereignty and why it has sought to promote its liberal values to non-liberal states. Briefly, however, I argue that the international community's commitment to liberal democracy can be explained on the basis that it considers that international peace and security can be only maintained between liberal states.

It is important to highlight that only non-liberal states become legitimate targets for reformative action by the international community. What I am suggesting here is that whilst liberal states have demonstrated a consistent trend of denigrating non-liberal states as illegitimate this does not necessarily mean that they will be subject to a campaign by the international community for their liberal reformation. Thus, it does not necessarily follow that as a conceptual tool the doctrine of the international community is somehow weakened because its international defence of liberal values appears sporadic and inconsistent. What is required is that we clearly distinguish between the will of the international community in its normative and operational form.[136] The normative refers to the international community's perception of non-liberal states (or their governments) as ideologically inferior, as *illegitimate*. In its normative capacity, the will of the international community is generally consistent, ie that states failing to respect liberal democratic standards are considered illegitimate.[137]

[134] M Mazarr, 'George W. Bush, Idealist' (2003) 79 *International Affairs* 503. 507.

[135] As the Vienna Declaration explains, the objective of the international community is to 'support the strengthening and promoting of democracy, development and respect for human rights and fundamental freedoms in the entire world': 1993 Vienna Declaration and Plan of Action, 8, A/CONF.157/23 (12 July 1993) para 8.

[136] N Tsagourias, 'The Will of the International Community as a Normative Source of International Law' in I Dekker and W Werner (eds), *Governance and International Legal Theory* (Leiden, Martinus Nijhoff, 2004) 120.

[137] As former British Prime Minister Tony Blair explained, '[w]hat amazes me is how many people are happy for Saddam to stay. They ask why we don't get rid of Mugabe, why not the Burmese lot. Yes, let's get rid of them all. I don't because I can't, but when you can, you should': quoted in P Stothard, *Thirty Days: Tony Blair and the Test of History* (New York, Harper Collins, 2003) 42.

In its operational form, however, it is not always possible for the normative will of international community to be 'translated into material action because the capacity of producing will and the capacity of exercising it are not always conterminous'.[138] Evidently, there is a plethora of practical obstacles that precludes a sustained global campaign for the liberal reformation of all non-liberal states;[139] operationally, this is impossible. Once these practical restraints are recognised, then, it becomes apparent that the international community must prioritise when committing its resources to reformative action against non-liberal states. For the normative will of the international community to be translated into material action a state must be not only non-liberal (illegitimate) but must also qualify as criminal, delinquent, or rogue,[140] whereby it exhibits characteristics that single it out as being of special concern. In chapter three I 'zero in' on what factors render a non-liberal state of special concern and thus make it a priority for liberal reformative action.

3.3 Disintegration of the International Community: Iraq 2003

The defining feature of the international community is its determination to promote liberal values to non-liberal states. However, because the international community has not institutionalised its association no centralised decision-making procedure has been established that allows for decisions to be taken by, and thus imputed to, the international community as a whole. Decisions relating to the promotion of its liberal values, such as which non-liberal states should be prioritised for reformative action and how the reformative action is to be conducted (which sanctions to deploy, when they should be deployed, how they should be deployed etc), are therefore taken by liberal regional organisations (such as the EU) or unilaterally by individual liberal states (or as multilateral action by ad hoc alliances of willing liberal states). However, where liberal states intervene in a non-liberal state in order to promote respect for liberal values, for the action to be considered legitimate other liberal states (the community as a whole) must provide at least 'hypothetical consent'[141] to the action. This is because 'the very fact of membership empowers those

[138] Tsagourias, 'The Will of the International Community' in Dekker and Werner (eds), *Governance and International Legal Theory* (n 136) at 120.

[139] Not least because the reconstruction of autocratic states upon a liberal democratic basis is a protracted and costly process, to which the recent peacebuilding missions in Afghanistan and Iraq are testament.

[140] R Litwak, *Rogue States and US Foreign Policy: Containment after the Cold War* (Baltimore MD, The Johns Hopkins University Press, 2000).

[141] N Tsagourias, 'International Community, Recognition of States and Political Cloning' in C Warbrick and S Tierney (eds), *Towards an International Legal Community?* (London, British Institute of International and Comparative Law, 2006) 213.

included in it to contribute to the shaping of a shared destiny'.[142] Thus, it is the arrival at, and the adherence to, a consensus which enable unilateral or multilateral actions to be legitimated and attributed to the 'political consciousness'[143] of the community, which is then perceived to act on the international plane as a bona fide community with a shared feeling of collective destiny. Indeed, it was precisely this agreement amongst liberal states that clothed NATO's intervention in Kosovo with community legitimacy. However, what if this consensual position cannot be achieved? What if internal disagreements cannot be reconciled yet individual members nevertheless act unilaterally without the support of the community members? Does this have a pernicious impact upon the community, or at least indicate that the community is a 'chimera',[144] a 'fictitious conceptual entity'[145] employed by states in a vain attempt to legitimise unilateral actions?[146]

Significantly, it was this notion of consensus that was so manifestly absent from the United States and the United Kingdom's decision to invade Iraq in 2003. This fuelled claims that the international community, which had reacted collectively to events in Kosovo and Afghanistan, had disintegrated. Cox notes that

> [a] few years ago, it was normal to refer to something called the West: liberal theorists could also talk (and did) about a 'security community'. Today, it is doubtful whether we can talk of either with the same degree of confidence.[147]

However, this deduction is based on a misunderstanding of the community dynamic. Instead, it must be recognised that the notion of community does not imply a zero sum game. As Tsagourias rightly identifies, '[c]ommunity

[142] R Beiner, *What's the Matter with Liberalism?* (Berkeley CA, University of California Press, 1992) 105. In this sense, '[G]*emeinschaft* [community] is an aim in itself; *Gesellschaft* [society] serves the individual purposes of its members. Community is prior to its members; society is subordinate to their interests'; A Paulus, 'The Influence of the United States on the Concept of the International Community' in M Byers and G Nolte (eds), *United States Hegemony and the Foundations of International Law* (Cambridge, Cambridge University Press 2003) 62.

[143] B Cronin, *Community under Anarchy: Transnational Identity and the Evolution of Cooperation* (New York, Columbia University Press, 1999) 4.

[144] Tsagourias (n 136) at 116.

[145] P Allot, 'The True Function of Law in the International Community' (1998) 5 *Journal of Global Legal Studies* 391, 411.

[146] Paulus questions whether 'the use of the term "international community" serves nothing but the rhetorical purpose of masking the pursuit of power': Paulus, 'The Influence of the United States on the Concept of the International Community' in Byers and Nolte (eds), *United States Hegemony* (n 142) at 63.

[147] M Cox, 'Beyond the West? Terror in Transatlantica' (2005) 11 *European Journal of International Relations* 203, 209. See generally J Anderson, GJ Ikenberry and T Risse (eds), *The End of the West? Crisis and Change in the Atlantic Order* (Ithaca NY, Cornell University Press, 2008). Rather, the world order is subject to a hegemonic power, namely the US; or, according to Hardt and Negri's neo-Marxist critique of international relations, a US-led transnational bourgeoisie that comprises powerful corporations and international organisations: M Hardt and A Negri, *Empire* (Cambridge MA, Harvard University Press, 2000)).

does not mean pure and total conformity'.[148] Where the community is composed of separate physical units, each with their own independent government responsible for its polity, states may have particular national interests which cannot be reconciled through mediation and community politics. Certain national interests may be sufficiently strong that unilateral action is considered necessary. The disagreement over the Kyoto Protocol, the Israel-Palestinian dispute and the International Criminal Court are prime examples in this context. Consequently, it is important to realise that where members act without a consensual position being formed, the corollary is not the demise of the community. Rather, what is essential is that we clearly identify the *nature* and *extent* of the disagreement and any subsequent *corrective* action that may confirm the member's commitment to the community ideal and thus the integrity of the community as a whole. It is these issues that are pertinent to our discussion of the invasion of Iraq in 2003.

Whether because of its heinous Ba'ath regime, its waging of aggressive wars against its neighbours, the attempted annexation of Kuwait, the brutal treatment of its own nationals, or the duplicity that it exhibited towards the UN, 'for over a decade Iraq has been the indispensable pariah of the international system'.[149] With this in mind, it is unsurprising that in the period leading up to invasion of Iraq in 2003 there was widespread agreement over the threat that Iraq posed to international peace and security, not just within the international community but also within the international society.[150] As UN Security Council Resolution 1441 (8 November 2001) made clear, Iraq would continue to pose a threat until UN weapons inspectors could confirm that Saddam Hussein was no longer in possession of weapons capable of mass destruction (biological, chemical and nuclear weapons).[151] Despite the comprehensive inspection regimes established under Resolution 1441, the US and the UK (prominent members of the international community) became increasingly disillusioned with the lack of effective progress being made by the weapons inspectors, which was accredited largely to the lack of Iraqi cooperation.[152] The consequence

[148] Tsagourias (n 136) at 116.

[149] N Tsagourias, 'The Shifting Laws on the Use of Force and the Trivialization of the UN Collective Security System: The Need to Reconstitute It' (2003) XXXIV *Netherlands Yearbook of International Law* 55, 56. See generally D Malone, *The International Struggle over Iraq: Politics in the United Nations Security Council 1980-2005* (New York, Oxford University Press, 2006).

[150] D McGoldrick, *From '9-11' to the Iraq War 2003: International Law in an Age of Complexity* (Oxford, Hart Publishing, 2004) ch 4.

[151] In 1988 Saddam Hussein used biological and chemical weapons against Iraqi Kurds in Halabja.

[152] As former British Prime Minister Tony Blair explained, 'it is actually an 11-year history: a history of UN will flouted, of lies told by Saddam about the existence of his chemical, biological and nuclear weapons programmes, and of obstruction, defiance and denial': T Blair, *Iraq and Weapons of Mass Destruction*, Statement to the House of Commons (24 September 2002), available at: www.publications.parliament.uk/pa/cm200102/cmhansrd/vo020924/debtext/20924-01.htm.

of Iraqi obfuscation was that the US and the UK inferred that Iraq continued to possess prohibited weapons,[153] concluding that military intervention was necessary to disarm Iraq and neutralise the threat that it posed. Although the use of military force was deplored by members of the international society, significantly, it was also resisted by members of the international community. In particular, France and Germany voiced strong disapproval of the proposed military intervention, instead preferring to continue with diplomatic procedures, allowing the weapons inspectors more time to complete their inspections, waiting for independent verification of weapons of mass destruction before military intervention could be considered. Irrespective of this disagreement, the US and the UK refused to wait and commenced hostilities against Iraq on 21 March 2003 (although it was the US which spearheaded the attack and, throughout the campaign, possessed strategic control).[154]

Both politically and academically, this division was considered to be the product of 'deep disagreement' within the international community,[155] reflective of 'two visions of the world order'.[156] Indeed, Kagan suggested that 'these disagreements reflected more than just differing tactical and analytical assessments of the situation in Iraq . . . The differences over Iraq were not only about policy. They were also about first principles'.[157] For Kagan, the conclusion is self-evident: any notion of community propounded in the years preceding Iraq had demised when the invasion commenced, being replaced by a US hegemony no longer constrained by the need to mediate its proposed conduct consensually within the community. To this end, the US no longer considers itself subject to authority outside its own domestic institutions and has become 'unfettered except by its own sense of restraint'.[158]

However, I submit that this conclusion derives from an erroneous analysis of the nature and extent of the disagreement. Rather than being a 'deep disagreement' pertaining to the core principles of the international community ie commitment to, and the promotion of, liberal values, the disagreement was instead rather more superficial, focused upon the necessity of military force, and thus can be explained on the basis of *personal physical*

[153] According to Blair, 'Iraq has chemical and biological weapons, that Saddam Hussein has continued to produce them, that he has existing and active military plans for the use of chemical and biological weapons, which could be activated within 45 minutes . . . and that he is actively trying to acquire nuclear weapons capability': ibid.

[154] Indeed, the German Foreign Minister Joschka Fischer asked whether the other coalition members 'can have or ever did have any influence at all': quoted in R Kagan, 'America's Crisis of Legitimacy' (2004) 83 *Foreign Affairs* 65, 83.

[155] ibid at 65.

[156] Address by French Foreign Minister of Affairs Dominique de Villepin (19 March 2003), quoted in Kagan (n 154).

[157] Kagan, 'America's Crisis of Legitimacy' (n 154) at 67.

[158] ibid at 70.

security. It must be appreciated that within the international community each member has its own physical dominion for which primary responsibility remains with the government. Thus, whilst an attack on a community member will represent a wider attack on the values for which that member (and thus the community) epitomises, the *principal* victim will be the individual state which is attacked because it will endure the material, physical damage that is inflicted. This is particularly relevant in relation to the US, which had already been the victim of a catastrophic terrorist attack (9/11) and the direct recipient of further threats; in short, 'because America was No. 1, they were target No. 1'.[159] From the perspective of national security, therefore, the US could not afford to wait whilst the weapons inspectors pursued their investigations: for the US, the only inference that could be drawn from Iraq's lack of transparency in relation to the weapons inspectors was that it actually possessed weapons of mass destruction, and that such weapons would be aimed directly at the them (indeed, this threat was compounded because of Saddam Hussein's history of waging aggressive wars and using chemical and biological weapons). For Europeans, however, they 'never fully shared Washington's concerns about WMD in Iraq . . . [because] they do not believe that those weapons will be aimed at them'.[160] States such as France and Germany could afford to wait for the weapons inspectors to complete their task because, even if Iraq did possess such weapons, if they were to be used they would not be used against them. To this end, 'the community cannot expect America to exercise self-restraint . . . if the community trivializes the risks, costs and dangers that inhere in the US leadership role'.[161]

Kagan's contention, then, that the US and Europeans represented 'two peoples living on separate strategic and ideological planets'[162] fails to adequately capture the nature of the disagreement. This misunderstanding is then perpetuated when Kagan suggests the demise of the transatlantic alliance (and presumably the international community). Instead, it is clear that the responses by the US and dissenting community members were motivated by, and remained committed to, the same ideology. Thus, whilst the failure to reach consensus prevented the invasion being 'legitimated' by the community, where the community acted in unity against a common adversary, its sense of shared identity was nevertheless preserved and so any relations damaged by the disagreement were capable of rehabilitation. Indeed, we can look to post-conflict reconstruction of Iraq, where the community members united over its liberal design, as providing an important

159 F Zakaria, 'Our Way: The Trouble with Being the World's Only Superpower', *The New Yorker* (14–15 October 2002).

160 Kagan (n 154) at 69.

161 M Leffler, '9/11 and the Past and Future American Foreign Policy' (2003) 79 *International Affairs* 1054, 1062.

162 Kagan (n 154) at 65.

cathartic experience for the international community after the disagreement over the invasion.[163] In a telling paragraph Gersham explains:

> It is important to emphasise, though, that the Iraq debate was not about democracy promotion, but focused instead on the decision to use military force to end Saddam Hussein's regime, largely because it was suspected of having weapons of mass destruction that could threaten the United States. On the issue of helping Iraqis establish a democratic system following Saddam's removal from power, however, the consensus has held firm.[164]

4. CONCLUSION

The objective of this chapter has been to clearly distinguish between the international society and the international community, employing these concepts as descriptive tools to capture two differing conceptions of sovereign statehood that operate within the world order. The concept of the international society has been deployed in order to describe a legal framework based upon the legal principle of sovereign equality. I have suggested that with the end of the Second World War all states of the world order, determined to maintain their individual security and prevent the recurrence of another world war, subscribed to the legal principle that all states are sovereign equals and entitled to determine their internal affairs without external intervention irrespective of their political constitution. By requiring mutual abstention this regulatory framework would enable the maintenance of international peace and security.

With the end of the Cold War, however, an international community of liberal states has emerged within this pluralist international society. For this international community 'it is not enough to have the corporate identity of a state' but it must also 'conform to type identity criteria which define only certain forms of state as legitimate'.[165] For liberal states, therefore, since the end of the Cold War it is liberal democracy that has become 'the only model of governance with any broad ideological legitimacy and appeal in the world';[166] only those states that exhibit respect for human rights, the rule of law and democracy are considered legitimate.[167] More

[163] B Buzan and A Gonzalez-Pelaez, 'International Community after Iraq' (2005) 81 *International Affairs* 31.

[164] C Gersham, 'Democracy as Policy Goal and Universal Value' (2005) 6 *The Whitehead Journal of Diplomacy and International Relations* 19, 19–20.

[165] A Wendt, *A Social Theory of International Politics* (Cambridge, Cambridge University Press 1999) 291.

[166] L Diamond, J Linz and S Lipset (eds), *Politics in Developing Countries: Contemporary Experiences with Democracy*, 2nd edn (Boulder CO, Lynne Rienner, 1995) x.

[167] Thus, in contrast to the international society where there are 'no barbarians, savages, infidels, or pagans standing outside', the international community demonstrates a visible trend towards exclusion, where non-liberal states are 'typically deprecated as rogue states . . . little more than international outlaws': W Bain, 'The Political Theory of Trusteeship and the Twilight of International Equality' (2003) 17 *International Relations* 59, 71.

importantly, as only liberal states are legitimate, only liberal states are considered sovereign. Non-liberal illegitimate states become vulnerable to being denied sovereignty and the protection this confers against external intervention. Indeed, motivated by the liberal peace thesis, I have suggested that the international community embraces a desire to promulgate its liberal values to non-liberal states.

It is important to emphasise that the emergence of the international community has not resulted in the abandonment of the international society and its constitutive norms of sovereign equality and non-interference.[168] Non-liberal states continue to advocate these norms. The significance of this is that the contemporary world order is now composed of two distinct forms of state association, which I have termed the international society and the international community, which embrace conflicting understandings of what qualities a state must demonstrate in order to be regarded as sovereign. As Simpson explains, the consequence is that '[t]he global political order [is] now composed of enemies and friends, not sovereign equals'.[169] Indeed, it is the interface between these enemies and friends that can account for the current tensions that are experienced within the world order. Specifically, whilst the international society maintains that all states are sovereign equals and are entitled to determine their internal affairs without external intervention, the international community perceives non-liberal states of the international society as illegitimate and consequently strips them of their previously held internationally recognised sovereign rights, campaigning for their liberal reformation. I argue that it is this determination of the international community to steer non-liberal states towards liberal democracy that can account for why violations of international peace and security occur in the contemporary era.

[168] As Clark explains, '[w]hat we are witnessing is not so much an abandonment of international society per se. Instead, this [international community] amounts to an attempted invention of a more restricted international society to take the place of a universal one': Clark (n 18) at 187.

[169] Simpson, Great Powers and Outlaw States (n 55) at ix.

2

The Role of International Law in the International Society and the International Community

1. INTRODUCTION

THE MAXIM PROVIDES that *ubi societas, ubi jus*: where there is society, there is law. What this means is that by definition any association will comprise individual members that are bound together by a particular normative framework. It is their commitment to this normative framework that provides the members with a sense of collective identity; a sense of 'we-ness'. As the maxim indicates, somewhat necessarily, associations will create rules (regulatory frameworks) in order to protect and, in certain instances promote, their normative frameworks. In addition, rules will be both internal and external facing. Internal rules will relate to the identity that members must maintain, for example, or to the expected conduct of members. External rules will dictate how members interact with those excluded from the association. Certainly, these rules will differ in character between associations. Whilst one association may require rules to be formally passed through stipulated procedures and be written down in formal documents, other associations may construct rules more informally, having not passed through any formal procedure or been enshrined in a written document. But this absence of formality does not mean that such associations do not construct rules that seek to regulate the conduct of their members.

As international associations, the international society and the international community have produced rules in order to protect and promote their normative associations. In short, the international society has created rules in order to protect the sovereignty of its member states. The international community, on the other hand, has formulated rules that require the protection and promotion of fundamental human rights. With this in mind, the purpose of this chapter is to assess the role and impact that the regulatory frameworks established by the international society and international community have had (and, especially in the case of the international community, are having) upon international law; or to put the matter differently, an inquiry as to how the international society and the international community have used international law to protect and promote their own normative agendas. This will be achieved by identifying principles of international law and, on the basis of their content and character, demonstrating that they are expressions of the international society and the international community. In this sense, when the normative content of international legal rules map onto and mirror the normative frameworks embraced by the international society and the international community, these legal rules can be regarded as an expression of these associations and thus a product of them.[1]

Accordingly, this chapter will be structured as follows. In Section 2, I identify the principle of non-intervention and the prohibition on the threat or use of force as particularly important examples of international legal rules created by the international society in order to protect its normative association. In Section 3, I argue that the emergence of the international community since the end of the Cold War has had a dramatic impact upon the international legal framework formulated by the international society. In particular, that the international community has sought to adapt existing legal principles in order to allow for the protection and promotion of fundamental human rights, democracy and the rule of law. In this context I focus upon the changing scope of the principle of non-intervention and the prohibition on the threat or use of force since the end of the Cold War. In addition, I submit that the international community has created new legal rules in order to facilitate the protection of liberal values. Here I identify the emerging right to democratic governance in customary international law and the responsibility to protect doctrine. Section 4 will draw some conclusions.

2. THE INTERNATIONAL SOCIETY AND INTERNATIONAL LAW

As I already noted, the overriding objective of the international society is the maintenance of international peace and security. In order to achieve this objective the international society has created international legal principles such as the principle of state sovereignty and the sovereign equality of states. Importantly, the international society has sought to transplant these principles into concrete principles of international law. Given the (eventual) universality of the international society in the years following the end of the Second World War, this association has been successful in crafting an international legal framework that is able to protect the sovereignty of its member states. Indeed, and as the International Court of

[1] For a similar approach see R Müllerson, *Ordering Anarchy: International Law in International Society* (The Hague, Martinus Nijhoff, 2000) and AC Arend, *Legal Rules and International Society* (Oxford, Oxford University Press, 1999).

Justice (ICJ) has explained, the consequence is that 'the fundamental principle of State sovereignty, [is the basis] on which the whole of international law rests'.[2] For Cassese, '[t]he conclusion is therefore warranted that sovereign equality constitutes the linchpin of the whole body of international standards, the fundamental premise on which all international relations rest'.[3] In Fassbender's words the UN Charter, which has as its primary objective the protection of state sovereignty (and indeed represents the formal institutionalisation of the international society),[4] 'is the supporting frame of all international law and, at the same time, the highest layer in a hierarchy of norms of international law'.[5] In this sense, the principle of state sovereignty has become a constitutional norm of international law; as such, all other international laws are premised upon the principle of state sovereignty and are orientated towards its protection.[6] As Brus notes,

> [t]he national Sovereign state has constituted the backbone of the world order for a long time. International law as we know it today has been developed on the basis of this notion . . . [Thus] rules of international law, whether related to non-intervention, the use of force, economic cooperation, diplomatic and consular relations, or the functional cooperation through inter-governmental organizations, to mention just a few areas, have a reciprocated State interest [protecting state sovereignty] as their rationale.[7]

In light of this, in this section I focus my attention upon the principle of non-intervention and the prohibition against the threat or use of force, arguing that these can be regarded as particularly important examples of the international society utilising international law to protect state sovereignty and thereby achieve its objective of maintaining international peace and security.

[2] *Military and Paramilitary Activities in and against Nicaragua (Nicaragua v United States of America)* (1986) ICJ Rep at para 263.

[3] A Cassese, *International Law in a Divided World* (Oxford, Clarendon Press, 1989) 130.

[4] 'The Charter adopted in 1945 was only a slightly modified Westphalian model since its thrust was to consecrate the inviolability of the society of sovereign states': Müllerson, *Ordering Anarchy* (n 1) at 163–64.

[5] B Fassbender, 'The United Nations Charter as Constitution of the International Community' (1998) 36 *Columbia Journal of Transnational Law* 529, 585. The principle of sovereignty is described as 'the most basic axiomatic premise of the international order': C Tomuschat, 'Obligations Arising for States Without or Against their Will' (1993-IV) 241 *Recueil Des Cours* 195, 237.

[6] 'The sovereignty and equality of states represent the basic constitutional doctrine of [international law], which governs a community consisting primarily of states having a uniform legal personality': I Brownlie, *Principles of Public International Law*, 7th edn (Oxford, Oxford University Press, 2008) 289.

[7] M Brus, 'Bridging the Gap between State Sovereignty and International Governance: The Authority of Law' in G Kreijin (ed), *State, Sovereignty and International Governance* (Oxford, Oxford University Press, 2002) 3–4.

2.1 The Principle of Non-Intervention

Although the principle of non-intervention does not feature in the UN Charter, it is nevertheless 'part and parcel' of customary international law.[8] Indeed, the principle of non-intervention is a fundamentally important legal principle in the context of the international society and is regarded as the 'corollary' of the principle of the sovereign equality of states.[9] Quite explicitly, the principle of non-intervention 'is designed to ensure that each State respects the sovereignty of the other members of the community'.[10]

In order to protect state sovereignty, the scope of the non-intervention principle is impressively wide. In essence, the non-intervention principle means 'that what takes place within the boundaries of a state is nobody else's business, and that for one state to insert itself into the internal affairs of another is a hostile act'.[11]

The UN General Assembly has passed many resolutions dealing with the principle of non-intervention and has sought to define the scope of its application.[12] In the Friendly Relations Declaration (1970) the General Assembly explained that the principle of non-intervention means that

> [n]o State may use or encourage the use of economic, political or any other type of measures to coerce another State in order to obtain from it the subordination of the exercise of its sovereign rights and to secure from it advantages of any kind.[13]

Similarly, the ICJ has explained that a

> prohibited intervention must . . . be one bearing on matters in which each State is permitted, by the principle of State sovereignty, to decide freely. One of these is the choice of a political, economic, social and cultural system, and the formation of foreign policy. Intervention is wrongful when it uses methods of coercion in regard to such choices, which must remain free ones.[14]

Consequently, an act will constitute a prohibited intervention where two requirements are met. First, there must be the intentional application of

[8] *Nicaragua* (n 2) at para 202. As Judge Jennings explained in his dissenting opinion, '[t]here can be no doubt that the principle of non-intervention is an autonomous principle of customary law': para 534.

[9] 'The principle of non-intervention has been said to flow logically and inevitably from the doctrine of sovereignty': T Redmond, 'The Rules, And How they Were Broken: The Changing Face of State Sovereignty' (2002) 10 *Irish Student Law Review* 50.

[10] Cassese, *International Law in a Divided World* (n 3) at 143

[11] R Haas, *Intervention: The Use of American Military Force in the Post-Cold War World* (Washington DC, Brookings Institution Press, 1999) 12.

[12] For a discussion of the impact of these resolutions see M Jamnejad and M Wood, 'The Principle of Non-Intervention' (2009) 22 *Leiden Journal of International Law* 345, 349 ff.

[13] GA Res 2625 (24 October 1970).

[14] *Nicaragua* (n 2) at para 205.

coercion: 'the essence of intervention is coercion . . . [o]nly acts of a certain magnitude are likely to qualify as "coercive", and only those that are intended to force a policy change in the target state will contravene the principle'.[15] In this sense, what is key is to distinguish between the mere exertion of influence (which, although perhaps unfriendly, is not unlawful) and the imposition of real coercion.[16]

Secondly, once the application of coercion is established, it must relate to a matter that the state is freely entitled to determine itself. Clearly, this requirement has the potential to severely restrict the scope of protection afforded by the non-intervention principle. If international law narrowly defines those areas that states are freely entitled to determine themselves, the scope of the non-intervention principle would be contracted and ultimately fail to adequately protect state sovereignty.

Importantly, this issue was dealt with by the ICJ in the *Nicaragua* judgment in 1986. In this case the ICJ had to determine whether the principle of non-intervention had been violated in relation to the US's support for internal opposition groups operating in Nicaragua. In essence, this required the ICJ to determine whether customary international law had evolved to the extent that it was recognised that one state could intervene in the internal affairs of another state in order to encourage political reform. After reviewing state practice in the area the ICJ concluded that 'no such general right of intervention, in support of the opposition within another State, exists in contemporary international law'.[17] In fact, the ICJ went so far as to say that '[t]he Court *cannot contemplate* the creation of a new rule opening up a right of intervention by one State against another on the ground that the latter has opted for some particular ideology or political system' (emphasis added).[18] Indeed, the ICJ explained that '[f]or such a general right to come into existence would involve a fundamental modification of the customary principle of non-intervention'.[19] Thus, in 1986 at least, the practice of members of the international society demonstrated a determination to ensure that the principle of non-intervention possessed a wide scope and thus enabled state sovereignty to be comprehensively protected.

[15] Jamnejad and Wood, 'The Principle of Non-Intervention' (n 12) at 348. The use of the word coercion is significant because it is clearly broader than the notion of 'dictatorial interference' that had been traditionally employed in order to determine an unlawful intervention: R Jennings and A Watts (eds), *Oppenheim's International Law*, 9th edn (Oxford, Oxford University Press, 2008) 418 ('the interference must be forcible or dictatorial, or otherwise coercive, in effect depriving the state intervened against of control over the matter in question. Interference pure and simple is not intervention'). Although do note Judge Schwebel's dissent in *Nicaragua* where he suggested that the court had erred when applying a weaker standard (coercion) than 'dictatorial interference': *Nicaragua* (n 2) at para 98.

[16] '[T]he requirement of coercion properly delimits the principle': Jamnejad and Wood (n 12) at 348.

[17] *Nicaragua* (n 2) at para 209.

[18] ibid at para 263 (emphasis added).

[19] ibid at para 206.

2.2 The Use of Force Prohibition

As the ICJ explained in the *Nicaragua* decision, the use of force by one state against another constitutes a 'particularly obvious' form of intervention.[20] However, because of the pernicious impact that the use of force can have against the sovereignty of a state, the international society developed an autonomous legal rule that specifically prohibits the threat or use of force against a state. Article 2(4) of the UN Charter, which is considered to be reflective of customary international law,[21] provides that '[a]ll Members shall refrain in their international relations from the threat or use of force against the territorial integrity or political independence of any state, or in any manner inconsistent with the Purposes of the United Nations'. In order to fully appreciate the protection that this prohibition affords state sovereignty it is necessary to inquire further into the meaning of the term 'force'.

Since the UN Charter came into force there has been considerable debate as to whether the Article 2(4) prohibition covers only the use of armed force or whether the prohibition extends more widely to the use of political and economic coercion. Certainly during the Cold War years Latin American and Middle Eastern states in particular argued that because Article 2(4) employed the term force without any qualification, it therefore extended to political and economic coercion.[22] To further support this approach, they explained that at other points in the UN Charter the term *armed* force is expressly used. For example, the preamble to the UN Charter explains that 'armed force shall not be used, save in the common interest'. In addition, Articles 41 to 46 provide that the Security Council can employ 'measures not involving the use of armed force' or, if such measures prove inadequate, 'armed force'. Thus, the argument was that if the framers of the UN Charter were minded to expressly state armed force in certain articles then that would indicate that the use of the term force without qualification in Article 2(4) meant that the prohibition should apply beyond armed force and include economic and political force.

In contrast, Western states contended that such an interpretation militated against the wider purposes and objectives of the UN Charter.[23] Their argument was that the UN Charter makes it quite clear that the overriding

[20] ibid at para 205.

[21] ibid at para 181.

[22] See generally G Tunkin, *Law and Force in the International System* (Moscow, Progress Publishers, 1985).

[23] Article 31(1) Vienna Convention on the Law of Treaties 1969 (VCLT) requires that the terms of a treaty must be interpreted in light of the purpose and objectives of the treaty. See generally A Aust, *Modern Treaty Law and Practice* (Cambridge, Cambridge University Press, 2007) 235.

purpose of the UN is to maintain international peace and security by removing the right of its member states to use armed force and instead locating it within the collective security system.[24] For example, the preamble to the Charter clearly states that the UN is an organisation determined to prevent 'the scourge of war' and that 'armed force shall not be used, save in the common interest'. Consequently, if curtailing the ability of its member states to use *armed* force is the purpose of the UN, this would indicate that the term force in Article 2(4) should be interpreted to mean armed force.

Ultimately, consensus seems to have cohered around an interpretation of Article 2(4) that only covers armed force. This is on the basis that when the UN was drafted members were in agreement that the term force would not include political or economic coercion.[25] This is demonstrated by the often cited proposal by the Brazilian delegation at the San Francisco conference that Article 2(4) should expressly prohibit 'the threat or use of force and the threat or use of economic measures in any manner inconsistent with the purposes of the Organization'.[26] As is well known, this proposal was vetoed by the drafting committee.[27] As a result, 'the *travaux préparatoires* also reveal that the drafters did not intend to extend the prohibition to economic coercion and political pressures'.[28] Thus, the generally accepted interpretation is that the term force within Article 2(4) is limited to *armed* force.[29] Of course, this does not mean that states are not protected from political and economic coercion. As I explained in the previous section, the principle of non-intervention prohibits states from using coercion (political, economic or otherwise) against another state. Thus, what has happened is that the international society has constructed different legal rules to combat different threats to state sovereignty. To recapitulate, the principle of non-intervention deals with non-forcible coercion, such as the imposition of political or economic coercion, whereas Article 2(4) is a specific prohibition against armed force.

[24] The exception is Article 51 UN Charter, which permits states to use force 'where an armed attack occurs'.

[25] Article 32 VCLT provides that where there is still ambiguity after the application of Article 31, the preparatory materials of a treaty can be taken into account.

[26] 6 UNCIO. Doc 559 (1945).

[27] 6 UNCIO. Doc 334–339, 405, 609 (1945).

[28] M Roscini, 'World Wide Warfare – Jus ad bellum and the Use of Force' (2010) 14 *Max Planck UNYB* 85, 105.

[29] 'The term does not cover any possible kind of force, but is, according to the correct and prevailing view, limited to armed force': A Randelzhofer, 'Article 2(4)' in B Simma (ed), *The Charter of the United Nations: A Commentary* (Oxford, Oxford University Press, 2002) 117. 'Unfortunately, "force" itself is a flexible term. Under modern conditions the threat or use of economic retaliation may be as effective against a weaker state as the threat or use of armed force. But it appears that the prohibition of Article 2(4) is directed exclusively at force in the sense of "armed force"': N Bentwich and A Martin, *A Commentary of the Charter of the United Nations* (London, Routledge & Kegan Paul, 1950) 12.

However, questions still remain as to the exact meaning of the term *armed* force. Clearly, the term armed requires that a weapon be used. *Black's Law Dictionary* defines 'armed' as meaning '[e]quipped with a weapon' or '[i]nvolving the use of a weapon'.[30] But the question then becomes how this weapon must be used in order for a violation of Article 2(4) to occur.

At first it was generally accepted that armed force required the use of a weapon that produced kinetic force,[31] ie the use of a weapon that had an 'explosive effect with shockwaves and heat'.[32] This approach was later criticised by Brownlie on the basis that it would seemingly exclude the use of chemical, biological and nuclear weapons. Clearly, such weapons do not necessarily result in an explosion that produces shockwaves or heat. In order to ensure that such weapons fell within the use of force prohibition, the definition of Article 2(4) moved away from the requirement of kinetic force and towards the *effects* that the weapon produced. In particular, Brownlie argued that the litmus test for determining whether an unlawful use has been committed is whether the weapon used caused 'destruction to life and property'.[33] This effects-based approach has since gained considerable traction in international legal literature. For example, Dinstein explains that '[i]t does not matter what specific means – kinetic or electronic – are used to bring it about, but the end result must be that violence occurs or is threatened'.[34]

Article 2(4) therefore prohibits the commission of acts that cause physical damage. It is important to note that unless authorised by the Security Council under Chapter VII of the UN Charter or pursuant to Article 51 of the UN Charter (the self-defence exception), Article 2(4) represents an 'absolute, all inclusive prohibition'.[35] In the words of Simma, '[i]t is clear, on the basis of both a teleological and historical interpretation of Article 2(4), that the prohibition enacted therein was, and is, intended to be of a comprehensive nature'.[36] Additionally, it is important to note that the use of force is generally regarded to be of *jus cogens* character,[37] which means that no state is permitted to derogate, via international agreement, from

[30] B Garner (ed), *Black's Law Dictionary*, 9th edn (West Group, 2009) 123.

[31] J Bond, *Peacetime Foreign Data Manipulation as One Aspect of Offensive Information Warfare: Questions of Legality under the United Nations Charter Article 2(4)* (US Dept of Commerce, National Technical Information Service, 1996) 78.

[32] I Brownlie, *International Law and the Use of Force by States* (Oxford, Clarendon Press, 1963) 362.

[33] ibid. Note that for Brownlie there was no requirement that the force be deployed by the military. Although cf B Roling, 'The Ban on the Use of Force and the U.N. Charter' in A Cassese (ed), *The Current Legal Regulation of the Use of Force* (The Hague, Martinus Nijhoff, 1986) 3 ('It seems obvious to the present writer that the "force" referred to in Art. 2(4) is military force').

[34] Y Dinstein, *War, Aggression and Self-Defence* (Cambridge, Cambridge University Press, 2010) 88 (footnotes omitted).

[35] US Delegate to San Francisco Conference, UNCIO, vi, 335.

[36] B Simma, 'NATO, the UN and the Use of Force: Legal Aspects' (1999) 10 *European Journal of International Law* 1, 2.

[37] See Articles 53 and 64 VCLT.

the prohibition. Indeed, any such agreement that is formed will be void.[38] Again, the *jus cogens* character of the prohibition on the use of force demonstrates the international society's commitment to establishing a legal regime that provides state sovereignty with comprehensive (or, for Simma, 'watertight'[39]) protection.

When asserting the comprehensive nature of the Article 2(4) prohibition one should not forget that Article 2(4) also prohibits the *threat* of force. This aspect of Article 2(4) was considered by the ICJ in *Nuclear Weapons Opinion*:

> the notion of 'threat' and 'use' of force under Article 2, paragraph 4, of the Charter stand together in the sense that if the use of force itself in a given case is illegal – for whatever reason – the threat to use such force will likewise be illegal. In short, if it is to be lawful, the declared readiness of a State to use force must be a use of force that is in conformity with the Charter.[40]

In the context of the international society the prohibition on threats of force is significant because threats of force can be just as damaging to state sovereignty as actual uses of force. Furthermore, threats of force are often the precursor to actual uses of force, as hostilities often escalate. In order to fully protect state sovereignty, therefore, the international society has created a prohibition that extends to threats of force.

In conclusion, when the legal rules relating to the principle of non-intervention and the threat and use of force are considered holistically, it is apparent that the international society has established a comprehensive international legal framework to protect state sovereignty from external intervention. As Cassese neatly puts it, these principles (non-intervention, non-use of force) are 'fundamental or "structural" standards (in de Visscher's terminology) in that they reflect the "political structure of the relations among States" and are "inherent in their coexistence" as sovereign entities'.[41]

3. THE INTERNATIONAL COMMUNITY AND INTERNATIONAL LAW

The central thesis of this book is that since the end of the Cold War liberal states have sought to profoundly redefine the principles of state sovereignty and the sovereign equality of states.[42] In essence, the international

[38] Article 52 VCLT.

[39] Simma, 'NATO, the UN and the Use of Force' (n 36) at 3.

[40] *Legality of the Threat or Use of Nuclear Weapons, Advisory Opinion* (1996) ICJ Rep at para 47.

[41] Cassese (n 3) at 128 (the quotations in inverted commas are from C de Visscher, *Théories et Réalités en Droit International Publique* (Paris, Pedone, 1970)).

[42] '[S]tate sovereignty, in its most basic sense, is being redefined – not least by forces of globalisation and international cooperation. States are now widely understood to be instruments at the service of their peoples, and not vice versa. At the same time, individual sover-

community has increasingly perceived only those states that demonstrate respect for liberal democratic standards as sovereign equals. Indeed, I argue that the international community has engaged in a sustained campaign to promote liberal values to non-liberal states.

As we shall see, the emergence of the international community has had a profound impact upon the nature and content of the international legal framework developed by the international society.[43] Stated succinctly, the international community has sought to transpose its own rules relating to the protection and promotion of liberal values into binding international law. As will become apparent from the following discussion of the post-Cold War international legal framework, this has been achieved with increasing success as the international community has acquired greater influence within the world order. The consequence is that international law is 'becoming an instrument of intervention; it is being used to transform international society in order to make up for economic, social, or equitable imbalances'.[44] For Jouannet, this has resulted in a 'moralisation of law'.[45] Meron describes this process as 'the humanization of international law'.[46] What this means is that the international community is now adapting existing legal rules and developing new legal rules so as to allow for the effective protection and promotion of human rights.[47] Several examples will serve to illustrate this point.

3.1 Adapting Existing Principles of International Law

3.1.1 Non-Intervention Principle

As the ICJ recognised in the *Nicaragua* judgment, the scope of the non-intervention principle can be modified by customary international law. Thus, where there is sufficient state practice and *opinio juris* to demonstrate that the application of coercion is permissible against a state when it

eignty – and by this I mean human rights and fundamental freedoms of each and every individual as enshrined in our Charter – has been enhanced by a renewed consciousness of the right of every individual to control his or her own destiny': UN Secretary-General Kofi Annan, *Annual Report to the General Assembly*, SG/SM/7136 (20 September 1999).

[43] As Friedmann notes, 'the move of international society, from an essentially negative code of rules of abstention to positive rules of cooperation . . . is an evolution of immense significance for the principles and structure of international law': W Friedmann, *The Changing Structure of International Law* (London, Stevens & Sons, 1964) 62.

[44] E Jouannet, 'What is the use of International Law? International Law as a 21st Century Guardian of Welfare' (2007) 28 *Michigan Journal of International Law* 815, 821.

[45] ibid at 820.

[46] T Meron, *The Humanization of International Law* (The Hague, Martinus Nijhoff, 2006).

[47] The international community has therefore taken up Brus's challenge: 'the international community has to develop new concepts and theories on the basis of which the failure of States to perform their role as sovereigns can be addressed at the international level': Brus, 'Bridging the Gap' in Kreijin (ed), *State, Sovereignty and International Governance* (n 7) at 10.

is acting in a particular manner, there will be no violation of the non-intervention principle.

Significantly, since the end of the Cold War there have been increasing claims that the non-intervention principle has undergone modification to the extent that it no longer prohibits a state from imposing coercion against another state where it is egregiously violating fundamental human rights. In this sense, the argument is that the deployment of coercion in order to protect fundamental human rights from serious infringement constitutes an exception to the non-intervention principle. In fact, the Institute of International Law advocated this argument as early as 1989. The Institute explained that

> [w]ithout prejudice to the functions and powers which the Charter attributes to the organs of the United Nations in case of violation of the obligations assumed by the member of the Organization, States, acting individually or collectively, are entitled to take diplomatic, economic and other measures towards any other State which has violated the obligation set forth in Article I [which requires states to respect human dignity], provided such measures are permitted under international law and do not involve the use of armed force in violation of the United Nations. These measures cannot be considered an unlawful interference in the internal affairs of States.[48]

Indeed, as the cause to protect human rights at the international level gained increasing momentum in the years following the end of the Cold War, there have been sustained claims that the non-intervention principle has been subject to profound modification and that it can no longer be used as a shield to protect states that violate fundamental human rights from external intervention.[49]

This being said, however, there is still debate as to whether sufficient state practice and *opinio juris* exists in order to substantiate this claim. As we know, there is an extremely high threshold for a norm to crystallise as customary international law.[50] Moreover, even if we concede that this human rights exception has passed into customary international law, the scope of this exception is still contested. As Jamnejad and Wood explain, '[t]he scope of a human rights "exception" to the principle of non-intervention is unclear'.[51] For example, does this exception only apply to the most serious

[48] Institute of International Law, 'The Protection of Human Rights and the Principle of Non-Intervention in the Internal Affairs of States', Yearbook of the Institute of International Law, Session of Santiago de Compostela (1989), available at: www.idi-iil.org/idiE/resolutionsE/1989_comp_03_en.PDF.

[49] See especially D McGoldrick, 'The Principle of Non-Intervention: Human Rights' in V Lowe and C Warbrick (eds), *The United Nations and the Principles of International Law: Essays in Memory of Michael Akehurst* (New York, Routledge, 1994).

[50] See generally A Perreau-Saussine and JB Murphy (eds), *The Nature of Customary International Law: Legal, Historical and Philosophical Perspectives* (Cambridge, Cambridge University Press, 2007).

[51] Jamnejad and Wood (n 12) at 376.

violations of human rights? If so, which human rights rank as sufficiently serious to justify the imposition of coercion against a sovereign state? Furthermore, what forms of coercion are considered permissible in order to put an end to the serious violation of these human rights?

Ascertaining whether a human rights exception forms part of customary international law and, if so, its scope, are clearly important questions. This would require a careful analysis of state practice and *opinio juris* since the end of the Cold War. However, this is a task that falls outside of the scope of this chapter. Instead, the purpose of this chapter is to suggest that the extent to which international lawyers are now debating a human rights exception to the non-intervention principle can be explained on the basis of an international community of liberal states that is increasingly prepared to intervene in the internal affairs of states in order to ensure the protection of human rights.

3.1.2 Use of Force Prohibition

Since the end of the Cold War the all-inclusive nature of the prohibition on the use of force contained in Article 2(4) has been subject to considerable challenge. This is particularly so where a state is committing egregious violations of human rights against its people and, because of lack of agreement between its members, the UN Security Council is unable to engage its Chapter VII powers and authorise (usually military) intervention.

In recent years the practice of members of the international community has indicated that a modification of customary international law has occurred. Specifically, that there now exists sufficient evidence (state practice accompanied by *opinio juris*) to substantiate the claim that where a government is systematically abusing the human rights of its citizens and the Security Council is unable to act, concerned states are able to use force to put an end to the human rights abuses. In this sense, customary international law has modified (or adapted) state obligations under Article 2(4) of the UN Charter.[52]

NATO's use of force against Kosovo in 1999 is seminal in this context. Following well documented reports that an ethnic cleansing campaign was being committed against Albanians in Kosovo, NATO launched air strikes in the name of the international community (and without Security Council authorisation) in order to put an end to these severe human rights abuses.[53] Clearly, the air strikes by NATO members constituted a prima

[52] See generally N Tsagourias, *Jurisprudence of International Law: The Humanitarian Dimension* (Manchester, Manchester University of Press, 2000).

[53] See Press Statement by Javier Solana, Secretary-General of NATO, 23 March 1999, cited in A Paulus, 'The Influence of the United States on the Concept of the International Community' in M Byers and G Nolte (eds), *United States Hegemony and the Foundations of International Law* (Cambridge, Cambridge University Press, 2003) 58.

facie violation of Article 2(4). Importantly, however, many of the NATO states participating in the air strikes argued that customary international law had evolved in such a way as to permit unilateral (ie without authorisation from the Security Council), humanitarian intervention. In relation to the Netherlands' role in NATO's intervention in Kosovo on 10 June 1999, the Dutch Representative explained to the Security Council that

> the [UN] Charter is not the only source of international law . . . The Charter, to be sure, is much more specific on respect for sovereignty than on respect for human rights, but since the day it was drafted the world had witnessed a gradual shift in that balance, making respect for human rights more mandatory and respect for sovereignty less absolute. Today, we regard it as a generally accepted rule of international law that no sovereign State has the right to terrorise its own citizens.[54]

In a similar vein, Belgium argued before the ICJ that its participation in the use of force in Kosovo was lawful on the basis of the doctrine of humanitarian intervention that was firmly established in customary international law.[55] The United Kingdom (UK)'s approach is of particular interest because in 1986 the UK Foreign Office was clearly of the opinion that customary international law did not recognise the doctrine of unilateral humanitarian intervention

> [T]he overwhelming majority of contemporary legal opinion comes down against the existence of a right of humanitarian intervention, for three main reasons: first, the UN Charter and the corpus of modern international law do not seem to specifically incorporate such a right; secondly, State practice in the past two centuries, and especially since 1945, at best provides only a handful of genuine cases of humanitarian intervention, and, on most assessments, none at all; and finally, on prudential grounds, that the scope for abusing such a right argues strongly against its creation . . . In essence, therefore, the case against making humanitarian intervention an exception to the principle of non-intervention is that its doubtful benefits would be heavily outweighed by its costs in terms of respect for international law.[56]

However, by 1999 the UK position had changed dramatically. In response to the UK's participation in the airstrikes in Kosovo the UK Defence Secretary explained that

> We are in no doubt that NATO is acting within international law. Our legal justification rests upon the accepted principle that force may be used in extreme circumstances to avert a humanitarian catastrophe. Those circumstances clearly exist in Kosovo.[57]

[54] UN Doc S/PV.4011, 12 (10 June 1999).

[55] Belgium, Oral Pleading in the Case *Legality of Use of Force (Yugoslavia v Belgium)*, ICJ Pleadings, (10 May 1999) CR 99/15 (translation).

[56] UK Foreign Office Policy Document No 148, reprinted in (1986) 57 *British Yearbook of International Law* 614.

[57] UK Secretary of State for Defence George Robertson, Statement to the House of Commons, Hansard, 25 March 1999 [Col 616]. See also the UK's statement to the UN: 'The action being

After contrasting these opposing statements, Simma points out that 'after the demise of the East-West conflict' and the increasing importance of human rights at the international level, the UK now subscribes to the view that customary international law recognises a right of unilateral humanitarian intervention.[58] The importance of the end of the Cold War is therefore clearly apparent.

Unsurprisingly, scholars are bitterly divided as to whether there exists sufficient evidence to support the contention that humanitarian intervention is now part of customary international law. Indeed, '[t]here have been no purported applications of this principle since 1999 [the Kosovo intervention] and a large number of states rejected the idea in the lead-up to the 2005 World Summit Outcome'.[59] However, as with the potential contraction of the principle of non-intervention, it is not the objective of this chapter to engage in a lengthy debate as to whether the doctrine of humanitarian intervention is now part of positivist international law. Rather, my claim is that the extent to which there is debate as to whether a doctrine of unilateral humanitarian intervention now exists in international law can be explained on the basis of an international community of liberal states that is agitating against an impermeable understanding of state sovereignty and thus attempting to adapt existing international legal rules in order to permit the protection of human rights.

3.2 The Development of New Legal Rules and Concepts

3.2.1 Democracy as a Customary Right

As I noted in the preceding chapter, international treaties have long made reference to democracy as a fundamental human entitlement: namely, a human right to 'meaningful participation by the governed in the formal political decisions by which the quality of their lives and societies are shaped'.[60] However, at least during the Cold War years, such was the international society's commitment to sovereign equality and non-intervention that democracy as a legal entitlement conferred by international treaties was never effectively enforced. Certainly, there was no credible suggestion that democracy as a fundamental entitlement had passed into customary international law.

taken is legal. It is justified as an exceptional measure to prevent an overwhelming humanitarian catastrophe': UN Doc S/PV.3989 (26 March 1999) 16.

[58] Simma (n 36) at 5.

[59] Jamnejad and Wood (n 12) at 360.

[60] T Franck, 'Legitimacy and the Democratic Entitlement' in G Fox and B Roth (eds), *Democratic Governance in International Law* (Cambridge, Cambridge University Press, 2000) 26.

This position has undergone profound transformation since the end of the Cold War. There are now sustained claims within academic literature that democracy as a system of political governance has emerged as a legal entitlement under customary international law. Thomas Franck has been the main proponent of this argument. In an important article published in 1992 Franck claimed that 'leaders of states constituting the international community vigorously asserted that *only* democracy validates governance';[61] 'both textually and in practice, the international system is moving toward a clearly designated democratic entitlement, with national governance validated by international standards and systematic monitoring of compliance'.[62] This assertion was based upon the increasing number of states that had opted for democracy since the end of the Cold War[63] and the firm support for electoral democracy by the UN and many regional organisations.[64] It is important to underscore, however, that Franck's claim was that, in 1992, '[w]e are not quite there yet'.[65] What he was arguing was that 'what we can see [are] the outlines of this new world in which the citizens of each state will look to international law and organization to guarantee their democratic entitlement'.[66] As Koskemniemi notes, the right advocated by Franck 'was always falling short of the law of the moment, always "emerging", not quite yet there, though well under way'.[67]

More recently, others have contributed to this research agenda and have sought to determine whether developments in state practice indicate that democratic governance has crystallised as a legal entitlement under international law. Fox maintains that it is unlikely that democracy has emerged as a customary entitlement on the basis that there still remain considerable variations in the way that democracy is practised around the world. In essence, there is no single agreed definition of the term democracy at the international level and, consequently, there is little state practice to contribute to the formation of a customary international law recognising an international legal right to democracy.[68] More recently, Marks and d'Aspremont have concurred with this approach, suggesting that

[61] T Franck, 'The Emerging Right to Democratic Governance' (1992) 86 *American Journal of International Law* 46, 47.

[62] ibid at 91.

[63] ibid at 47–49.

[64] ibid at 63–69.

[65] ibid at 50.

[66] ibid.

[67] M Koskemniemi, 'Legal Cosmopolitanism: Tom Franck's Messianic World' (2003) 35 *NYU Journal of International Law and Policy* 417, 484.

[68] H Fox, 'Democracy, Right to, International Protection' (2008) *Max Planck Encyclopaedia of Public International Law* (www.mpepil.com). For a similar approach see C Pippan, 'International Law, Domestic Political orders, and the "Democratic Imperative": Has Democracy Finally Emerged as a Global legal Entitlement?' (2010) Jean Monnet Working Paper 02/10. This was also the opinion of the World Summit Outcome, GA Res 60/1 (24 October 2005) para 135 ('while democracies share common features, there is no single model of democracy').

insufficient state practice is available to argue with confidence that democracy as an international human right has made the transition from an emerging norm to one that is now an integral part of customary international law.[69] There are those that disagree, of course. Meron, for example, is of the opinion that 'on the balance, it is undeniable that democracy has become both an expectation of the people and a universal norm'.[70] Wheately adopts a more moderate position, arguing that although democracy may not have emerged as an international legal entitlement, it has crystallised as a regional customary international norm in regions such as Europe.[71]

However, putting the argument as to the customary status of democracy aside, the purpose of this section has been is to argue that the extent to which democracy is crystallising or perhaps has crystallised as a principle of customary international law can be regarded as an expression of the international community and its increasing dominance within the world order.

3.2.2. *Responsibility to Protect*

In chapter four I argue that in the post-Cold War era the UN Security Council, acting under the influence of the international community, has been increasingly prepared to engage its mandatory powers in order to protect and promote fundamental human rights. This is not to say, however, that since the end of the Cold War the UN Security Council has always been prepared to use its powers to protect human rights. This is well represented by the UN's failure to react to the humanitarian catastrophes that occurred in Somalia, Rwanda, Bosnia and Kosovo (amongst others). Indeed, the Security Council's response to these crises was heavily criticised for being 'erratic, incomplete or counterproductive'.[72] As a result, UN Secretary-General Kofi Annan explained that there needed to be a new international consensus on responding to massive violations of human rights and humanitarian law.[73] The task for determining the structure of this new framework was taken up by the Canadian-sponsored International Commission on Intervention and State Sovereignty. The

[69] S Marks, 'What has Become of the Emerging Right to Democratic Governance?' (2011) 22 *European Journal of International Law* 507 and J d'Aspremont, 'The Rise and Fall of Democracy Governance in International Law: A Reply to Susan Marks' (2011) 22 *European Journal of International Law* 549.

[70] Meron, *The Humanization of International Law* (n 46) at 497.

[71] S Wheatley, 'Democracy in International Law: A European Perspective' (2002) 51 *ICLQ* 225.

[72] G Evans, 'From Humanitarian Intervention to the Responsibility to Protect' (2006) 24 *Wisconsin International law Journal* 704, 706.

[73] K Annan, 'We the Peoples – The Role of the United Nations in the 21st Century' (27 March 2000, UN Doc A/54/2000)

Commission presented its report to the Secretary-General in 2001. The defining feature of this report was to frame the debate surrounding humanitarian intervention in terms of a *responsibility to protect*. The overarching theme was

> the idea that sovereign states have a responsibility to protect their own citizens from avoidable catastrophe – from mass murder and rape, from starvation – but that when they are unwilling to do so, that responsibility must be borne by the broader community of states.[74]

Thus, the Commission moved away from a pristine conception of state sovereignty which conferred on states an unfettered right to deal with their citizens in a manner that they saw fit and towards an approach that regarded states as being under a responsibility to protect their citizens.

Significantly, the Commission submitted that if a state fails to discharge its responsibility to protect its citizens then this responsibility will fall upon (or, in the words of the Commission, will be 'borne by') 'the broader community of states'. Two points are of importance here. First, who actually bears this responsibility in the event that the state fails to discharge it? Put simply, who is the 'broader community of states'? The Commission explains that 'the first port of call'[75] should always be the UN Security Council. However, implicit in this suggestion is the recognition that another body, such as the General Assembly, a regional organisation or even a coalition of willing states, could perhaps intervene in order to discharge the responsibility to protect.[76] Secondly, what is the nature of the responsibility that passes to the Security Council? Is the Commission suggesting that the Security Council would be legally obligated ie under a positive duty, to protect where a human catastrophe is threatened or occurring? This is not particularly clear from the Commission's report. But as the quotation above reveals, the Commission does explicitly state that 'the responsibility *must be borne* by the broader community of states' (emphasis added). This sounds very much like the Commission seeing a positive duty residing with the Security Council to protect human rights in the event that the national government has failed to do so.

Subsequent to the Commission's report in 2001, the concept of a responsibility to protect was adopted on two occasions: in 2004 in the UN

[74] International Commission on Intervention and State Sovereignty, *The Responsibility to Protect* (December 2001) Foreword, VIII.

[75] ibid at para 6.28.

[76] As Stahn says, the Commission 'did not categorically exclude the possibility that the responsibility to protect doctrine might ultimately be assumed by the General Assembly, regional organizations, or coalitions of states if the Security Council fails to act': C Stahn, 'Responsibility to Protect: Political Rhetoric or Emerging Legal Norm?' (2007) 101 *American Journal of International Law* 99, 104.

High-Level Panel Report *A More Secure World*[77] and the UN Secretary-General's Report in 2005 entitled *In Larger Freedom*.[78] This being said, whilst both of these reports confirmed the existence of an international legal rule imposing a responsibility upon states to protect their citizens against avoidable catastrophes, in contrast to the 2001 report these two reports firmly regarded this responsibility as passing to (and only to) the Security Council in the event that it was violated.

Importantly, this position was broadly adopted by the General Assembly in 2005.[79] It is worth quoting the critical passages of the General Assembly verbatim:

> Each individual State has the responsibility to protect its populations from genocide, war crimes, ethnic cleansing and crimes against humanity. This responsibility entails the prevention of such crimes, including their incitement, through appropriate and necessary means. We accept that responsibility and will act in accordance with it . . .
>
> The international community, through the United Nations, also has the responsibility to use appropriate diplomatic, humanitarian and other peaceful means, in accordance with Chapters VI and VII of the Charter, to help protect populations from genocide, war crimes, ethnic cleansing and crimes against humanity. In this context, we are prepared to take collective action, in a timely and decisive manner, through the Security Council, in accordance with the Charter, including Chapter VII, on a case-by-case basis and in cooperation with relevant regional organizations as appropriate, should peaceful means be inadequate and national authorities are manifestly failing to protect their populations from genocide, war crimes, ethnic cleansing and crimes against humanity.[80]

In this sense, the 'responsibility to protect' doctrine was adopted by the UN. Significantly, since 2005 the Security Council has identified the responsibility of states to protect the human rights of their citizens in two resolutions, both adopted under Chapter VII of the UN Charter: once in relation to Darfur (2006)[81] and the other in relation to Libya (2011).[82]

Interestingly, Stahn argues that the responsibility to protect doctrine displays little uniqueness or innovation. By 2007, he argues, the re-characterisation of sovereignty as control to sovereignty as responsibility was well underway, if not complete. Particularly since the end of the Cold War, customary international human rights law has developed

[77] Report of the UN High-Level Panel on Threats, Challenges and Change, 'A More Secure World: Our Shared Responsibility', UN Doc A/59/565 (2 December 2004).

[78] Report of the Secretary-General of the United Nations, 'In Larger Freedom: Towards Security, Development and Human Rights for All', UN Doc A/59/2005 (21 March 2005)

[79] UN General Assembly, World Summit Outcome, A/RES/60/1 (24 October 2005).

[80] ibid at paras 138–39.

[81] SC Res 1706 (31 August 2006).

[82] SC Res 1973 (17 March 2011). The Security Council's articulation of the responsibility to protect doctrine in Libya will be dealt with in detail in chapter 4 of this volume.

considerably, placing a plethora of legal obligations upon states to respect and protect the human rights of their citizens. Thus, when perceived in this light a doctrine that imposes a responsibility upon states to protect their citizens from severe human rights abuses does not place upon states any additional legal obligation.

Indeed, Stahn argues that the contention that the responsibility to protect will pass to an international organisation in the event that it is violated by a state also lacks novelty. First, Stahn submits that, as the General Assembly Resolution explains, the responsibility to protect will pass to the Security Council under Chapter VII.[83] But as he rightly notes, since the end of the Cold War the Security Council has frequently engaged Chapter VII in order to protect populations against severe violations of human rights, even if sometimes haphazardly.[84] Secondly, Stahn argues that it is clear from the General Assembly Resolution that although states are under a responsibility to protect, where this responsibility is breached it does not pass to the Security Council in the form of a *positive duty* to protect. Instead, it is within the *discretion* of the Security Council to act. Again, this seems to be a correct reading of the resolution, not least because US Secretary of State John Bolton explained in a letter dated 30 August 2005 that the US would 'not accept that either the United Nations as a whole, or the Security Council, or individual states, have an obligation to intervene under international law'.[85] Moreover, as we shall see in chapter four, the Security Council recently engaged the doctrine of the responsibility to protect in the context of the Libya crisis. Although the Security Council declared in Resolution 1973 (2011) that the Libyan government was subject to an international legal responsibility to protect, importantly the Council did not regard this responsibility as passing to itself when it was violated by the Libyan government. If the responsibility to protect doctrine would impose an obligation upon the Security Council to intervene, this would indeed represent a significant development in international law and in particular the responsibilities of the Security Council. However, this does not seem to be the case.[86]

[83] It is interesting to note that General Assembly Resolution 60/1 (24 October 2005) makes it quite clear that in the context of the responsibility to protect the power to protect populations from egregious human rights abuses resides exclusively with the Security Council.

[84] See chapter 4 of this volume.

[85] Quoted in Stahn, 'Responsibility to Protect' (n 76) at 108.

[86] Indeed, that the responsibility to protect doctrine does not impose an obligation to act on the Security Council seems also to be the position of current UN Secretary-General Ban Ki Moon: 'The Charter gives the Security Council a *wide degree of latitude* to determine the most appropriate course of action. The Council should continue to respond flexibly to the demands of protecting populations from crimes and violations relating to RtoP [responsibility to protect]' (emphasis added): UN Secretary-General's Report, 'Responsibility to Protect: Timely and Decisive Response', UN Doc A/66/874-S/2012/578 (25 July 2012).

Substantively, then, Stahn seems to be correct that the responsibility to protect doctrine is 'old wine in new bottles'.[87] This being said, this does not mean that the emergence of the concept of responsibility to protect is without significance. On the contrary, the deployment of the concept of a responsibility to protect allows for an important *conceptual development* in international law: namely, that a concrete legal principle now exists that subjects states to a positive and affirmative responsibility to protect the fundamental human rights of their citizens and, in the event that this responsibility is not discharged, it will pass to an international body.

In light of this, the purpose of this section is to argue that this significant development in international law can be explained on the basis of the influence exercised by the international community over international law. This is indeed recognised by Stahn, who notes that the inauguration of the responsibility to protect doctrine

> is testimony to a broader systemic shift in international law, namely, a growing tendency to recognize that the principle of state sovereignty finds its limits in the protection of 'human security'. Under the concept of responsibility to protect, matters affecting the life of the citizens and subjects of a state are no longer exclusively subject to the discretion of the domestic ruler but are perceived as issues of concern to the broader international community (e.g., third states, multilateral institutions, and nonstate actors). This development is part and parcel of a growing transformation of international law from a state and governing-elite-based system of rules into a normative framework designed to protect certain human and community interests.[88]

4. CONCLUSION

The objective of this chapter has been to illustrate that the political associations of the international society and the international community have each sought to develop legal rules in order to protect and promote their defining principles. The international society has created rules such as non-intervention and the non-use of force in order to protect state sovereignty. Emerging in the years following the end of the Cold War and finding itself situated within this international legal framework, the international community has attempted to adapt existing international law and create new international laws in order to protect human rights. In this sense, 'the will of the international community has emerged as a

[87] Stahn (n 76) at 102. According to Ponzio, 'the norm of an "international responsibility to protect" gathered momentum – albeit not necessarily in name – since the end of the cold war in response to human suffering caused by internal war and state failure': R Ponzio, *Democratic Peacebuilding: Aiding Afghanistan and other Fragile States* (Oxford/New York, Oxford University Press, 2011) 112.

[88] Stahn, (n 76) at 100–101 (footnotes omitted).

normative source of international law'.[89] In fact, by reformulating international law to allow for the promotion of liberal values to non-liberal states we can go so far as to say that the international community has instituted a form of global governance into the world order.[90] As Brus observes,

> [i]nternational [global] governance, then, is used to restore the capacity and authority of States to exercise their sovereign powers on the basis of restrictions and expectations of the international community within the context of shared values and interests incorporated in existing international, in particular those norms relating to peace and security and respect for human rights and human dignity.[91]

Thus, all in all, what emerges is two political associations whose normative frameworks have profoundly influenced the development of international law; or to be more precise, the international community is attempting to modify the international legal framework that was successfully implemented by the international society in the aftermath of the Second World War. This is what Cassese calls 'international law in a divided world'; 'certain fundamental principles reflect the "Westphalian model" whereas others are indicative of the new trends which emerged in the world community after the decline of that model'.[92] Thus, the human rights doctrine that has emerged since the end of the Cold War 'is, in fact, competing – if not at loggerheads – with the traditional principles of respect for the sovereign equality of States and of non-interference in the domestic affairs of other States'.[93] Müllerson seems to hit the nail of the head when, in response to Cassese's remarks, he argues that

> [t]his conflict is not only a conflict between different legal norms, but also reflects the underlying conflict between a strictly state-centric world-view and a more humanistic world-view that pierces the veil of state sovereignty and is concerned with human beings, peoples and various minorities.[94]

Consequently, whilst the primary objective of this chapter has been to reveal the way in which the international society and the international community utilise international law to achieve and realise their normative objectives, it is equally apparent that a thorough understanding of the structure and dynamic of the contemporary world order (specifically, the

[89] N Tsagourias, 'The Will of the International Community as a Normative Source of International Law' in I Dekker and W Werner (eds), *Governance and International Legal Theory* (Leiden, Martinus Nijhoff, 2004) 120.

[90] '[Global governance is] the process by which the international community on the basis of shared values and interests collectively manages resources, issues, conflicts in a world that is increasingly a "global *neighbourhood*"': Brus (n 7) at 5.

[91] ibid at 10.

[92] Cassese (n 3) at 163.

[93] ibid at 148.

[94] Müllerson, *Ordering Anarchy* (n 1) at 161.

interface between the international society and the international community) is crucial to understanding the complexities of contemporary international law. Indeed, '[i]t seems that the future of international law will depend on the outcome of the contest between Westphalian and post-Westphalian principles'.[95]

[95] ibid at 169.

3

The International Community and the Liberal Peace

1. INTRODUCTION

IN THE PREVIOUS chapter I argued that the defining feature of the international community is its desire to promote its liberal values to non-liberal states. With this in mind, the objective of this chapter is to uncover the ideological factors that motivate this 'messianic'[1] campaign for liberal development.

In the years following the end of the Cold War the international community principally sought to justify this liberal campaign on the basis that liberal democracy, as a system of governance that is devoted to protecting fundamental human rights, is universally desired. The international community therefore considered its promotion of liberal democracy to non-liberal states as being an attempt to liberate repressed populations from tyranny and suffering. Indeed, the international community's sustained intervention in the Balkans and its determination to reconstruct the region upon a liberal basis was largely justified on (altruistic) humanitarian grounds.[2]

However, in recent years it has become apparent that the primary motive that sustains the international community's campaign is the belief that the spread of liberal democracy enhances the security of its members. Sure, and as I reveal below, the international community clearly considers liberal democracy to represent a universally desired system of governance. Thus, the international community can (and often does) appeal to

[1] D Simes, 'America's Imperial Dilemma' (2003) 82 *Foreign Affairs* 94, 97. The use of the word 'missionary' to describe the international community's liberal endeavour also seems appropriate here. In the context of America's role in the international community, Keller wrote in the *New York Times* that the Bush Administration embraces 'an optimism about America's ability to build a better world. [They have] an almost missionary sense of America's role': B Keller, 'The Sunshine Warrior', *New York Times* (22 September 2002), available at: www.nytimes.com/2002/09/22/magazine/22WOLFOWITZ.html?pagewanted=all.

[2] Former British Prime Minister Tony Blair, *'Doctrine of International Community', Speech to the Economic Club of Chicago* (22 April 1999), available at: http://webarchive.nationalarchives.gov.uk/20040308042406/http://pm.gov.uk:80/output/Page1297.asp ('This is a just war, based not on any territorial ambitions but on values. We cannot let the evil of ethnic cleansing stand. We must not rest until it is reversed').

this humanitarian dimension in order to justify its liberal campaign.[3] However, at best this is a supplementary justification. Certainly since the war on terror began the international community's commitment to promoting liberal democracy to non-liberal states is firmly located in the desire to ensure 'the maintenance of order over barbarian threat'.[4] '[S]ince 11 September 2001, the liberating dimension of regime change has been downgraded, being replaced by a new emphasis on security'.[5] That the promotion of liberal democracy enhances the security of the international community is firmly rooted in the empirical claim that liberal states enjoy a zone of peace where any disputes that emerge between them will be resolved without recourse to force. This phenomenon is known as the liberal peace thesis.

2. THE LIBERAL PEACE THESIS

The significance the international community accords to the liberal peace thesis can be traced directly to the perceived failing of the international society to maintain international peace and security. The primary objective of the international society is to prevent states from intervening in the sovereign affairs of other states.[6] In particular, the international society is determined to eradicate the threat or use of armed force between sovereign states, as this is considered a particularly pernicious form of intervention.[7] The raison d'être of the international society is to create a regulatory framework that engenders an environment where, despite their political differentiation, states can enjoy a peaceful coexistence. However, for the international community, history reveals that the international society has failed to eliminate inter-state intervention and has thus failed to accomplish

[3] For example, in relation to the UK's military involvement to protect human rights in Libya in 2011, British Prime Minister David Cameron explained that 'Britain could not stand by as Qadhafi slaughtered his people. Nor could we allow a failed pariah state festering on Europe's southern borders, with the potential to threaten our own security': D Cameron, *Statement on Libya* (5 September 2011), available at: www.number10.gov.uk/news/statement-on-libya/.

[4] 'The ostensible motive that sustains these nation-building projects may be humanitarian, but the real principle is imperial: the maintenance of order over barbarian threat': M Ignatieff, *Empire Lite: Nation-Building in Bosnia, Kosovo and Afghanistan* (London, Vintage, 2003) 22. Indeed, Ignatieff argues that even the reconstruction of the Balkans, often cited as a prime example of the international community's most altruistic humanitarian operation, was in reality motivated by the international community's desire to protect its own security. 'The reconstruction of the Balkans has not been an exercise in humanitarian social work. It has always been an imperial project, driven by a clear, if reluctantly grasped imperative to replace the new collapsed Communist imperium of Tito's era with a new architecture of states that would bring stability to a combustible corner of Europe' (ibid at 32).

[5] L Whitehead, 'Democratization with the Benefit of Hindsight' in E Newman and R Rich (eds), *The UN Role in Promoting Democracy: Between Ideals and Reality* (New York, United Nations University Press, 2004) 161.

[6] GA Res 34/101 (14 December 1979).

[7] Article 2(4) UN Charter (signed 26 June 1945, San Francisco, in force 24 October 1945).

its objective of maintaining international peace and security. Since the crystallisation of the international society in 1945, such has been the frequency with which states have resorted to the use of force that 'the practice of these states has so severely shattered the mutual confidence which would have been the *sine qua non* of an operative law embodying the precepts of article 2(4) that, as with Ozymandias, only the words remain'.[8] The prohibition on the use of force is only pious aspiration in the face of its continual transgression. Moreover, the Security Council, responsible for maintaining international peace and security under Chapter VII of the UN Charter, has failed effectively to respond to these violations of Article 2(4) and thus restore state sovereignty. Indeed, at least during the Cold War the Security Council was frequently described as being in a state of paralysis.[9] Consequently, for the international community inter-state conflict remains an endemic feature of the world order, which has had a destructive impact upon the legal framework that the international society sought to establish. In short, its attempt to surmount the security dilemma of the anarchic world order by establishing a legal framework premised upon mutual abstention has abjectly failed. In the words of Franck, although the legal structure that the international society represents endures, 'it mocks us from the grave'.[10]

Franck therefore perceives a lawless world where the international society's attempt to substitute the rule of law for the rule of the jungle has been proved largely ineffective.[11] However, for the international community Franck's conclusions are misleading because 'there nevertheless exists an island of peace in an ocean of conflicts and wars'.[12] In particular, the international community subscribes to the robust empirical 'fact'[13] that notwithstanding the continual inter-state violence experienced within the international society, liberal states have experienced a stable peace where any disputes that have emerged between them have been resolved without recourse to violence.[14] That liberal states have managed to forge a

[8] T Franck, 'Who Killed Article 2(4)?' (1970) 64 *American Journal of International Law* 809, 809. 'Since 1945, so many states have used armed force on so many occasions, in flagrant violation of the charter, that the regime can only be said to have collapsed': M Glennon, 'Why the Security Council Failed' (2003) 82 *Foreign Affairs* 16, 18.

[9] See generally ND White, *Toward International Justice: The United Nations System* (Boulder CO, Lynne Rienner, 2002).

[10] Franck, 'Who Killed Article 2(4)?' (n 8) at 809.

[11] cf L Henkin, 'The Reports of the Death of Article 2(4) are Greatly Exaggerated' (1971) 65 *American Journal of International Law* 544.

[12] T Risse-Kappen, 'Democratic Peace – Warlike Democracies? A Social Constructivist Interpretation of the Liberal Argument' (1995) 1 *European Journal of International Relations* 491, 492.

[13] B Russett, 'The Fact of Democratic Peace' in M Brown, S Lynn-Jones and S Miller (eds), *Debating the Democratic Peace* (Cambridge MA, MIT Press, 1996).

[14] Indeed, much empirical research is available to substantiate the claim that liberal states have always enjoyed peaceful relations. Indeed, Levy explains that the absence of war between liberal states is 'the closest thing we have to an empirical law in the study of international relations': J Levy, 'Domestic Politics and War' in R Rotberg and T Rabb (eds), *The Origin and Prevention of Major Wars* (Cambridge, Cambridge University Press, 1989) 88.

zone of peace is most often explained on the basis of the normative structure of liberal states.[15] The argument runs that at the heart of a liberal state is the belief 'that individuals everywhere are fundamentally the same, and are best off pursuing self-preservation and material well-being. Freedom is required for these pursuits, and peace is required for freedom; coercion and violence are counter-productive'.[16] If freedom is to be preserved, violence as a form of political adjudication must be forgone at all costs; the peaceful reconciliation of these disputes has to be not just pursued but actually achieved if freedom and autonomy are to be maintained. As a result, '[m]odern democratic societies foster the internalization of norms for regulating and reconciling competing interests and values in public affairs in ways that are neither violent nor coercive'.[17] The consequence is that 'if the norms regulating the decision-making processes in a

Risse-Kappen argues that 'there is no other empirical finding in the realm of international relations that has reached a similar consensus among scholars': Risse-Kappen, 'Democratic Peace' (n 12) at 494. Similarly, Russett has observed that the liberal peace proposition constitutes 'one of the strongest nontrivial or nontautological generalizations that can be made about international relations': B Russett, *Controlling the Sword: the Democratic Governance of National Security* (Cambridge MA, Harvard University Press, 1990) 123. That said, there are still a few dissenting voices over the empirical robustness of the liberal peace thesis: see K Waltz, 'The Emerging Structure of International Politics' (1993) 18 *International Security* 44; C Layne, 'Kant or Cant: The Myth of the Democratic Peace' (1994) 19 *International Security* 5; and D Spiro, 'The Insignificance of the Democratic Peace' (1994) 19 *International Security* 50.

[15] Historically, the liberal peace thesis was explained on the basis of the democratic institutions within liberal states (often referred to as the institutional account). The argument runs that because a democratic government is responsive to the people, a democratic government will not sanction violence because it is aware that this will be acutely unpopular with the population, who will have to both pay for and fight in any ensuing violence. Thus, democratic governments will not initiate violence because they fear loss of office at the next election. Consequently, between democratic governments there will be an institutional deadlock in favour of peace. As Kant explained, '[i]f the consent of the citizens is required to decide whether or not war is to be declared, it is very natural that they will have great hesitation in embarking on so dangerous an enterprise. For this it would mean calling down on themselves all the miseries of war, such as doing the fighting themselves, supplying the costs of war from their own resources, painfully making good the ensuing devastation, and, as the crowning evil, having to take upon themselves a burden of debt which will embitter peace itself and which can never be paid off on account of the constant threat of new wars': I Kant, 'Perpetual Peace' (translation by H Reiss), *Kant's Political Writings* (Cambridge, Cambridge University Press, 1991) 100. However, this theory is unconvincing because it assumes democratic governments are inherently peaceful in the international sphere. As history reveals, democratic governments frequently initiate violence against non-liberal states. Indeed, some suggest that democratic governments may be *more* aggressive than non-democratic governments: M Small and D Singer, 'The War-Proneness of Democratic Regimes' (1976) 1 *Jerusalem Journal of International Relations* 50. This notwithstanding, liberal states have nevertheless maintained a robust peace between themselves. To this end, I suggest that the normative account provides a far more convincing explanation for why liberal states have achieved a stable peace but are nevertheless prepared to act aggressively towards non-liberal states.

[16] J Owen, 'How Liberalism Produces Peace' in Brown, Lynn-Jones and Miller (eds), *Debating the Democratic Peace* (n 13) at 118.

[17] W Dixon, 'Democracy and the Peaceful Settlement of International Conflict' (1994) 88 *American Political Science Review* 14, 16.

democratic system are orientated toward non-violence and the peaceful resolution of political conflicts, one could expect that democracies externalise these norms when dealing with one another'.[18] If a norm exists that requires the peaceful resolution of disputes *within* states, it will also require the peaceful resolution of disputes *between* them.[19] Thus, when two liberal states come into contact in the international sphere and, after observation and scrutiny of each other's political constitution, perceive each other to be genuinely liberal a mutual trust of peaceful exchange will be established. 'In this way, a culture of [liberal] democracy is fundamentally a culture of peace'.[20] Indeed, this liberal peace thesis has become a recurring theme in the rhetoric of liberal policy-makers since the end of the Cold War. In 1994 US President Bill Clinton declared emphatically that 'democracies do not attack each other'.[21] More recently, in 2004 President George W Bush explained that 'the reason why I'm so strong on democracy is that democracies don't go to war with each other'.[22] Again in 2006 he explained that 'democracies yield the peace we all want. History has taught us democracies don't war . . . Democracies yield peace'.[23]

[18] Risse-Kappen (n 12) at 500. 'Liberals contend that peace is required to advance the basic common interests in self-preservation and material well-being. They see war as a wasteful diversion of resources to destruction that is both irrational and unnatural': C Kahl, 'Constructing a Separate Peace: Constructivism, Collective Liberal Identity, and Democratic Peace' (1999) 8 *Security Studies* 94, 112.

[19] '[Thus] the culture, perceptions and practices that permit compromise and the peaceful resolution of conflicts without the threat of violence within countries come to apply across national boundaries toward other democratic countries': Dixon, 'Democracy and the Peaceful Settlement of International Conflict' (n 17) at 15–18. '[T]he norms and rules of behaviour internationally . . . [are] extensions of the norms and rules of the domestic political behaviour': B Russet, 'Why Democratic Peace?' in Brown, Lynn-Jones and Miller (eds), (n 13) at 82.

[20] UN Secretary-General Boutros Boutros-Ghali, *An Agenda for Democratization*, UN Doc A/51/761 (20 December 1996) para 17. In this report the UN Secretary-General further explained that liberal democratic institutions 'provide a means of compromise which can be respected by all participants in debates, thereby minimizing the risk that differences or disputes will erupt into armed conflict' and that democratic institutions 'may likewise be conducive to peace among States' (para 18).

[21] B Clinton, 'Confronting the Challenges of a Broader World', *US Department of State, Bureau of Public Affairs, Dispatch* (21 September 1993), available at: dosfan.lib.uic.edu/ERC/briefing/dispatch/1993/html/Dispatchv4no39.html.

[22] GW Bush, 'President and Prime Minister Blair Discussed Iraq, Middle East' (12 November 2004), available at: georgewbush-whitehouse.archives.gov/news/releases/2004/11/20041112-5.html.

[23] GW Bush, 'President Thanks US and Coalition Troops in Afghanistan', *The White House* (1 March 2006), available at: www.gpo.gov/fdsys/pkg/WCPD-2006-03-06/html/WCPD-2006-03-06-Pg373.htm. The careful reader will notice that throughout this chapter I refer most frequently to statements made by US administrations. This does not mean that it is only the US that subscribes to the liberal peace thesis. I use statements by the US because in material terms this is the most powerful member of the international community and thus most able to operationalise the liberal peace thesis. In this sense, the US has become the leader of the international community and therefore its representative. For a comprehensive review, however, of how the liberal peace thesis dominates the rhetoric of liberal states and liberal regional organisations see S Talbott, 'Democracy and the National Interest' (1996) 75 *Foreign Affairs* 47.

This being said, that the international community is able to enjoy a liberal peace does not in itself explain why liberal states seek to promote liberal democracy to non-liberal states. Why cannot liberal states simply enjoy their peace to the exclusion of non-liberal states? Risse-Kappen argues that the reason why the international community seeks to promote liberal democracy to non-liberal states can be adequately explained by classic realist theory. 'The presumption of potential enmity, however, creates a realist world of anarchy when democratic states interact with authoritarian regimes'.[24] In essence, the argument runs that whilst liberal states are able to 'know'[25] the peaceful intentions of other liberal states (liberal states are able to trust that other liberal states will be committed to resolving a dispute peacefully in the event that they fall into dispute), conversely liberal states are unable to discern the intentions of non-liberal states. To put the matter differently, liberal states are unable to trust that a non-liberal state will not seek recourse to force if they fall into dispute. When this uncertainty of intention is combined with the fact that all states are assumed to possess some form of military capability, the only safe course of action for the international community is to assume that all non-liberal states are potential aggressors.[26] In short, although in their relations between themselves liberal states have been able to supplant the anarchic structure of the world order, their relationship with non-liberal states can be nevertheless characterised as a 'state of nature'.[27] For this reason, the only way that the international community can avert the threat posed by non-liberal states is to encourage (or even coerce) them into adopting peace-mandating liberal norms, thereby becoming a member of the international community, contributing to the liberal peace rather than existing as a threat to it.

[24] Risse-Kappen (n 12) at 492.

[25] 'The key point to remember, when we seek to explain peaceful exchange, is that the identity factor allows peoples from different states to know each other better. This reduces the uncertainty spawned by the anarchic nature of the international system and increases mutual responsiveness. The corollary to this argument is that when it comes to democratic norms, states not only can know each other better, but they can know each other as states that tend to solve their internal and external problems by peaceful means': E Alder, 'Imagined (Security) Communities: Cognitive Regions in International Relations' (1997) 26 *Millennium: Journal of International Studies* 249, 249.

[26] For a good overview of realist theory see H Morgenthau, *Politics Among Nations* (New York, McGraw-Hill, 1985) and K Waltz, *A Theory of International Politics* (London, McGraw-Hill, 1979).

[27] As Hobbes observed, in the state of nature the intentions of other states cannot be discerned. Consequently, all states must assume that violence could be used against them at any moment: '[b]ut though there had never been any time, wherein particular men were in a condition of warre against another; yet in all other times, Kings, and Persons of Soveraigne authority, because of their Independency, are in continuall jealousies, and in the state and posture of Gladiators; having their weapons pointing, and their eyes fixed on one another; that is, their Forts, Garrisions, and Guns upon the Frontiers of their Kingdomes; and continual Spyes upon their neighbours, which is a posture of war': T Hobbes, *Leviathan* (Peterborough, Ont, Broadview Press, 2002) 89–90.

In this chapter, however, I argue that the international community relies upon a stronger justification for regarding non-liberal states as a threat to the liberal peace. Rather than assuming that non-liberal states may be a potential threat, the international community instead identifies non-liberal states to be a real and imminent threat because of their failure to embrace liberal democracy.[28] This is an important recognition because according to this justification non-liberal states are identified as actual threats because of their non-liberal constitution, rather than assumed threats because of the anarchic structure of the world order. In other words, the origin of the threat resides in the political structure of non-liberal states rather than the anarchic structure of the world order. By labelling non-liberal states as actual threats the international community is able to enhance its justification for taking liberal reformative action against non-liberal states. According to this justification, the threat represented by non-liberal states is more imminent and pressing and thus deserving of a more robust response.

In this chapter I argue that the reason why the international community identifies non-liberal states as representing an actual (rather than potential) threat to their security is because non-liberal states are considered to exist in a state of aggression with their own people. As Doyle explains, 'the atmosphere of suspicion can be attributed to the perception by liberal states that nonliberal states are in a permanent state of aggression against their own people'.[29] Importantly, I argue that liberal states consider domestic behaviour to be an indicator of likely international behaviour. Thus, non-liberal states are expected to externalise this domestic aggressive behaviour when interacting in the international sphere. Consequently, 'their foreign relations become deeply suspect for liberal governments'.[30]

Significantly, however, Doyle does not provide any guidance on why liberal states consider non-liberal states to be in a permanent state of aggression with their own people. Of course, where a government employs overt violence against its citizens and flagrantly violates their human rights it is rational to assume that a state of aggression accurately defines the relationship between ruler and ruled. But as I have already noted, the international community considers *all* non-liberal states to be in a state of aggression. What is the theoretical basis for this perception? Why does the international community consider all non-liberal states to

[28] As former British Prime Minister Tony Blair explained, '[t]he threat [to the international community] comes because, in another part of the globe, there is shadow and darkness where not all the world is free': T Blair, *Prime Minister's Speech to the US Congress* (18 July 2003), available at: http://webarchive.nationalarchives.gov.uk/20040105034004/http://number10.gov.uk/output/Page4220.asp.

[29] M Doyle, 'Kant, Liberal Legacies, and Foreign Affairs: Part II' (1983) 12 *Philosophy and Public Affairs* 323, 325.

[30] M Doyle, 'Liberalism and World Politics' (1986) 80 *American Political Science Review* 1151, 1161.

be in a state of aggression with their own people even in the absence of violent abuses of human rights? Doyle does not help us answer this question. Thus, it is this question that I address in the following section. In addition, by contrasting the international community's reaction to the nuclear programmes being pursued by India and Iran, I illustrate that the international community regards domestic politics (or more specifically the non-liberal constitution of a state) as being the primary indicator of its likely aggressiveness in the international sphere. For this reason non-liberal states are regarded as a threat to the security of the international community. After revealing why the international community perceives non-liberal states to be a threat to the liberal peace, in section 4 I address a second research question: if all non-liberal states represent a threat to the international community what are the factors that will determine which non-liberal states the international community will prioritise for liberal reformative action?

3. NON-LIBERAL STATES AND THE STATE OF AGGRESSION

Liberal states consider non-liberal states to be in a state of aggression because non-liberal governments deny the realisation of a system of governance that is universally desired. Liberal democracy is cast as a universally desired system of governance because it constructs a political structure that is devoted to protecting individual liberty and freedom (or more specifically those human rights that are considered necessary in order for liberty and freedom to be enjoyed), which are considered to be universal values. Certainly since the end of the Cold War leaders of liberal states have consistently and unambiguously claimed that liberal democracy represents a universally desired system of governance. For example, in 2006 US President George W Bush explained that

> I believe in the universality of freedom. That's what I believe. Much of my foreign policy is driven by my firm belief that everybody desires to be free; that embedded in the soul of each man and women on the face of the Earth is this deep desire to live in liberty. That's what I believe.[31]

Indeed, the international community's perception that liberal democracy is a universally desired system of governance is revealed by its reaction to the 'Arab Spring' that swept across Northern Africa and the Middle East from late 2010. In essence, the Arab Spring represented mass demonstrations in

[31] GW Bush, 'President Discusses Democracy in Iraq with Freedom House', The White House (29 March 2006), available at: georgewbush-whitehouse.archives.gov/news/releases/2006/03/images/20060329-6_d-0197-3-515h.html. Former US Secretary of State Condoleezza Rice also explained that '[l]iberty is the universal longing of every soul': C Rice, *Speech at the American University in Cairo* (20 June 2005), available at: 2001-2009.state.gov/secretary/rm/2005/48328.htm.

many Northern African and Middle Eastern states in favour of democracy and good governance.

On 19 May 2011 US President Barack Obama explained that

> [w]e support a set of universal rights. Those rights include free speech; the freedom of peaceful assembly; freedom of religion; equality for men and women under the rule of law; and the right to choose your own leaders – whether you live in Baghdad or Damascus; Sanaa or Tehran.[32]

In the same month, Australian Foreign Minister Kevin Rudd stated that '[t]he Arab democratic revolutions have made it clear that democracy is not something called for by the West. The call for democracy came resoundingly from within and to the complete surprise of the outside world'.[33] One month later, French Foreign Minister Alain Juppe determined that '[a]bove all, we must not be afraid of the Arab Spring because it embodies universal values: dignity, freedom, respect for human rights, the right of people to choose their own leaders'.[34]

The claim that liberal democracy represents a universally desired system of governance has attracted substantial criticism. In particular, critics argue that the human rights which a liberal democracy seeks to protect are culturally specific in their appeal.[35] Perhaps unsurprisingly with the liberal reconstructions currently being pursued in Afghanistan and Iraq, critics in particular argue that the human rights protected by liberal democracy are not necessarily compatible with the Islamic world. The argument runs that the values which liberal democracy protects, such as secularism and equality, are incompatible with Islam. As Lee explains, 'different civilizations or societies have different conceptions of human well-being. Hence they may have a different attitude toward human rights issues'.[36] To put the matter bluntly, '[t]he universality of international human rights norms is called fallacious'.[37]

[32] B Obama, 'Remarks by the President on the Middle East and North Africa', *The White House* (19 May 2011), available at: www.whitehouse.gov/the-press-office/2011/05/19/remarks-president-middle-east-and-north-africa.

[33] K Rudd, 'Keeping the Faith with the Arab Spring', *The Australian* (20 May 2011), available at: www.theaustralian.com.au/national-affairs/opinion/keep-the-faith-with-the-arab-spring/story-e6frgd0x-1226059172816.

[34] A Juppe, 'Speech to the Brookings Institute', Washington DC, *France Diplomatie* (6 June 2011), available at: www.diplomatie.gouv.fr/en/country-files/united-states/visits-4563/article/visit-of-alain-juppe-to-the-united.

[35] See, for example, the now-famous statement made by the Saudi Arabian representative to the United Nations: UN Doc A/C.3/32/SR.43 (1977) 11–13.

[36] M Lee, 'North Korea and the Western Notion of Human Rights' in J Hsiung (ed), *Human Rights in East Asia: A Cultural Perspective* (New York, Paragon House Publishers, 1985) 131. See generally S Huntington, *The Clash of Civilizations and the Remaking of World Order* (London, Touchstone, 1998).

[37] A Bayefsky, 'Cultural Sovereignty, Relativism, and International Human Rights: New Excuses for Old Strategies' (1996) 9 *Ratio Juris* 42, 43.

The international community has unambiguously rejected this claim of cultural relativism, asserting that the values that constitute a liberal democracy are desired by all individuals irrespective of culture or religion.[38] Indeed, that liberal democracy and Islam are compatible has been a consistent and dominant theme in the rhetoric of liberal policy-makers. As former US President George W Bush noted

> [t]he requirements of freedom apply fully to Africa and Latin American and the entire Islamic world. The peoples of the Islamic nations want and deserve the same freedoms and opportunities as people in every nation. And their governments should listen to them.[39]

These claims also resonate with the language of former British Prime Tony Blair, who explained that

> [t]here is a myth. That though we love freedom, others don't, that attachment to freedom is a product of our culture. That freedom, democracy, human rights, the rule of law are American values or Western values. That Afghan women were content under the lash of the Taliban. That Saddam was beloved by his people. That Milosevic was Serbia's saviour. Ours are not Western values. They are the universal values of the spirit.

Thus, '[w]hen we removed the Taliban and Saddam Hussein, this was not imperialism. For those oppressed people, it was their liberation'.[40]

In this chapter it is not my intention to engage in any normative judgement about whether or not liberal democracy can be correctly regarded as a universal desire.[41] Rather, my intention is to reveal that, rightly or wrongly, the international community clearly regards liberal democracy as

[38] See also the statement made by former UN Secretary-General Boutros Boutros-Ghali, who he stated that there 'is no one set of European rights, and another of African rights . . . They belong inherently to each person, each individual': quoted in T Franck, 'Are Human Rights Universal?' (2001) 80 *Foreign Affairs* 191, 197.

[39] GW Bush, 'Graduation Exercise of the United States Military Academy', *The White House* (1 June 2002), available at: georgewbush-whitehouse.archives.gov/news/releases/2002/06/20020601-3.html. As former French President Françoise Mitterrand explained: '[n]otre conception des droits de l'homme ne varie pas selon les latitudes ni selon es circonstances': quoted in F Teson, 'International Human Rights and Cultural Relativism' (1984–85) 25 *Virginia Journal of International Law* 869, 869.

[40] Blair (n 28). Former British Foreign Secretary Jack Straw also explained that '[w]e're sometimes told that democracy is a Western value; and that promoting it reflects a Western agenda which we are seeking to impose on others. I utterly reject that': J Straw, 'Promoting Democracy: A Progressive Foreign Policy Agenda' (10 March 2005), available at: news.bbc.co.uk/1/hi/uk_politics/4336159.stm.

[41] Although for a good discussion of the liberal democracy/cultural relativism debate see J Donnelly, *Universal Human Rights in Theory and Practice* (Ithaca NY, London, Cornell University Press, 2003). Indeed, the question of whether liberal democracy is a universally desired system of governance is important because if it is then the international community's promotion of liberal democracy can be regarded as an act of liberation. If it is not universally desired then the promotion of these (Western) values becomes an act of imperialism and, in the words of Hardt and Negri, represents the revival of Empire: M Hardt and A Negri, *Empire* (Cambridge MA, Harvard University Press, 2000).

representing a universally desired system of political governance. This is so significant, I argue, because it yields important implications for the way in which the international community perceives states that do not demonstrate respect for liberal democratic standards. Specifically, that where a state fails to embrace liberal democracy and respect the universal desires of its population the international community will perceive the government to exist in a state of aggression with its own citizens. This is because the population of a non-liberal state is perceived to be in a constant and determined struggle for liberal reformation and the realisation of its universal desires.[42] Consequently in order to deny calls for liberal reform and therefore maintain its sphere of control and influence, members of the international community believe that a non-liberal government will inevitably be required to exercise some degree of repression over the population.[43] Sure, some states are more non-liberal than others. Contrast the non-liberal regimes in Singapore[44] and Iran, for example. Thus, the more repressive a non-liberal state is (or rather the greater the restriction upon fundamental human rights) the more aggressive the international community will consider it to be domestically. As I reveal in the next section, where the international community considers a state to be highly aggressive domestically it will expect that state to be highly aggressive internationally.[45] The international community is therefore more likely to prioritise these extremely non-liberal states for reformative action. However, the objective of this section is to reveal why the international community considers *all* non-liberal states to be in a state of aggression with their populations even in the absence of violent abuses of human rights. I suggest that this is because non-liberal governments are perceived as denying their citizens a just and legitimate system of governance.

Importantly, I submit that liberal states consider domestic behaviour to be the primary indicator of likely international behaviour.[46] Indeed, the fact that liberal states enjoy a stable peace is explained on the same basis; the norms that demand peaceful exchange *within* liberal states are expected to

[42] As former British Prime Minister Tony Blair explained, 'in many Arab and Muslim states, similar, though less publicised, struggles for democracy dominate their politics': T Blair, *Clash of Civilizations* (21 March 2006), available at: www.guardian.co.uk/politics/2006/mar/21/iraq.iraq1.

[43] As Franck remarks, '[i]t often turns out that oppressive practices defended by leaders of a culture, far from being pedigreed, are little more than the current self-interested preferences of a power elite': Franck, 'Are Human Rights Universal?' (n 38) at 197.

[44] Zakaria refers to Singapore as a 'soft authoritarian regime': F Zakaria, 'The Rise of Illiberal Democracies' (1997) 76 *Foreign Affairs* 22, 31.

[45] This argument is developed further in section 4 below.

[46] Russett agrees, arguing that '[p]erhaps major features of the international system can be socially constructed from the bottom up; that is, norms and rules of behaviour can become extensions of the norms and rules of domestic political behaviour': Russett (n 13) at 114.

be externalised in exchanges *between* liberal states.[47] Consequently, if non-liberal states are considered to be aggressive in the domestic sphere, liberal states expect non-liberal states to externalise these aggressive tendencies when acting in the international sphere:

> [g]overnments which systematically disregard the rights of their own people are not likely to respect the rights of other nations and people and are likely to seek their objectives by coercion and force in the international field.[48]
>
> In non-democracies, decision-makers use, and may expect their opponents to use, violence and the threat of violence to resolve conflicts as part of their domestic political processes . . . Therefore non-democracies may use violence and the threat of violence in conflicts with other states, and other states may expect them to use violence and the threat of violence in such conflicts.[49]

It is important to point out here that liberal states *perceive* non-liberal states to be likely aggressive international actors because of their non-liberal structure. Thus, the international community's determination that non-liberal states represent a threat to the liberal peace is premised upon theoretical considerations, rather than empirical evidence which indicates that non-liberal states *are* inherently aggressive.[50] 'It is irrelevant in this context whether dictatorships are inherently aggressive or not. It is enough to set a security dilemma in motion if one side perceives the other as potentially violent'.[51] For the international community, the source of the threat is derived from the dual premise that non-liberal states are considered aggressive domestically and that this aggressive domestic behaviour is an indicator of likely aggressive international conduct.

[47] For liberal states, 'malignant as well as benign norms – violent as well as pacific norms – should transfer as readily from the domestic environment to the international': M Caprioli and P Trumbore, 'Identifying 'Rogue' States and Testing their Interstate Conflict Behaviour' (2003) 9 *European Journal of International Relations* 377, 379.

[48] Former US Secretary of State George Marshall, quoted in BV Cohen, 'Human Rights under the UN Charter' (1949) 14 *Law and Contemporary Problems* 430, 436.

[49] B Russett, *Grasping the Democratic Peace* (Princeton NJ, Princeton University Press, 1993) 35. Raymond also explains that 'democracies view the world as an extension of domestic politics . . . [w]hat functions at home is assumed to be viable abroad': G Raymond, 'Democracies, Disputes, and Third Party Intermediaries' (1994) 38 *Journal of Conflict Resolution* 24, 27.

[50] 'In other words, states that typically exhibit discrimination and violence in their domestic relations will, theoretically, exhibit similar behaviour in the international arena and vice versa': Caprioli and Trumbore, 'Identifying 'Rogue' States' (n 47) at 379. It is interesting to point out, however, that, Burke-White has reviewed instances of international aggression since the end of the Cold War and suggests that non-liberal states are *empirically* more likely to be aggressive in the international sphere. He concludes that '[e]vidence from the post-Cold War period indicates that states that systematically abuse their own citizens' human rights are also those most likely to engage in aggression': W Burke-White, 'Human Rights and National Security: The Strategic Correlation' (2004) 17 *Harvard Human Rights Journal* 249, 250.

[51] Risse-Kappen (n 12) at 507.

3.1 Case Study: Contrasting the US's Differing Responses to India and Iran's Nuclear Programmes

That the international community regards the non-liberal constitution of a state to be an indicator of likely aggressive behaviour in the international sphere is vividly illustrated by contrasting the way in which the international community has responded to the nuclear programmes being pursued by India and Iran. In particular, the United States' differing reactions to India and Iran are informative. In 2006 US President George W Bush concluded an agreement with the Indian Prime Minister to share US nuclear technology and fuel with India. This is despite the fact that India has not signed the Non-Proliferation Treaty, which imposes an obligation upon signatory states to use nuclear energy for exclusively peaceful purposes. Contrast this, however, with the way in which the US has reacted to Iran's nuclear programme. Iran was one of the original signatories to the Non-Proliferation Treaty and is thus subject to the obligation to use nuclear energy for peaceful purposes.[52] Notwithstanding this obligation, the US (in conjunction with other members of the international community) has sought to censure and frustrate Iran's programme for nuclear development. The question becomes how can we explain these different approaches? I suggest that the answer to this question is located in how the US perceives these states to be politically constituted. Consistently, the US has reiterated the liberal credentials of India. In 2005 President Bush explained:

> I'm proud to stand here today with Prime Minister Singh, the leader of one of the world's great democracies . . . India and the United States share a commitment to freedom and a belief that democracy provides the best path to a more hopeful future for all people. We also believe that the spread of liberty is the best alternative to hatred and violence. Because of our shared values, the relationship between our two countries has never been stronger. We're working together to make our nations more secure, deliver a better life to our citizens and advance the cause of peace and freedom throughout the world.[53]

The US therefore clearly regards India to be a functioning liberal democracy. As a result, the US is prepared to facilitate the development of India's nuclear capabilities irrespective of the fact that it is not bound by the Non-Proliferation Treaty's obligation to use nuclear power for peaceful purposes. This is because the US considers India to be a member of the international community and therefore committed to liberal peace. Thus,

[52] Article III Non-Proliferation Treaty 1968.

[53] GW Bush, 'President, Prime Minister of India Discuss Freedom and Democracy', *The White House* (18 July 2005), available at: georgewbush-whitehouse.archives.gov/news/releases/2005/07/20050718-6.html.

even if India were to use its nuclear power to develop nuclear weapons[54] the US can be certain (they can trust) that these weapons would not be used against them (or indeed the wider international community).

By contrast, the US regards Iran to be an extremely aggressive state domestically because it denies its own citizens the most basic human rights. In 2003 President Bush explained that '[i]n Iran, we continue to see a government that represses its people, pursues weapons of mass destruction, and supports terror'.[55] In 2006 President Bush explicitly linked Iran's non-liberal political character to the threat it poses. He explained that

> Iran [is] a nation now held hostage by a small clerical elite that is isolating and repressing its people. The regime in that country sponsors terrorists in the Palestinian territories and in Lebanon . . . The Iranian government is defying the world with its nuclear ambitions, and the nations of the world must not permit the Iranian regime to gain nuclear weapons. American will continue to rally the world to confront these threats.[56]

Iran's failure to embrace liberal democracy is thus considered to be an indicator of likely international aggression and Iran is therefore considered to be a threat to the US and the wider international community. For this reason, President Bush determined that 'Iran would be very dangerous with nuclear weapons';[57] '[t]he most destabilizing thing that can happen is for Iran to have a nuclear weapon'.[58] The US is therefore determined to prevent Iran from developing nuclear power because it cannot trust Iran to use nuclear power peacefully, ie not to use nuclear power to develop nuclear weapons. This lack of trust exists irrespective of Iran's obligations under the Non-Proliferation Treaty. The US's inability to trust Iran on the basis of its non-liberal character is evident from the following quotation from President Bush:

> And the good news is most of the world recognizes that Iran, being the non-transparent society that it is, a government that had violated IAEA [International Atomic Energy Association] rules, is one that cannot be trusted with technology that could enable it to develop a nuclear weapon.[59]

[54] In fact, India already possesses nuclear weapons, having successfully tested them in 1978.

[55] GW Bush, 'State of the Union Address', *The White House* (28 January 2003), available at: whitehouse.georgewbush.org/news/2003/012803-SOTU.asp.

[56] GW Bush, 'State of the Union Address', *The White House* (31 January 2006), available at: georgewbush-whitehouse.archives.gov/stateoftheunion/2006/.

[57] G W Bush, 'President Discusses Medicare, Iraq, Iran and the Middle East', *The White House* (18 June 2003), available at: georgewbush-whitehouse.archives.gov/newsreleases/2003/06/20030618-6.html.

[58] GW Bush, 'President Meets with President Hamid Karzai in Kabul, Afghanistan'. (1 March 2006), available: 2001-2009.state.gov/p/sca/rls/rm/2006/62285.htm.

[59] GW Bush, 'President Bush Delivers State of the Union Address', *The White House* (2006), available at: www.whitehouse.gov/news/releases/2006/01/print/20060131-10.html.

It is important to reiterate that the source of the threat is not the possibility that Iran could possess nuclear weapons. Rather, the source of the threat is Iran's aggressive political regime, the 'unelected few [that] repress the Iranian people's hope for freedom'.[60] Fundamentally, it is the nature of Iran's political regime that is the repository of the threat. As Hayes explains, '[it is] the nature of the country's government [that] makes it aggressive, untrustworthy, and a threat to the democratic United States . . . the political character of Iran is the central referent point in the threat discussion'.[61] Indeed, I submit that this explanation can be also applied to account for why the US (and the coalition of the willing) intervened in Iraq in 2003. The source of the threat was not Iraq's (assumed) possession of weapons of mass destruction per se. Rather, it was the fact that a regime *like* the one in Iraq, ie extremely aggressive domestically, could be in possession of weapons of mass destruction that created the threat.[62]

Thus, because of their non-liberal constitutions all non-liberal states are considered to be 'dangerous'[63] international actors. 'The main threat to the security of the international community is the weakness of states owing to a lack of democratic structures'.[64] Although some non-liberal states represent a greater threat than others (see Section 4), I contend that for the international community all non-liberal states represent at the very least an existential threat to the liberal peace. In the famous words of Immanuel Kant,

> man (or an individual people) in a mere state of nature robs me of any such security and injures me by virtue of this very state in which he coexists with me. He may not have injured me actively (*facto*), but he does injure me by the very lawlessness of his state (*statu iniusto*), for he is a permanent threat to me, and I can require him either to enter into a common lawful state along with me or to move away from my vicinity.[65]

[60] GW Bush, 'President Delivers State of the Union Address', *The White House* (2002), available at: www.whitehouse.gov/news/releases/2002/01/20020129-11.html.

[61] J Hayes, 'Identity and Securitization in the Democratic Peace: The United States and the Divergence of Response to India and Iran's Nuclear Programs' (2009) 53 *International Studies Quarterly* 977, 991.

[62] Consider, for example, the following statement by US Senator John Kerry. In justifying his vote in the US Senate to authorise the US President to use force against Iraq he explained 'without question, we need to disarm Saddam Hussein. He is a brutal, murderous dictator, leading an oppressive regime . . . He presents a particularly grievous threat because he is so consistently prone to miscalculation. And now he has continued deceit and his consistent grasp for weapons of mass destruction . . . So the threat of Saddam Hussein with weapons of mass destruction is real': J Kerry, *Speech at Georgetown University* (23 January 2003), available at: kerry.senate.gov/text/cfm/record.cfm?id=189831.

[63] J Owen, 'How Liberalism Produces Democratic Peace' (1994) 19 *International Security* 87, 103.

[64] A Rotfeld, 'The Organizing Principles of Global Society' in *Stockholm International Peace Research Institute Yearbook* (2001) 1, 3.

[65] Kant, 'Perpetual Peace' (n 15) at 98.

For the international community, the only way that this threat can be averted is by steering non-liberal states towards liberal democratic reform; by replacing their aggressive domestic political structure with one that is based upon cooperation, mediation and conciliation, ie liberal democracy.[66] In US President Woodrow Wilson's celebrated caption, 'the world must be made safe for democracy'.[67] After this process of liberalisation the state will contribute to the liberal peace rather than existing as an existential threat to it. Consequently, and as Kant explained, this liberal peace will only become a perpetual peace where the world order is composed of exclusively liberal states.[68] For the international community, peace can be only achieved where all states of the world order embrace liberal norms that mandate peaceful exchange.[69]

4. QUANTIFYING AND PRIORITISING THREATS TO THE INTERNATIONAL COMMUNITY

Propelled by the liberal peace thesis, liberal states have engaged in an 'aggressive push to bring freedom and democracy to countries where evil

[66] According to President GW Bush in 2002, '[w]e will defend the peace against the threats from terrorists and tyrants. We will preserve the peace by building good relations among the great powers. And we will extend the peace by encouraging free and open societies on every continent': GW Bush, 'President's Commencement Address', *The White House* (1 June 2002), available at: georgewbush-whitehouse.archives.gov/news/releases/2002/06/20020601-3.html. '[U]ltimately the best strategy to ensure our security and to build a durable peace is to support the advance of [liberal] democracy elsewhere': former US President Bill Clinton, 'State of the Union Address' (25 January 1994), available at: www.washingtonpost.com/wp-srv/politics/special/states/docs/sou94.htm.

[67] President Wilson further explained, '[a] steadfast concert of peace can never be maintained except by a partnership of democratic nations. No autocratic government could be trusted to keep faith within it or its covenants. It must be a league of honour, a partnership of opinion': W Wilson, 'Declaration for War' (2 April 1917). See also the speech delivered by the President of the American Society of International Law and the former Secretary of State Elihu Root at the Annual Meeting of the Society in 1917: 'So long as military autocracy continues, democracy is not safe from attacks, which are certain to come sometime, and certain to find it unprepared. The conflict is inevitable and universal; and it is *a l'outrance*. To be safe democracy must kill its enemy when it can and where it can. The world cannot be half democratic and half autocratic': E Root, 'The Effect of Democracy on International Law' (1917) 11 *Proclamation American Society of International Law* 10.

[68] It should be noted here that although Kant refers to 'republican' government in his discussion of a perpetual peace, in contemporary politics this approximates to what we understand today to be liberal democracy: see M Doyle, 'Kant, Liberal Legacies, and Foreign Affairs: Part I' (1983) 12 *Philosophy and Public Affairs* 205, 207.

[69] 'Peace is understood to lie in the establishment of reconstructive and transformative processes that culminate in a state that mirror the liberal-democratic state': O Richmond, 'UN Peace Operations and the Dilemmas of the Peacebuilding Consensus' (2004) 11 *International Peacekeeping* 83, 87. As former British Prime Minister Tony Blair noted, 'the best defence of our security lies in the spread of our values': T Blair, 'Speech on the Threat of Global Terrorism' (5 March 2004), available at: webarchive.nationalarchives.gov.uk/20040308042406/http://pm.gov.uk:80/output/Page5470.asp.

lurks'.[70] However, as I suggested in chapter one, the international community is not physically capable of engaging in a sustained campaign for liberal reform in all non-liberal states. Operationally, this is impossible. As former British Prime Minister Tony Blair stated in 1999,

> [l]ooking around the world there are many regimes that are undemocratic and engaged in barbarous acts. If we wanted to right every wrong that we see in the modern world then we would do little else than intervene in the affairs of other countries. We would not be able to cope.[71]

Thus, many non-liberal states do not feature in the immediate security concerns of the international community and there is little attempt by liberal states to induce these states into liberal reform. Sure, the fact that the international community now articulates a standard of legitimate statehood imposes substantial political pressure upon non-liberal states to undergo reform and thereby join the international community. But beyond this political pressure, many non-liberal states remain outside of the international community's sphere of concern.

This being said, other non-liberal states do attract the attention of the international community and become actual targets for liberal reformative action. Specifically, the international community deploys coercive measures against certain non-liberal states with the clear objective of engendering liberal reform. The measures available to the international community exist on a continuum of coerciveness. Practice illustrates a range of weak and strong methods of coercion.[72] An example of a weak method of coercion is excluding non-liberal states from liberal international organisations (and consequently the benefits that these organisations confer), on the basis that the required standards of liberal democracy have not been attained. These excluded non-liberal states are then informed of the measures that they must adopt in order to reach the requisite political standard and thus be permitted admission to the organisation. The exclusion of Turkey from the EU, for example, has been consistently justified on the basis of its poor human rights practices. As the President of the European Commission explained,

[70] J Ikenberry, 'The End of the Neo-Conservative Moment' (2004) 46 *Survival* 7, 7.

[71] Blair (n 2).

[72] '[C]oercive measures . . . can vary in intensity from non-recognition through diverse economic sanctions to the threat or use of force, a category further subdividable in various important ways': T Farer, 'The Promotion of Democracy: International Law and Norms' in E Newman and R Rich (eds), *The UN Role in Promoting Democracy: Between Ideals and Reality* (New York, United Nations University Press, 2004) 41–42. As Franck explains, 'the international community has many sanctions that can be deployed to protect universal values. These range from diplomatic non-recognition to the suspension of air traffic and the withholding of World Bank loans, International Monetary Fund credits, and bilateral trading privileges': Franck (n 38) at 204.

> [w]e are concerned about Turkey because the pace of reforms is rather slow from our point of view. I believe it would be great to have Turkey if Turkey respects all the economic and political criteria. This is not the case.[73]

The use of development aid is another example of a 'weak' coercive measure that is deployed by the international community in order to cajole non-liberal states into liberal reform. In this context it is interesting to consider the EU's Cotonou Agreement 2000 with the American, Caribbean and Pacific (ACP) states. This Agreement states that the EU will only make development aid available to ACP states where it is linked to sustainable development. The Cotonou Agreement makes it quite clear that '[r]espect for human rights and fundamental freedoms, including respect for fundamental social rights, democracy based on the rule of law and transparent and accountable governance are an integral part of sustainable development'.[74] To this end, the EU will only make aid available to ACP states where they demonstrate a commitment to improving their human rights practices and the quality of their governance.

Political and economic sanctions are additional examples of coercive measures deployed by the international community in order to encourage non-liberal states to adopt liberal democratic reforms. Consider, for example, the EU's comprehensive sanctions regime against Zimbabwe. As a direct response to Zimbabwe's record of human rights abuses and its sham elections the EU imposed sanctions against government officials (including President Robert Mugabe) and Zimbabwean companies that were complicit in the human rights abuses and the frustration of democratic practices.[75] This has included the freezing of assets and preventing specified governmental officials from visiting any EU state, and also preventing EU-based companies from engaging in commercial ventures with

[73] President of the European Commission, Jose Manuel Barroso, 'EU Relations', *The Times* (16 October 2006), available at: news.bbc.co.uk/1/hi/programmes/sunday_am/6052808.stm.

[74] Cotonou Agreement (signed 23 June 2000, Cotonou), Articles 9 (political dialogue) and 96 (consultation procedure on human rights). See further the EU's 2006 Consensus on Development, which explained that development aid would be available to those ACP states that embrace the EU's 'common values of . . . respect for human rights, fundamental freedoms, peace, [and] democracy . . .': 'European Consensus on Development' (Joint statement by the Council and the representatives of the governments of the Member States meeting within the Council, the European Parliament and the Commission on European Union Development Policy: 'The European Consensus'), 24 February 2006 ([2006] OJ C46/01) point 13. In the case that one of the parties fails to fulfil an obligation relating to the respect for human rights, democratic principles or the rule of law, a consultation procedure can be initiated followed by 'appropriate measures' to be taken if necessary. Suspension of the agreement can occur as a last resort: Article 96.

[75] In imposing sanctions the EU condemned 'the ongoing violations of human rights, in particular the abduction and detention of those exercising a democratic right to express opposition to the regime and of those defending human rights': Brussels – Council of the European Union, 2920th General Affairs Council Meeting, *Conclusions on Zimbabwe* (26 January 2009).

embargoed Zimbabwean companies. The EU has made it clear to Zimbabwe that these sanctions will only be lifted when human rights are respected and power is passed to democratically elected representatives.[76] Indeed, more recently the EU has imposed a similar sanctions regime against individuals and institutions in Syria that have been linked to human rights abuses since the start of the conflict in 2011.[77]

Albeit in the most extreme of circumstances, the international community has been prepared to use military force in order to encourage non-liberal states to undergo liberal reform. Indeed, this is undoubtedly the most coercive sanction available to the international community. In certain instances liberal states have intervened militarily in non-liberal states, often toppling a regime in the process, and then assuming responsibility over the state, reconstructing it upon a liberal basis (see Kosovo, East Timor, Afghanistan and Iraq). However, this raises the question of how the international community prioritises which non-liberal states should be singled out for liberal reformative action? Against which non-liberal states will the international community concert their efforts and engage in a sustained endeavour to reconstruct them upon a liberal basis? The answer to this question can be again located in the political structure of non-liberal states. For the international community, because liberal democracy represents a universal aspiration, the more repressive a non-liberal regime is in the domestic sphere the greater the aggression perpetrated by the non-liberal regime against the population. Indeed, when the abuse of human rights is flagrant and widespread, perhaps spilling over into violence, a non-liberal government will be considered to be in a highly aggressive relationship with its population. Furthermore, the extent of the government's aggressiveness in the domestic sphere will be an indicator of how aggressive it is likely to be in the international sphere. In sum, the more aggressive a regime is domestically, the greater the threat it poses to the security of the international community.[78] This is clearly reflected in the language and justifications used by leaders of liberal states. Consider, for example, former US President George W Bush's famous determination that there exists an 'axis of evil' within the world

[76] 'The Council reaffirms that the European Union stands ready to support the economic and social recovery of Zimbabwe once a government reflecting the will of the Zimbabwean people has been formed and shows tangible signs of a return to respect for human rights, the rule of law and macroeconomic stabilization': ibid.

[77] For an overview of this sanctions regime see: www.consilium.europa.eu/uedocs/cms_data/docs/pressdata/EN/foraff/132847.pdf.

[78] The corollary is that '[s]ignficant improvements in a previously repressive state's human rights policy can signal an intent not to engage in international aggression . . . States of concern can utilize the linkage between human rights and international aggression as a means to send unambiguous signals of the lack of aggressive intent through institutionalized improvements in human rights practices': Burke-White, 'Human Rights and National Security' (n 50) at 272.

order that poses the greatest threat to the security of the international community (and in particular the US).[79] It is not surprising that this axis was constituted by Iran, North Korea and Iraq, states that were considered to be extremely repressive in their domestic spheres.[80]

At this juncture it is prudent to point out that there are other factors that will affect how threatening a non-liberal state appears to be to the international community. It is necessary to bring in here the seminal work of Alexander Wendt, for his work has been highly influential in explaining threat perception since the end of the Cold War. In particular, Wendt argues that perceived threats to state security are constructed on the basis of the conduct, acts and gestures that materialises between states as they interact with each other.[81] He argues that when states (or rather the governments of each state) come into contact in the international sphere one state will make an act or gesture and the other state will then interpret this act and respond to it. In light of this 'social act'[82] each state will form a perception of the other and determine whether or not they are to be regarded as a threat; in essence, whether they are considered to be a friend or enemy. During interaction a state may commit a whole array of acts that will contribute towards how it is perceived. This may include, for example, the political language the state is using. Is its rhetoric bellicose or is it benign? Another factor may include whether or not a state has previously committed an internationally wrongful act, particularly an act of aggression. If so, how has that state addressed these previous international wrongs? Does it deny that the wrongful act happened or does it seek to displace blame onto others? Does it glorify the act or is it in fact apologetic?[83] Does it participate in international organisations? This is important because such participation demonstrates a preparedness to engage in dialogue and compromise in order to confront international problems.[84] Other acts and gestures that could be germane to the calculation of threat perception include how a state organises its military forces. Is the military organised in a defensive fashion or is it positioned close to the border of a state with which it experiences uneasy relations? Moreover, is the state under scrutiny increasing its weapons arsenal, such as seeking to develop long-range missiles or nuclear weapons? For constructivists,

[79] GW Bush, 'State of the Union Address' (29 January 2002), available at: georgewbush-whitehouse.archives.gov/news/releases/2002/01/20020129-11.html.

[80] 'Iran's human rights record alone would place it near the top of the US policy agendas as a potential aggressor state': Burke-White (n 50) at 276.

[81] A Wendt, *A Social Theory of International Politics* (Cambridge, Cambridge University Press, 1999) 33.

[82] A Wendt, 'Anarchy is What States Make of It: A Social Construction of Power Politics' (1992) 46 *International Organization* 391, 405.

[83] N Kristof, 'The Problem of Memory' (1998) 77 *Foreign Affairs* 37.

[84] R Keohane and L Martin, 'The Promise of Internationalist Theory' (1995) 20 *International Security* 20, 39.

such conduct, acts and gestures will determine whether or not a state is considered a threat. Indeed, Wendt argues quite vigorously that although threat perception is constructed on the basis of state identity, state identity is defined by reference to the acts and conduct of a state (its 'corporate identity'),[85] not its political constitution (political identity).[86] For Wendt, the reference point of threat perception (whether the state is a friend or enemy) is not the political constitution of the state but its actions and conduct.[87] Significantly, Wendt then argues that in order for security threats to be deconstructed states must be prepared to transform their corporate identity, ie where they modify their acts and conduct towards each other so as to engender peaceful perceptions. Wendt uses Mikhail Gorbachev's policy of 'New Thinking' towards the West (which constituted a fundamental change of attitude from the Soviet Union's previous aggressive stance) as 'an example of how states might transform a competitive security system into a cooperative one'.[88]

This is at odds with the approach I have developed here. As I explained in the previous section, when a liberal state interacts with other states in the world order its primary concern is to make the crucial determination of whether or not that state is liberal: as Owen explains, liberal democracies 'assess threat through an ideological prism'.[89] If the state being scrutinised demonstrates respect for liberal values then peaceful relations will be enjoyed. In recognising each other as liberal, these liberal states will modify their behaviour/actions to ensure peaceful intentions are manifestly communicated. In contrast, if a liberal state determines that the other state is not liberal, however, by its very nature it will be regarded as a threat; its actions, conduct and gestures notwithstanding.[90] However, in making the determination that a state is non-liberal the liberal state will further assess the extent to which liberal values are denied. The extent to

[85] A Wendt, 'Constructing International Politics (1995) 20 *International Security* 71, 73 ff.

[86] 'Actors do not have a "portfolio" of interests that they carry around independent of social context; instead, they define their interests in the process of defining situations': Wendt, 'Anarchy is What States Make of It' (n 82) at 398.

[87] In using the example of alter and ego (two fictional states) meeting each other in the international sphere, Wendt explains that 'there is no reason for it [alter] to assume a priori – before the gesture – that ego is threatening, since it is only through a process of signalling and interpreting that the costs and probabilities of being wrong can be determined': Wendt (n 82) at 405. Thus, for Wendt ultimately perceptions of enmity (and perceptions of amity) are determined by the acts and conduct of other states, as opposed to their domestic political composition.

[88] Wendt (n 82) at 420.

[89] J Owen, 'Perceptions and the Limits of the Liberal Peace: Mexican-American and Spanish-American Wars' in M Elman (ed), *Paths to Peace: Is Democracy the Answer?* (Cambridge MA/London, MIT Press, 1997) 186.

[90] Thus, there is a 'dualism in a democracy's foreign conduct with one set of norms characterizing its relations with other democracies and another set applying to those with non-democracies': S Chan, 'In Search of Democratic Peace: Problems and Promise' (1997) 41 *Mershon International Studies Review* 59, 77.

which individual liberty is restricted by the regime will be a prima facie indicator of the magnitude of the threat that the non-liberal state poses to the security of the international community. Thus, the degree of the restriction upon individual liberty and human rights will signal which non-liberal state(s) should be prioritised for liberal reform.

Of course, the magnitude of this threat can be elevated or reduced depending upon the actions/conduct of the non-liberal state. The corporate identity of a non-liberal state is therefore very important to the approach that I develop here. Although I ultimately reject Wendt's submission that the international community determines whether a non-liberal state is threatening or not on the basis of its corporate identity, I accept that a non-liberal state's corporate identity does play a significant role in determining the extent to which the international community considers it threatening. For example, a non-liberal state may be not particularly aggressive in the domestic sphere but its 'threat status' nevertheless elevated if it makes hostile statements against a member of the international community. Alternatively, the threat posed by a state whose government is an inherently aggressive regime in the domestic sphere may be reduced if it is benign in its interactions with liberal states. It is for this reason, I believe, that the international community has failed effectively to intervene in states such as Zimbabwe and Sudan in order to put an end to the violent abuses of human rights that are being perpetrated by these governments against their populations. Although these states commit violent abuses of human rights in the domestic setting and, prima facie, can be assumed to be highly aggressive in the international sphere, the fact that they have not supported international terrorism, pursued weapons of mass destruction or made credible threats to the international community has meant that they have remained generally outside of the international community's sphere of concern. If, however, such a state exhibits aggressive tendencies in its relations with members of the international community (for example, it has previously committed acts of aggression (like Saddam Hussein's Iraq), or has directed aggressive rhetoric towards members of the international community (Iran's claim that Israel does not deserve to exist comes to mind), harbours terrorist organisations (like the Taliban in Afghanistan), or perhaps has sought to bolster its material power (such as pursuing weapons of mass destruction (like Iraq[91] and now Iran)) then, when combined with the inherently aggressive nature of its regime, it will become a priority for liberal reformation.

Fundamentally, however, and as the previous discussion of the international community's differing reactions to the nuclear programmes

[91] Of course, weapons of mass destruction have not been found in Iraq. However, at the time of the intervention the US, the UK and their allies were convinced that Iraq possessed weapons of mass destruction and that they were operational: see news.bbc.co.uk/1/hi/uk_politics/2277352.stm.

being pursued by liberal India and non-liberal Iran illustrates, for the international community the reference point of threat perception is the failure of a non-liberal state to embrace liberal norms. The consequence is that for liberal states a non-liberal state will inevitably be considered a threat regardless of its actions and conduct. This is because it is its internal political nature that renders it a threat. Thus, a non-liberal state may modify its actions in order to make itself appear less threatening (such as when Libya handed over for trial individuals suspected of being involved in the Lockerbie bombings). Alternatively, members of the international community may force a non-liberal state to modify its conduct in order to alleviate the extent of the threat it poses (Israel's pre-emptive attack on Iraq's nuclear reactor in 1981 comes to mind). However, for the international community a change of actions/conduct will not eliminate the threat posed by that non-liberal state. This will not allow peace to be enjoyed. Rather, in order to achieve a genuine peace liberal states believe that they must alter the domestic political structure of non-liberal states, ie non-liberal states must undergo internal political (liberal) reform. In sum, for the international community the antidote to the threat is political, not material.

5. CONCLUSION

The principal objective of this chapter has been to provide a fuller, more convincing explanation for why the international community has sought to promote (at times aggressively) its liberal values to non-liberal states. The answer to this question can be located in the empirical finding that liberal states are able to enjoy a durable peace whilst any disputes that emerge between them can be resolved without recourse to force. Significantly, I have argued that the international community considers non-liberal states to represent a threat to this liberal peace on the basis that they exist in a state of aggression with their own people. In essence, the governments of non-liberal states deny the realisation of a form of governance (liberal democracy) that is universally desired. From this domestic aggression liberal states infer likely aggressive conduct in the international sphere. Although the more aggressive a non-liberal regime is in the domestic sphere (the greater the denial of individual liberty) the greater the threat it is regarded as representing to the security of members of the international community, I have suggested that for the international community all non-liberal states exist as a threat to the liberal peace. In line with Immanuel Kant's observations, for the international community its liberal peace will only be perpetual where all states are constituted upon a liberal basis. This is the theory, I argue, that sustains and motivates the international community's campaign for liberal development.

4

The International Community and the Security Council

'The United Nations . . . has always been and continues to be a Western organization in the sense that the policies of the organization most often coincide with Western preferences . . . The "West", moreover, never was, nor is it now, solely the United States. It is a multinational entity . . . politically, it is a club of democracies; ideologically, it is the source and center of liberal internationalism; hegemonically, it is a transnational coalition of elites sharing interests, aims, and aspirations stemming from similar institutions and a common ideology'.[1]

1. INTRODUCTION

THE SECURITY COUNCIL possesses a fundamentally important position within the United Nations (UN) system. Under Article 24 of the UN Charter the Security Council is conferred the primary responsibility for maintaining international peace and security. In order to discharge this objective, Chapter VII of the UN Charter confers upon the Security Council the power to take mandatory enforcement action against member states to the extent that it is considered necessary to maintain or restore international peace and security. In this context, enforcement action includes forcible or non-forcible measures.[2] Importantly, in order to engage Chapter VII, at least nine of the 15 Security Council members, including at least the permanent five,[3] must agree that there exists 'a threat to international peace and security, a breach of the peace or an act of aggression'.[4]

[1] D Puchala, 'World Hegemony and the United Nations' (2005) 7 *International Studies Review* 571, 577.

[2] Articles 41 and 42 UN Charter.

[3] Article 27 UN Charter.

[4] Article 39 UN Charter. Whilst Article 39 distinguishes between situations that constitute a threat to international peace and security, a breach of international peace and security and an act of aggression, in practice the Security Council has not made such a systematic distinction. Instead it has opted to declare the minimum that is necessary in order to engage Chapter VII: 'a threat to international peace and security': T Franck, 'The Security Council and "Threats to the Peace": Some Remarks on Remarkable Recent Developments' in R-J Depuy (ed), *Peace-Keeping and Peace-Building: The Development of the Role of the Security Council* (Boston, Martinus Nijhoff, 1993) 83, 86.

As the UN is the formal institutionalisation of the international society, the Security Council was always intended to interpret Chapter VII in accordance with the principles of sovereign equality and non-intervention. Specifically, the Security Council was always intended to use its mandatory enforcement powers under Chapter VII in order to preserve the territorial integrity and political independence of its member states from external intervention. I submit that the framers of the Charter never intended the Security Council to employ its enforcement powers in order to interfere in matters that were essentially domestic in nature. Articles 2(1) and 2(7) of the UN Charter expressly reserve this competence for each member state. Indeed, in section 2 of this chapter I illustrate that, at least during the Cold War, this is how the Security Council interpreted Chapter VII. By reviewing Security Council practice until the end of the Cold War I reveal that the Security Council was only prepared to declare a threat to international peace and security where state sovereignty was threatened or violated.

As I suggested in previous chapters, with the end of the Cold War liberal states altered their ideological commitments, largely rejecting the principle of the sovereign equality of states and instead subscribing to the view that liberal democracy represents the only legitimate form of political governance. The consequence is that those liberal states on the Security Council have sought to encourage the Council to engage its mandatory powers in order to promote liberal democracy to those states that do not adhere to liberal democratic standards. Significantly, however, the Security Council still comprises non-liberal states that remain loyal to the principles of sovereign equality and non-intervention. Presumably, these non-liberal states would prevent the Security Council from engaging Chapter VII in order to intervene in the domestic affairs of a member state and promote a particular form of political governance (liberal democracy).[5] This point is particularly salient in relation to those non-liberal states that occupy a permanent seat on the Security Council who can therefore unilaterally veto any resolution. Consequently, because of the disparate political composition of the Security Council (specifically liberal and non-liberal states), it would appear that the international community would be forced to act *outside* of the Security Council if it is to promote respect for liberal values.

This was certainly the case in relation to the ethnic cleansing campaign that was being perpetrated in Kosovo in 1999. Despite attempts by liberal states to encourage the Security Council to engage its collective security system to address the ethnic cleansing campaign, Russia and China

[5] Fidler considers it axiomatic that in order 'for collective security to work through the Security Council, the great powers would have to share identical interests in preserving the peace and pursue such shared interests collectively': D Fidler, 'Caught between Traditions: The Security Council in Philosophical Conundrum' (1995–96) 17 *Michigan Journal of International Law* 411, 427.

prevented the Security Council from authorising forcible intervention.[6] For Russia and China the situation in Kosovo was considered to be an essentially domestic matter in which the UN had no appropriate role. In the face of a worsening humanitarian crisis the international community (acting through NATO) took the decision to use force without prior Security Council authorisation in order to put an end to the violent abuses of human rights being perpetrated. As Sadeniemi observes, the consequence is that '[i]n our day . . . democratically legitimated states have shown a growing . . . tendency to restrict some forms of international discourses and co-operation to their own circle'.[7] If non-liberal states are prepared to block Security Council decisions that seek to promote liberal values then the international community will decide for itself when and how liberal values are to be promoted. This is justified on the basis that 'dictators cannot be treated as the pinnacle of international legitimacy'. Instead, 'democracies must band together to reflect their true power and legitimacy'.[8]

Interestingly, this also seems to the position playing out in Syria at the time of writing (January 2013). As is well known, with the on-going fighting between President Al-Assad's government and rebel forces, a severe humanitarian crisis is occurring in Syria. Despite international condemnation of the human rights abuses being perpetrated against civilians, Russia and China continue to veto any UN Security Council resolution which authorises the deployment of tougher measures against the Syrian regime.[9] In response, United States (US) Secretary of State Hilary Clinton has stated that

> we haven't seen eye-to-eye with Russia on Syria and that may continue and if it does continue we will work with like-minded states to support the Syrian opposition to hasten the day when Assad falls and to help prepare Syria for a democratic future.[10]

This being said, however, in this chapter I argue that the international community has remained (generally) committed to the UN's collective security system and has actually achieved a large degree of success in convincing the Security Council to use Chapter VII of the UN Charter to promote respect for its liberal values. Section 3 below argues that with the end of the Cold War there has been a fundamental transformation in how

[6] See L Henkin, 'Kosovo and the Law of "Humanitarian Intervention"' (1999) 93 *American Journal of International Law* 824.

[7] P Sadeniemi, *Principles of Legitimacy and International Relations* (Helsingfors, Helsingfors Universitet, 1995) 227–28.

[8] Editorial, *Jerusalem Post* (4 October 2002) 6A, quoted in I Clark, *Legitimacy in International Society* (Oxford, Oxford University Press, 2005) 187.

[9] 'Friction at the UN as Russia and China Veto Another Resolution on Syria Sanctions', *The New York Times* (19 July 2012), available at: www.nytimes.com/2012/07/20/world/middleeast/russia-and-china-veto-un-sanctions-against-syria.html?_r=0.

[10] Quoted in 'US Doesn't need UN to Oust Assad-Clinton', *Question More* (10 September 2012), available at: rt.com/news/clinton-syria-un-unnecessary-755/.

the Security Council interprets the concept of a threat to international peace and security. Indeed, in section 3, I review Chapter VII decisions taken by the Security Council since the end of the Cold War and demonstrate that the Security Council has exhibited an increased willingness to declare a threat to international peace and security where there has been a violation of liberal values, and taken enforcement action against member states to ensure their compliance with such standards. In addition, I examine the nature of the enforcement action authorised by the Security Council because this demonstrates the extent of the normative commitment of the Security Council to the realisation of liberal objectives.

2. THE COLD WAR YEARS: PROTECTING STATE SOVEREIGNTY

As an organ of the UN the Security Council must discharge its responsibilities 'in accordance with the Purposes and Principles of the United Nations Charter'.[11] As I explained in chapter one, although the Charter makes sporadic references to the protection of human rights as an objective of the UN,[12] as the formal institutionalisation of the international society the UN was created with the ultimate objective of protecting the sovereignty of its member states from external intervention, particularly from the threat or use of force. It is clear from the structure and wording of the Charter that human rights are allocated a subservient role in the UN's hierarchy of principles and objectives, being subordinated to the principle of the sovereign equality of states; '[that] the protection of nation states from each other, and that not of individuals from their own government, is given pride of place in UN Purposes and Principles'.[13] Thus, the 'original plan'[14] was that a threat to international peace and security would only emerge where the territorial integrity or political independence of another state was threatened or violated. The concept of a threat to

[11] Article 24(2) UN Charter. This has been reaffirmed in the *Tadić* case where the Appeals Chamber explained that the Security Council does not have 'a totally unfettered discretion, as it has to remain, at the very least, within the Purposes and Principles of the Charter': *Prosecutor v Dusko Tadić*, Case No IT-94-1-AR72 (2 October 1995) para 27. Cf Kelsen who explains that 'it is completely within the discretion of the Security Council to decide what constitutes a "threat to the peace"': H Kelsen, *The Law of the United Nations* (New York: Frederick A Praeger 1964).

[12] See Article 1(3) and Articles 55–56 UN Charter. See also the Preamble of the Charter which states that 'the United Nations [is] determined . . . to reaffirm faith in fundamental human rights, in the dignity and worth of the human person'.

[13] J Alvarez, 'Constitutional Interpretation in International Organisations' in J-M Coicaud and V Heiskinman (eds), *The Legitimacy of International Organizations* (Tokyo, United Nations University Press, 2001) 107. '[W]hile the Charter's human rights provisions are aspirational and future orientated, Article 2(4) is emphatic and unconditional': ME O'Connell, 'Regulating the Use of Force in the 21st Century: The Continuing Importance of State Autonomy' (1998) 36 *Columbia Journal of Transnational Law* 473.

[14] Kirgis, 'The Security Council's first 50 Years' (1995) *American Journal of International Law* 506 at 506.

international peace and security therefore had a principally military connotation. 'The United Nations Charter was drafted in the belief that the danger to be dealt with was the orthodox war between clear sovereign states'.[15] Indeed, I suggest that at least during the Cold War years this was how the Security Council interpreted the concept of a threat to international peace and security; international peace and security was defined negatively,[16] being confined to the absence of inter-state intervention. The consequence was that the Security Council was indifferent to what happened within states, refusing to enforce human rights against recalcitrant governments, declining to engage Article 39 in relation to matters that were essentially domestic.

> The whole system was tilted to stop transborder aggressions. It therefore had nothing to do with what happened within any member state, such as a certain part of a country striving for independence and perhaps seeking outside help, or civil wars between ethnic or religious groups.[17]

Although Article 2(7) does not technically impose any restrictions upon the Security Council when deciding whether to declare a threat to international peace and security and thus take enforcement action under Chapter VII, in actuality Article 2(7) defines the limits of appropriate Security Council involvement: 'in a rather circumlocutory way, Article 2(7) of the United Nations defines the limits of the Organization's delegated powers'.[18] Glennon makes a similar point when he explains:

> [t]rue, this provision [Article 2(7)] does indicate that it ought not be construed as prejudicing the application of enforcement measures under Chapter VII; but that proviso need merely be read as requiring that the two provisions be construed together, as allowing only those enforcement measures that do not conflict with a state's domestic jurisdiction.[19]

This understanding of Chapter VII was reflected in the practice of the Security Council until the end of the Cold War. In 1946, for example, the Security Council refused to declare that President Francisco Franco's fascist regime in Spain constituted a threat to international peace and security. In fact, the Council even refused to discuss the human rights violations being committed by the fascist government, believing that placing the

[15] R Jennings, 'Broader Perspectives in International Law' in A Anghie and G Sturgess (eds), *Legal Visions of the 21st Century: Essays in Honour of Judge Christopher Weeramantry* (The Hague, Kluwer Law International, 1998) 501.

[16] The concept of 'negative peace' is borrowed from J Galtung, 'Peace: Negative and Positive' (1964) 1 *Journal of Peace Research* 1.

[17] P Kennedy, *The Parliament of Man: The United Nations and the Quest for World Government* (London, Allen Lane, 2006) 78.

[18] T Franck, *Fairness in International Law and Institutions* (Oxford, Clarendon Press, 1998) 219.

[19] M Glennon, 'Sovereignty and Community after Haiti: Rethinking the Collective Use of Force' (1995) 89 *American Journal of International Law* 70, 72.

matter on the Security Council's agenda would result in unlawful intervention in Spain's domestic affairs.[20] As the matter was devoid of an international dimension it was beyond the Security Council's jurisdiction. In what was very significant language, the Security Council refused to engage Chapter VII on the basis that the collective security system was a 'very sharp instrument' and that care should be taken that 'this instrument is not blunted or used in any way which would strain the intentions of the Charter'.[21]

Contrast this, however, with the preparedness of the Security Council to engage its collective security system where a member state's sovereignty had been violated. Significantly, at the same time that the Security Council refused to respond to the human rights abuses being perpetrated in Franco's Spain the Security Council declared 'a threat to the peace within the meaning of Article 39' in response to the outbreak of violence between Israel and surrounding Arab states after Israel declared its statehood on 14 May 1948. Acting under Chapter VII, the Security Council made the mandatory determination that all sides 'desist from further military action'.[22] In 1950 the Security Council declared that the 'armed attack upon the Republic of Korea by forces from North Korea constitutes a breach of the peace' and demanded 'an immediate cessation of hostilities', calling upon 'the authorities in North Korea to withdraw forthwith their armed forces to the 38th parallel', thereby enabling South Korea's sovereignty to be restored.[23] In response to North Korea's failure to comply with the Security Council's demands, in Resolution 84 (1950) the Security Council again declared a breach of the peace but this time recommended that '[m]embers of the United Nations furnish such assistance to the Republic of Korea as may be necessary to repel the armed attack and to restore international peace and security'. Pursuant to this resolution, an international force was deployed in order to repel North Korean forces to the 38th parallel, thereby enabling South Korea's sovereignty to be restored and international peace and security maintained.[24] The Security Council reacted in a similar manner to Iraq's invasion of Iran in 1980. In Resolution 514 the Security Council declared that the military conflict

[20] Also consider the Security Council's failure to engage Chapter VII in relation to Pol Pot's murderous regime in Cambodia, for example, or Idi Admin's commission of massive human rights abuses in Uganda.

[21] UN Doc S/75 (1946) 12, quoted in L Goodrich, E Hambro and AP Simons, *Charter of the United Nations: Commentary and Documents*, 3rd edn (New York, Columbia University Press, 1969) 266. Although note that the General Assembly did adopt a resolution recommending that Spain be banned from the UN and its specialised agencies: GA Res 39 (12 December 1946).

[22] SC Res 54 (15 July 1948) UN Doc S/902.

[23] SC Res 83 (27 June 1950) UN Doc S/1511.

[24] SC Res 84 (7 July 1950) UN Doc S/1588. Although note that in the resolutions dealing with the invasion of South Korea the USSR was absent from the Security Council and therefore did not vote.

between these two states endangered international peace and security and, acting under Chapter VII of the UN Charter, called 'for a cease-fire and an end to all military operations'.[25] Furthermore, in this resolution the Security Council called 'for a withdrawal of forces to international recognised boundaries', thereby preserving the sovereignty of Iran and Iraq and restoring international peace and security.[26]

The Security Council's response to Apartheid in South Africa and Southern Rhodesia are often cited as notable exceptions during the Cold War. In particular, these cases are cited as examples of the Security Council being prepared to declare a threat to international peace and security on the basis of the domestic policies being pursued by both regimes. In this sense, the Security Council was prepared to use its Chapter VII powers in order to intervene in matters that were essentially domestic rather than to protect state sovereignty. In 1960 the Security Council warned South Africa that the 'situation arising out of the large-scale killings of unarmed and peaceful demonstrators against racial discrimination and segregation . . . might endanger international peace and security'.[27] In 1963 the Security Council determined that South Africa's endorsement of Apartheid policies had created a situation that was 'seriously disturbing' the peace.[28] In 1965 the Security Council condemned Southern Rhodesia's unilateral declaration of independence from the United Kingdom (UK). In particular, the Security Council condemned Ian Smith's regime as a 'usurpation of power by a racist settler minority' and determined that the situation was 'a threat to international peace and security', imposing severe economic sanctions.[29]

How, then, can this practice be explained? Are these to be regarded as examples of the Security Council engaging Chapter VII in order to protect human rights *within* member states? One should not rush to this conclusion. It is important to point out that the Security Council's reaction to South Africa and Southern Rhodesia can also be explained on the basis of traditional concerns of preventing inter-state conflict. In particular, it was likely that the Security Council was aware of the negative implications that these racist regimes would yield for peace and security within the region. Indeed, in relation to South Africa the Security Council stated in Resolution 134 that the racist policies being endorsed by the government

[25] SC Res 514 (12 July 1982).

[26] The Security Council went on to reiterate this demand in SC Res 598 (20 July 1987). For further examples of the Security Council engaging Chapter VII during the Cold War in order to respond to the infringement of a state's sovereignty see South Africa's attack on Zambia (SC Res 393 (30 July 1976)), the Falkland's conflict (SC Res 502 (3 April 1982)) and Israel's attack on Tunisia (SC Res 573 (4 October 1985) and SC Res 611 (25 April 1988)).

[27] SC Res 134 (1 April 1960).

[28] SC Res 181 (7 August 1963). The General Assembly had also condemned South Africa's racist policies and had asked the Security Council to impose mandatory sanctions: GA Res 1598 (15 April 1961).

[29] SC Res 217 (20 November 1965).

might lead to 'international friction'. The Security Council appeared concerned over how fellow African states would react to a white racist regime that was committing such violent abuses of human rights against an indigenous black population. Moreover, in Resolution 282 (1970) the Security Council also expressed concern that South Africa had exploded a nuclear device and that its defence forces were making frequent military incursions into surrounding states.[30] In relation to Southern Rhodesia, analysis of Resolutions 202, 216 and 217 indicates that a major concern of the Security Council was to prevent a territory of the UK from unilaterally declaring independence. In this sense, it is almost certainly correct that the Security Council's decision to engage Chapter VII in relation to South Rhodesia was at least in part motivated by a desire to protect the territorial integrity of the sovereign state of the UK.

This being said, however, it is incontrovertible that the text of the resolutions adopted in relation to South Africa and Southern Rhodesia reveal that the Security Council was concerned with the human rights abuses that both regimes were committing. In short, in determining a threat to international peace and security, the words 'racism', 'discrimination' and 'Apartheid' featured prominently in the language of the Security Council.

I argue that the extent to which the Security Council engaged Chapter VII in order to protect human rights can be imputed to a nascent international community that was beginning to form within the international society and which utilised its influence within the Security Council in order to respond to the violent human rights abuses that were being perpetrated by these two regimes. As I suggested in chapter one, the international community did not emerge instantly with the end of the Cold War. Rather, liberal states within the world order had begun to express an interest in protecting human rights at the international level for many decades before the end of the Cold War, albeit without forming a cohesive association as they did with the end of the Cold War. For this reason, I submit that the Security Council's intervention in South African and Southern Rhodesia is to a certain extent illustrative of an embryonic international community of liberal states that was becoming increasingly prepared to enforce human rights at the international level and which was enjoying a growing influence over the policies adopted by the Security Council. Thus,

[30] '[T]he sanctions imposed by the Security Council under Chapter VII were formally justified and justifiable as means for dealing with a threat to the peace and were plainly responsive to the country's explosion of a nuclear device and to the proliferating cross-border military operations executed by the South African defence forces': T Farer, 'Promoting Democracy: International Law and Norms' in E Newman and R Rich (eds), *The UN Role in Promoting Democracy: Between Ideals and Reality* (New York, United Nations University Press, 2004) 35.

the anti-human rights nature of the policy was clearly at the bottom of Security Council actions, in which sense the two cases can be seen as a precursor to the post-Cold War tendency to give serious human rights abuses the status of the threat to the peace.[31]

The Security Council's reaction to the racist regimes in South Africa and Southern Rhodesia notwithstanding, I suggest that just as human rights were largely subordinated to the preservation of state sovereignty in the UN Charter, during the Cold War human rights abuses were also largely neglected by the Security Council within the context of collective security. As I sought to illustrate in the preceding discussion, this is the consistent (albeit not uniform) trend within the Security Council's Cold War practice. However, it is also true that during the Cold War the Security Council failed to respond to many instances where state sovereignty was violated. Recall Franck's study that I referred to in chapter three and his identification of the numerous violations of state sovereignty that occurred during the Cold War.[32] Does this mean that in these instances the Security Council was not prepared to engage Chapter VII in order to protect state sovereignty? Moreover, does this mean that in those instances where the Security Council *did* declare a threat to international peace and security, the Security Council was not really motivated by the determination to protect state sovereignty but instead because intervention satisfied other national interests of the Security Council members, who employed the language of state sovereignty as a mask for intervention? I reject this explanation. Rather, I suggest that the explanation for the Security Council's failure to intervene more consistently in response to violations of state sovereignty lies in the fact that the two Cold War superpowers were locked in bitter conflict and both possessed permanent seats on the Security Council. Thus, both the US and USSR could unilaterally prevent the Security Council from taking any decisions. As rival superpowers, each seeking to protect and extend its power and influence throughout the world, both the US and USSR intervened in the domestic affairs of other states, be it directly (such as the US's armed intervention in Vietnam or the USSR's invasion of Afghanistan) or by sponsoring intervention by other states (what is known as 'proxy war').[33] Are we surprised that the Security Council did not declare a threat to international peace and security in these instances? I suggest, therefore, that the Security Council's

[31] H Yamashita, 'Reading "Threats to International Peace and Security" 1946–2005' (2007) 18 *Diplomacy and Statecraft* 551, 554.

[32] T Franck, 'Who Killed Article 2(4)?' (1970) 64 *American Journal of International Law* 809.

[33] 'The Cold War bipolarity meant that most uses of force, affecting the sensitive East-West balance of power or simply involving the states which were closer to one or the other superpower, necessarily raised immediate and fierce criticism from one side and apologetic justification from the other side': R Müllerson, *Ordering Anarchy: International Law in International Society* (The Hague, Martinus Nijhoff, 2000) 292.

failure to engage Chapter VII more consistently can be imputed to the tensions that existed between these two permanent members and their reluctance to allow the Security Council to condemn interventions that they were either directly or indirectly responsible for (or at least had an interest in). The Security Council's failure to intervene cannot, I believe, be explained on the basis that the Security Council *as an organ* lacked a normative commitment to protect state sovereignty. Thus, in those (admittedly few)[34] areas outside of the concern of these two superpowers (or where the USSR was absent from the Security Council, like in relation to the Korean war) and where the Security Council was able to act, I have argued that the Security Council engaged Chapter VII in order to protect state sovereignty. The protection of state sovereignty from external violation was thus the overriding concern of the Security Council. As I have sought to reveal, the Security Council consistently failed to engage Chapter VII in order to protect against the violation of human rights. In the words of Taylor, '[d]uring the Cold War sovereignty was usually interpreted by the United Nations members . . . to mean that the rule of non-intervention was to be rigidly applied, and that what happened within states was no concern of outsiders'.[35]

3. POST-COLD WAR: PROMOTING LIBERAL DEMOCRACY

Since the end of the Cold War the Security Council has invoked Chapter VII with increasing frequency. What is more important, however, is the nature of these resolutions. I suggest that with the end of the Cold War there has been a qualitative shift in the meaning that the Security Council has ascribed to the concept of a threat to international peace and security.[36] In particular, the Security Council has demonstrated a preparedness to declare a threat to international peace and security in circumstances where a state fails to demonstrate respect for liberal values (or rather the human rights that a liberal democracy protects). The consequence is that the Security Council has adopted a definition of state sovereignty modified from the largely pristine conception it endorsed during the Cold War. Where a state fails to respect human rights the Security Council has

[34] 'There was virtually no corner of the world that did not define itself with reference to the Cold War': E Aksu, *The United Nations, Intra-State Peacekeeping and Normative Change* (Manchester, Manchester University Press, 2003) 44.

[35] P Taylor, 'The United Nations in the 1990s: Proactive Cosmopolitanism and the Issue of Sovereignty' (1999) 47 *Political Studies* 538, 538.

[36] '[T]he threat-to-the-peace concept has been steadily expanded from initial focus on interstate relations to include new situations and issues that go well beyond it': Yamashita, 'Reading "Threats to International Peace and Security" 1946–2005" (n 31) at 552. Thus, after the Cold War 'there was less emphasis on trans-border effects, and the suffering of the population as such became increasingly decisive': B Simma, *The Charter of the United Nations: A Commentary* (Oxford, Oxford University Press, 2002) 724.

demonstrated a preparedness to engage Chapter VII and enforce respect.[37] As Glennon notes, '[t]he Security Council became a more active promoter of humanitarian values as democracy and the protection of human rights became widespread, challenging longstanding principles of sovereignty'.[38] Malone makes a similar point when he explains that 'the [Security] Council's decisions have eroded conceptions of state sovereignty firmly held during the Cold War years, altering the way in which many of us see the relationship between state and citizen'.[39]

This is not to say, however, that in the post-Cold War era the Security Council is only concerned with promoting respect for human rights and thus refuses to act in order to protect state sovereignty in the event that it is violated. When Iraq invaded Kuwait in 1990 the Security Council was quick to declare a threat to international peace and security, condemning Iraq's unlawful violation of Kuwait's sovereignty and authorising a coalition of the willing to use force in order to expel Iraqi forces from Kuwait.[40] But what I am arguing in this chapter is that the Security Council is increasingly passing resolutions which declare a threat to international peace and security on the basis that human rights (rather than state sovereignty) are being violated, and taking mandatory measures in order to ensure that human rights are protected.[41]

When juxtaposed with the activities of the Security Council during the Cold War it becomes apparent that '[t]his is indeed a dramatic change'.[42] The end of the Cold War has been 'the single most formative experience in the existence of the Security Council'.[43] In fact, in the post-Cold War era '[w]e can justifiably describe it as a new Council'.[44] Indeed, that the Security Council can be regarded as a new Council strikes at the heart of my argument; that in the post-Cold War era the Security Council is now dominated by members of the international community who exert substantial influence over the other members. I suggest that the Security

[37] Thus, '[h]uman rights have revolutionalized state sovereignty and collective security': B Frederking, *The United States and the Security Council: Collective Security since the Cold War* (London/New York, Routledge, 2007) 126.

[38] Glennon, 'Sovereignty and Community after Haiti' (n 19) at 70.

[39] D Malone, 'The Security Council in the Post-Cold War Era: A Study in the Creative Interpretation of the UN Charter' (2003) 35 *NYU Journal of International Law and Politics* 487, 487.

[40] SC Res 660 (2 August 1990). In 2000, for example, the Security Council declared a threat to international peace and security on the basis of 'continued fighting' between Ethiopia and Eritrea: see SC Res 1298 (17 May 2000).

[41] See generally S MacFarlane and YF Khong, *Human Security and the UN: A Critical History* (Bloomington IN, Indiana Press, 2006). In this sense, since the end of the Cold War the Security Council has been pursuing a positive, as opposed to negative, conception of peace: see Galtung, *Peace: Negative and Positive* (n 16).

[42] P Wallenstein and P Johansson, 'Security Council Decisions in Perspective' in D Malone (ed), *The UN Security Council: From the Cold War to the 21st Century* (Boulder CO, Lynne Rienner, 2004) 18.

[43] ibid at 17.

[44] ibid at 30.

Council's preparedness to declare a threat to *international* peace and security on the basis of domestic human rights violations and subsequently take enforcement action in order to ensure compliance can be explained on the basis that there now exists a powerful international community of liberal states within the world order which considers non-liberal states to represent a threat to their liberal peace. In essence, the Security Council has adopted the theory that international peace and security can only be maintained in a world of liberal states (the liberal peace thesis) and that the Security Council's adoption of this theory can be attributed to the international community.[45]

In order to illustrate the influence of the international community over the Security Council I examine the practice of the Security Council under Chapter VII since the end of Cold War. By doing so, I seek to reveal the Security Council's commitment to the promotion of liberal values.[46] In particular, the Security Council's determination to promote respect for liberal values is apparent through its peacebuilding activities, especially in Kosovo and East Timor, where the UN assumed responsibility for these territories and reconstructed them upon a liberal basis. Such is the importance of these peacebuilding missions in the context of the Security Council's newfound commitment to promoting respect for liberal democracy that I will dedicate an entire chapter to their discussion. For this reason, peacebuilding missions established under Chapter VII will not be discussed here.[47] Rather, in this chapter my intention is to call upon other instances where the Security Council has engaged Chapter VII in order to promote respect for liberal values in the post-Cold War era.

3.1 Promoting Human Rights: Iraq (1991), Somalia (1992) and Libya (2011)

Iraq can be regarded as a pivotal moment in the Security Council's turn towards the protection of human rights under Chapter VII. With the

[45] The liberal peace thesis featured prominently in the language of former UN Secretary-General Boutros-Ghali: 'The promotion of democracy is both an end in itself and part of the responsibility of the United Nations to maintain international peace and security. It should be pursued for its own sake, and also because democracy is one of the pillars on which a more peaceful, more equitable, and more secure would can be built': B Boutros-Ghali, 'Democracy: A Newly Recognised Imperative' (1995) 1 *Global Governance* 3, 3.

[46] The careful reader will notice that I do not examine in detail examples of humanitarian catastrophes that the Security Council failed to mount an adequate response to (such as the genocide in Rwanda in 1994). This is because the purpose of this chapter is to highlight a change in direction of the Security Council away from its Cold War approach of remaining indifferent in relation to human rights abuses within member states and, in the post-Cold War era, towards an approach where the Security Council is now prepared to engage Chapter VII in order to promote respect for liberal values.

[47] See chapter 6 of this volume.

successful expulsion of Iraq from Kuwait in 1991, US President George Bush Sr encouraged Iraqi citizens to take matters into their own hands and topple Saddam Hussein from power. In particular, the apparent defeat of the Iraqi army by coalition forces and the support of foreign leaders reignited the desire by Iraqi Kurds for independence in northern Iraq. Iraqi Kurds began to revolt, but the Iraqi army responded ruthlessly, attacking Kurdish towns and villages, forcing them to flee their homes, with reports of torture and non-judicial executions.[48]

In response, on 5 April 1991 the Security Council passed Resolution 688. This resolution explained that the Security Council was 'gravely concerned by the repression of the Iraqi civilian population in many parts of Iraq, including most recently in Kurdish populated areas, the consequences of which threaten international peace and security'. In light of this, the Security Council demanded that 'Iraq, as a contributor to removing the threat to international peace and security in the region, immediately end this repression', expressing 'the hope . . . that an open dialogue will take place to ensure that the human and political rights of all Iraqi citizens are respected'. In expressing their condemnation of the 'repression . . . of the civilian population' and 'the magnitude of human suffering', the Security Council clearly demonstrated that it considered such governmental acts to be outside of the domestic jurisdiction limitation and within the purview of Chapter VII. As Alexander explains,

> [t]he Security Council's approval of the use of force to protect the Kurds was unprecedented in international law. For the first time since the creation of the Charter, the goal of preventing the slaughter of non-nationals within a sovereign state's borders trumped that state's claim to sovereignty and non-intervention.[49]

For this reason, Tsagourias and White determine that '1991–92 was a seminal period for the UNSC in widening its concept of peace and security'.[50]

However, notwithstanding the importance of the Security Council's willingness to condemn Iraq's treatment of its citizens, we must nevertheless recognise that Resolution 688 was very cautious in its decision to protect human rights. Most notably, whilst the resolution employs language that we associate with Chapter VII (such as the concept of a 'threat to international peace and security'), the resolution never actually states that it is acting pursuant to Chapter VII, which is significant, as all 14 previous resolutions in relation to Iraq had explicitly declared that the Security Council was acting under Chapter VII. Indeed, even if we assume that the Council *was* acting under Chapter VII, the assumption that the declaration

[48] Proceedings of the Security Council, UN Doc S/PV.2982 (5 April 1991) 6.

[49] K Alexander, 'Ignoring the Lessons of the Past: The Crisis in Darfur and the Case for Humanitarian Intervention' (2005) 15 *Journal of Transnational Law and Policy* 1, 23.

[50] N Tsagourias and ND White, *Collective Security: Law, Theory and Practice* (Cambridge, Cambridge University Press, 2013) (forthcoming).

of a threat to international peace and security was made on the basis of the repression committed against Iraqi Kurds is disputed. In particular, whilst the Security Council condemned the repression committed against the Iraqi Kurds it went on to explain that it is 'the consequences [of the repression] which threaten international peace and security', which the Security Council identified as 'a massive flow of refugees' piercing the territorial integrity of surrounding states. Thus, in actuality it was the *consequences* of the repression that threatened international peace and security: specifically, the adverse implications that the repression yielded for the sovereignty of surrounding states. Even though the human rights abuses were deplored by the Security Council, it does not appear to be the repression per se that the resolution identifies as constituting the threat to international peace and security (indeed, Resolution 688 actually recalls Article 2(7) and the requirement that the UN respect the principle of non-intervention). For this reason, in its ultimate desire to protect the sovereignty of surrounding states Resolution 688 can be perceived as a product of the international society rather than the international community. As Alexander ultimately concedes, 'international security concerns in the border area between Iraq and Turkey were at the forefront of the Security Council's thinking'.[51]

That Resolution 688 gets so close to declaring a threat to international peace and security on the basis of human rights abuses but then shies away at the last moment is not surprising given that the Cold War had only just ended and so the international community was in the process of crystallisation.[52] In other words, at this stage the international community's influence over the Security Council was not particularly strong. Thus, although the international community could persuade the Security Council unequivocally to condemn the human rights abuses, in order for the resolution to achieve requisite agreement within the Security Council (and especially the agreement of non-liberal states) it was necessary that the declaration of a threat to international peace and security be located within traditional concerns over state sovereignty and that Article 2(7) be explicitly recalled. As Chesterman explains, that the Security Council

[51] Alexander, 'Ignoring the Lessons of the Past' (n 49) at 23.

[52] Whilst the Security Council was dealing with the repression in Iraq, widespread abuses of human rights were being committed in Yugoslavia. In response, the Security Council passed Resolution 713 (25 September 1991), which declared a threat to international peace and security on the basis of the 'heavy loss of human life and material damage, and . . . the consequences for the countries of the region, in particular the border areas of neighbouring countries'. Thus, like in Iraq, whilst the Security Council indicated a willingness to discuss human rights abuses in the context of Chapter VII the Security Council was only prepared to declare a threat to international peace and security on the basis that it was the international repercussions of these human rights abuses (specifically, that these abuses stimulated the flow of refugees that then had negative implications for the sovereignty of surrounding states) that constituted the threat.

identified the international repercussions as constituting the threat to international peace and security was 'necessary to secure the support of the USSR, Romania, and Ecuador, as well as the abstention of China'.[53] Security Council Resolution 688 therefore clearly demonstrates the tensions that existed between liberal and non-liberal states on the Security Council (and their opposing ideological commitments) during the early 1990s.

However, these issues notwithstanding, from Resolution 688 'one can see here a growing awareness [by the Security Council] that a serious humanitarian crisis may deserve some sort of collective response'.[54] In this sense, the need to protect human rights was integrated into the normative vocabulary of the Security Council. Consequently, the Security Council's response to the humanitarian crisis in Iraq is extremely significant. Indeed, it is likely that Resolution 688 provided the impetus for the Security Council's important Presidential Statement in 1991. Here the Security Council explicitly stated that a threat to international peace and security can arise not just where state sovereignty is breached but also in the event of a humanitarian crisis:

> the absence of war and military conflicts amongst States does not in itself ensure international peace and security. The non-military sources of instability in the economic, social, humanitarian and ecological fields have become threats to peace and security.[55]

Of course, this Presidential Statement was not adopted under Chapter VII. However, the nub of this Statement, that human rights abuses can constitute a threat to international peace and security, was soon transposed in Chapter VII when the Security Council declared a threat to international peace and security in relation to the civil unrest in Somalia. When President Mohammed Siad Barre was forced from power in January 1991 fierce fighting commenced between rival clans, resulting in civil war. By October 1992 the UN Secretary-General reported that 300,000 people had died, 1.5 million were at risk of imminent death and 4.5 million of Somalia's 6 million population were threatened by severe malnutrition and related diseases.[56]

The Security Council initially deployed a traditional peacekeeping force to assist in the delivery of humanitarian aid (UNOSOM I).[57] However, with the violence and human suffering increasing, the UN Secretary-General explained that Somalia had 'deteriorated beyond the point at

[53] S Chesterman, *Just War or Just Peace?: Humanitarian Intervention and International Law* (Oxford, Oxford University Press, 1999) 132.

[54] Yamashita (n 31) at 555.

[55] Security Council Summit, *Statement Concerning the Security Council's Responsibility in the Maintenance of International Peace and Security*, UN Doc S/23500 (31 January 1992).

[56] Report of the UN Secretary-General, UN Doc A/47/553 (22 October 1992).

[57] SC Res 746 (3 December 1992).

which it is susceptible to the peace-keeping treatment'.[58] The Secretary-General subsequently called upon more 'forcible measures' to facilitate humanitarian relief.[59] As a result, on 3 December 1992 the Security Council unanimously adopted Resolution 794 (1992), declaring that 'the magnitude of the human tragedy caused by the conflict in Somalia, further exacerbated by the obstacles being created to the distribution of humanitarian assistance, constitutes a threat to international peace and security'. 'Acting under chapter VII . . . the Security Council [authorises] member states . . . to use all necessary means to establish as soon as possible a secure environment for humanitarian relief operations in Somalia'. The US took the lead in creating a coalition of the willing to enforce Resolution 794 (which became known as UNITAF).[60]

Clearly, the decision of the Security Council is significant and marks a notable departure from the cautious response by the Security Council to the humanitarian crisis in Iraq. First, and importantly, any reference to Article 2(7) was omitted. Secondly, although the resolution stresses the 'unique character . . . [and] complex and extraordinary nature' of the crisis, the resolution forgoes any mention of international repercussions of the civil conflict.[61] Significantly, therefore, the determination of a threat to international peace and security is made *exclusively* upon the basis of human suffering. As Kirgis rightly identifies, Resolution 794 must be perceived as a direct response 'to the anarchy in Somalia and the desperate need to end the suffering of the people'.[62] Indeed, the UN Secretary-General explained that the Security Council had 'established a precedent in the history of the UN: it decided for the first time to intervene militarily for strict humanitarian purposes', for 'exclusively, humanitarian, internal reasons'.[63] Whereas in Iraq Resolution 688 was careful to maintain the formal integrity of Article 2(7) notwithstanding its direct references to the need to protect human rights, the Security Council's response to the civil war in Somalia waived such a formality. The consequence was that the Security Council reconceptualised its conventional understanding of sovereignty. Unlike during the Cold War, sovereignty no longer provided an unqualified shield

[58] Security Council Letter, Letter from the Secretary-General Addressed to the President of the Security Council, UN Doc S/24868 (1992).

[59] D Oberdorfer and J Lancaster, 'UN Chief Weighs Use of US Troops in Somalia; Security Council to Consider Options for Protecting Relief Supply Lines', *Washington Post* (27 November 1992) A1, available at: www.highbeam.com/doc/1P2-1036846.html.

[60] UNITAF was later transformed into UNOSOM II. Although established under Chapter VII UN Charter, UNOSOM II is more accurately characterised as a peace-building mission – as opposed to a Security Council peace enforcement action performed by a coalition of willing states – and for this reason will be discussed in chapter 6 of this volume.

[61] 'Unlike the intervention in Iraq a year earlier, the Security Council's decision to intervene in Somalia was made for predominantly humanitarian reasons': Alexander (n 49) at 24.

[62] Kirgis (n 14) at 513.

[63] Quoted in O'Connell, 'Regulating the Use of Force' (n 13) at 487.

against external scrutiny and intervention. Instead, 'sovereignty means responsibility'.[64]

It is therefore apparent that Somalia marked the turning point in the Security Council's willingness to place the promotion of human rights on its security agenda and to declare a threat to international peace and security on an exclusively human rights basis. Since Somalia the Security Council has frequently engaged Chapter VII in order to promote human rights, regardless of whether the sovereignty of a neighbouring state (or indeed any other state) was affected. The systematic violation of human rights is now considered to represent a clear threat to international peace and security. As the Security Council explained in 2000,

> [the] deliberate targeting of civilian populations or other protected persons and the committing of systematic, flagrant and widespread violations of international humanitarian and human rights law in situations of armed conflict may constitute a threat to international peace and security.[65]

When confronted with the persecution of ethnic Muslims in Darfur by the government-backed Janjaweed militia, the UN Security Council passed a number of resolutions recognising that these violations of human rights constituted a threat to international peace and security.[66] Importantly, not only was reference to Article 2(7) again omitted but these resolutions were passed without determining that the situation was unique or exceptional in any way. Citing 'indiscriminate attacks on civilians, rape, forced displacements, and acts of violence especially those with an ethnic dimension', the Security Council declared a threat to international peace and security and established an 'international commission of inquiry in order to investigate reports of violations of international humanitarian law and human rights law in Darfur'.[67] In light of the reports by the Commission, mandatory arms embargoes, travel bans and economic sanctions were imposed.[68] Tracing the Security Council's response to these humanitarian crises illustrates that the Council has become far more comfortable with the terminology of human rights in the context of collective security: 'Council resolutions on

[64] 'The Charter protects the sovereignty of peoples. It was never meant as a license for governments to trample human rights and human dignity. Sovereignty means responsibility': UN Secretary-General Kofi Annan, 'Intervention', Ditchley Foundation Lecture XXXV (1998) 2.

[65] SC Res 1296 (19 April 2000). Although do note that in the preamble to this resolution the Security Council recalled Article 2(7) UN Charter and the principle of the sovereign equality of states. Again, the tension between then liberal members of the Security Council and the non-liberal members (or more specifically their opposing ideologies) is evident.

[66] See for example SC Res 1556 (30 July 2004); SC Res 1564 (18 September 2004); SC Res 1590 (24 March 2005); SC Res 1591 (29 March 2005); SC Res 1651 (21 December 2005); SC Res 1706 (31 August 2006).

[67] SC Res 1556 (30 July 2004).

[68] SC Res 1591 (29 March 2005). It should be noted here that although the Security Council has deployed sanctions under Chapter VII in relation to the human rights abuses in Darfur these have been criticised as being both late and ineffective: see generally Alexander (n 49).

the recent Darfur crisis in fact reflect this shift towards unqualified recognition of humanitarian crises as international threats'.[69]

The Security Council's intervention in Libya in 2011 further demonstrates its preparedness to engage Chapter VII in order to protect human rights. In early 2011 protests broke out across Libya calling for the end to Colonel Muammar Gaddafi's 41-year reign and for democratic elections to be held. Gaddafi's regime refused to stand down and fiercely resisted democratic reform, engaging in a prolonged and bloody campaign against those that were considered hostile to the government. As the violence intensified (and with war crimes and crimes against humanity being reported),[70] the Security Council responded by adopting Resolution 1970 on 26 February 2011. In particular, the Council

> deplor[ed] the gross and systematic violations of human rights, including the repression of peaceful demonstrations, expressing deep concern at the deaths of civilians, and rejecting unequivocally the incitement to hostility and violence against the civilian population made from the highest level of the Libyan government.

Importantly, the Council also recalled the Libyan government's 'responsibility to protect' its civilian population. As I noted in chapter two, in substance this declaration was not particularly novel. As we have seen from the discussion in this chapter, on numerous occasions since the end of the Cold War the Security Council has determined that governments must protect the human rights of their citizens. This notwithstanding, in symbolic terms by engaging Chapter VII and explicitly stating that governments are subject to a responsibility to protect, the Security Council has made a significant step in crystallising a transformation that has been evolving since the end of the Cold War; namely, the idea that sovereignty is invested in the people, not in the government.[71]

After citing the Libyan government's failure to discharge its responsibility to protect, the Council invoked Chapter VII of the UN Charter and demanded an 'immediate end to the violence' and called for 'steps to fulfil the legitimate demands of the population', which could arguably mean the holding of democratic elections (although the word democracy does not appear in Resolution 1970). In addition, the Council referred the situation in Libya to the International Criminal Court (ICC) for examination, imposed an arms embargo against Libya and implemented a comprehensive travel ban and freezing of assets against leading Libyan government officials.

[69] Yamashita (n 31) at 556.

[70] 'Libya Conflict: UN Accuses both sides of War Crimes', *BBC News* (1 June 2011), available at: www.bbc.co.uk/news/world-africa-13622965 .

[71] L Jubilut, 'Has the 'Responsibility to Protect' Been a Real Change in Humanitarian Intervention? An Analysis from the Crisis in Libya' (2012) 14 *International Community Law Review* 309.

With the violence against the citizens of Libya increasing, on 17 March 2011 the Security Council adopted Resolution 1973. After condemning this violence and 'reiterating the responsibility of the Libyan authorities to protect the Libyan population', the Security Council declared that a threat to international peace and security existed and again engaged Chapter VII. After demanding an immediate end to the violence against civilians the Security Council adopted several measures, the most important of which was the authorisation to use all necessary means, ie the use of military force, to protect civilians. In particular, the Security Council authorised member states 'to take all necessary measures . . . to protect civilians and civilian populated areas under threat of attack', although it excluded the possibility of 'a foreign occupation force'. Thus, the Security Council's decision to declare a threat to international peace and security on the basis of the human rights violations and to authorise the use of force to protect civilians represents yet another important step in the Security Council (subject to the influence of the international community) developing Chapter VII as an instrument to intervene in a state's internal affairs and protect fundamental human rights.

In the context of human rights protection it is also important to identify the Security Council's willingness to engage Chapter VII in order to refer situations involving human rights abuses to the ICC under Article 13 of the Rome Statute.[72] In 2005, after declaring that the humanitarian crisis constituted a threat to international peace and security, the Security Council referred the situation in Darfur to the ICC and issued warrants for the arrest of Ahmad Harun and Ali Kushayb Darfur – those considered to be primarily responsible for orchestrating the genocide.[73] Similarly, as I have already noted, in Security Council Resolution 1970 the Security Council referred the situation in Libya to the ICC so that criminal investigations could be carried out into reports that international crimes had been committed.

That the Security Council has been prepared to utilise Chapter VII in order to engage the jurisdiction of the ICC illustrates that the Security Council is concerned with punishing those responsible for human rights abuses and thereby deterring others from committing violations in the future. Indeed, in this context the Security Council has previously invoked Chapter VII of the UN Charter to establish ad hoc tribunals in order to

[72] Although do note that the Security Council can, under Article 16 of the Rome Statute, prevent an ICC investigation or prosecution for a period of 12 months where it determines that ICC intervention would constitute a threat to international peace and security according to Chapter VII UN Charter. Controversially, the Security Council exercised this power under Article 16 in 2002 in order to prevent UN personnel from being brought before the ICC even though they may have committed international crimes, ie severe abuses of human rights: see SC Res 1422 (12 July 2002). In fact, this resolution was renewed for another 12-month period in 2003: see SC Res 1487 (12 June 2003).

[73] SC Res 1593 (31 March 2005).

bring to account those responsible for serious violations of international human rights law in Rwanda and the former Yugoslavia. However, not only is this a recognition by the Security Council that serious violations of human rights law constitute a threat to international peace and security but also that the prosecution of these crimes and bringing those responsible to justice contributes to the restoration of international peace and security. For example, the Security Council declared a threat to international peace and security in Yugoslavia on the basis of 'reports of mass killings, massive, organised and systematic detention and rape of women . . . [and] the practice of "ethnic cleansing"'. The Security Council went on to establish the International Criminal Tribunal for the Former Yugoslavia (ICTY) on the basis that prosecution of those responsible for these violations of human rights would 'contribute to ensuring that such violations are halted and effectively addressed'.[74] Acting under Chapter VII the Security Council later established the International Criminal Tribunal for Rwanda (ICTR), noting that 'genocide and other systematic, widespread and flagrant violations of international humanitarian law' constituted a threat to international peace and security.[75] Again, the establishment of an international criminal tribunal was considered necessary to punish those responsible for these violations and thus contribute towards the restoration of international peace and security.

Although space has precluded a comprehensive review of all instances in the post-Cold War era where the Security Council has engaged Chapter VII in order to promote respect for human rights, the preceding examples strongly indicate that the Security Council has quite 'indisputably ventured into the field of justice and has taken on a "maximalist" role in recent years'.[76] Since the end of the Cold War the Security Council has demonstrated a progressive trend towards finding a threat to international peace and security where a government is implicated (through act or omission) in the perpetration of human rights violations. I argue that the Security Council's preparedness to engage its collective security system in order to promote respect for human rights can be explained on the basis that there now exists an international community of liberal states which exerts substantial influence within the world order and over the Security Council in particular.

[74] SC Res 827 (25 May 1993).
[75] SC Res 995 (26 May 1994).
[76] I Österdahl, *Threat to the Peace and the Interpretation by the Security Council of Article 39* (Stockholm, Iustus Forlag, 1998) 126.

3.2 Promoting Democracy: Haiti (1994) and Sierra Leone (1997)

The importance of the activities of the Security Council in relation to the civil unrest in Haiti can hardly be overstated. On 30 September 1991, nine months after the UN had monitored elections in Haiti and certified them to be free and fair,[77] the democratically elected President, Jean-Bertrand Aristide, was expelled from power and forced into exile. The military coup was bloody, with 3,000 deaths being reported.[78] Both the UN Secretary-General[79] and President Aristide[80] pleaded for the Security Council to engage Chapter VII in order to restore the elected government to power. At first the Security Council refused to act, principally because of the reluctance of India, Romania, Ecuador, Cuba, Yemen and China to intervene in what they considered to be an essentially domestic political matter.[81]

However, with the more flexible voting procedures in the UN General Assembly, the Assembly was able to pass a resolution expressing support for President Aristide, demanding the 'immediate restoration of the legitimate government' and 'the full observance of human rights in Haiti'.[82] In addition, the General Assembly encouraged UN member states to impose voluntary sanctions against Haiti.[83]

Irrespective of this, the Security Council refused to act. During this period of Security Council paralysis, human rights abuses continued in Haiti as the

[77] UN General Assembly, Electoral Assistance to Haiti: Note by the Secretary-General, UN Doc A/45/870 (1990).

[78] United Nations, Economic and Social Council, Commission on Human Rights: 'Situation of Human Rights in Haiti': Report submitted by Mr Marco Tulio Bruni Celli, Special Rapporteur, in accordance with Commission Resolution 1993/68, UN Doc E/CN.4/1994/55 (7 February 1994).

[79] Consider the statement by the then UN Secretary-General, Perez de Cuellar: 'I deeply regret the violent events which have just occurred in Haiti, and which have caused numerous victims. I am worried about the fate of President Jean-Bertrand Aristide and disturbed at the grave threats posed to democracy, which the people of Haiti have just established, with the assistance of the United Nations, by participating in such large numbers in free and fair elections. I hope that calm will soon be restored and that the democratic process will resume in accordance with the Constitution': UN Secretary-General Javier Perez de Cuellar, SG/SM/4627 HI/4 (1 October 1991). Later that day the Secretary-General went on to say 'I expressed deep regret because the United Nations must try to protect democracy in all countries in the world, and mainly in this particular case, because the United Nations has supervised the elections in Haiti' (transcript from the UN Department of Public Information).

[80] UN Doc S/23098 (30 September 1991) (letter to the Security Council from the Haitian Permanent Representative to the UN).

[81] 'Aristide Tells UNSC Coup is a Threat to All Democracies', *Washington Post* (4 October 1991) A22, available at www.highbeam.com/doc/1P2-1088169.html.

[82] GA Res 46/7 (11 October 1991).

[83] Although these were largely unsuccessful because member states did not effectively implement them: C Cerna, 'The Case of Haiti before the OAS' (1992) *American Society of International Law Proclamation* 378.

military dictatorship sought to consolidate its sphere of power.[84] In response, the Security Council finally intervened on 16 June 1993, adopting Resolution 841 under Chapter VII. Citing the usurpation of the 'legitimate government of President Aristide', the prevailing humanitarian crisis and the flood of refugees towards North America, the Council declared a threat to international peace and security. It is important to note that these three reasons were cited disjunctively; each independently constituted a threat to international peace and security. In order to restore international peace and security, the Council imposed mandatory economic sanctions.

The decision by the Security Council to engage Chapter VII forced the military dictatorship into communicating with President Aristide. As a consequence of their negotiations, the Governor's Island Agreement was concluded, which was designed to eventually allow for President Aristide to return to power. This led briefly to the lifting of the sanctions.[85] However, the de facto government failed to adhere to its promises under the Governor's Island Agreement. Following their forfeiture of the agreement and fearing UN enforcement action, human rights abuses worsened as the military became desperate to protect its sphere of control.[86] This prompted a series of measures by the Security Council, all taken pursuant to Chapter VII. The Council re-imposed the sanctions previously established by Resolution 841 and, in addition, imposed a complete naval blockade of Haiti.[87] However, in the face of the failure of the sanctions and blockade the Security Council passed Resolution 917, which imposed a full trade embargo. Principally, this was a result of the failure to restore President Aristide to power. The usurpation of the democratically elected government constituted a threat to international peace and security. As the Security Council explained, 'the goal . . . remains the restoration of democracy in Haiti and the prompt return of the legitimately elected President'.

However, these sanctions and embargoes proved ineffective, impacting more upon the population rather than the dictatorship, thus only serving to

[84] The UN Secretary-General reported that '[s]ince February 1992, repression and violence in Haiti have prevailed. Harassment, intimidation, attacks, arbitrary arrests, summary executions, and torture by members of the military and civilians working with them have continued since September 1991, increasing in mid-May 1992 in response to popular protests . . . The security forces have engaged in human rights violations . . . in its policy of so-called preventive repression, directed not so much at individuals as at entire sectors of society. So widespread is the fear of persecution in Haiti that many Haitians have gone into hiding': UN Secretary-General Boutros Boutros-Ghali, UN Doc A/47/621 (6 November 1992).

[85] SC Res 861 (27 August 1993).

[86] See the UN Security Council statement which condemned 'the recent upsurge in violence in Haiti, particularly the events of 11 and 12 September, when at least a dozen were assassinated, including a prominent supporter of President Aristide during a church service': UN Doc S/26460 (17 September 1993).

[87] SC Res 875 (16 October 1993).

exacerbate the existing humanitarian crisis.[88] With the humanitarian crisis worsening and the elected government still ousted from power, on 31 July 1994 the Security Council passed Resolution 940, which again determined that the continued disruption of democracy in Haiti and the widespread and flagrant abuses of human rights constituted a threat to international peace and security.[89] The Security Council reaffirmed 'that the goal of the international community remains the restoration of democracy in Haiti and the prompt return of the *legitimately* elected President, Jean-Bertrand Aristide' (emphasis added) and authorised 'all necessary means' to remove the military dictatorship (which the Council termed 'illegal' and 'illegitimate') and reinstall the democratically elected government.[90]

The importance of Resolution 940 cannot be overstated.[91] Quite transparently, the Security Council declared a threat to international peace and security on the basis of not just the human rights abuses (which, since Somalia, the Security Council had become comfortable discussing in the context of Chapter VII), *but in order to remove one regime and install another*; to dispose of the illegitimate military regime and reinstall the legitimate democratic representatives. This is clearly a significant departure from the Security Council's approach during the Cold War years, where changes to a state's constitutional framework (even if through violent means) fell within the domestic jurisdiction exclusion (Article 2(7) UN Charter) and thus outside of the concern of the Security Council. Thus, from this resolution it is possible to glean the Security Council's preference for democracy as the only form of legitimate governance.[92] Perhaps more importantly, by

[88] On 27 July, after the imposition of the embargo, MICIVIH (*Mission Civile Internationale en Haïti*) reported an 'unprecedented human rights crisis' in Haiti: UN Doc A/48/532/Add 3 (27 July 1994).

[89] The Security Council noted that it was 'gravely concerned by the significant further deterioration of the humanitarian crisis in Haiti, in particular the continuing escalation by the illegal de facto regime of systematic violations of civil liberties, the desperate plight of Haitian refugees and the recent expulsion of the staff of the International Civilian Mission': SC Res 940 (31 July 1994).

[90] Acting under Chapter VII of the Charter, the Security Council authorised 'all necessary means to facilitate the departure from Haiti of the military leadership . . . the prompt return of the legitimately elected President and the restoration of the legitimate authorities of the Government of Haiti': SC Res 940 (31 July 1994).

[91] J Leininger, 'Democracy and UN Peace-Keeping – Conflict Resolution through State-Building and Democracy Promotion in Haiti' (2006) 10 *Max Planck UNYB* 465.

[92] Although note that Resolution 940 does recognise 'the unique character of the present situation in Haiti and its deteriorating, complex and extraordinary nature, requiring an exceptional response'. Moreover, Uruguay strongly resisted Resolution 940, claiming that 'we do not believe that the internal political situation in Haiti projects externally in such a way as to represent a threat to international peace and security': cited in ND White, *Toward International Justice: The United Nations System* (Boulder CO, Lynne Rienner, 2002) 47. See also the concerns expressed by Mexico in the General Assembly, who considered it imperative to distinguish international problems that legitimately fall within the remit of the UN from national crises that are inherently domestic and thus beyond the competence of the UN. For a discussion of Mexico's position see R Gordon, 'United Nations Intervention in Internal Conflicts: Iraq, Somalia, and Beyond' (1993–94) 15 *Michigan Journal of International Law* 519, 558.

passing this resolution the Security Council made it quite clear that international peace and security would only be restored in the event that the democratic government was returned to power. In this way, the influence of the international community over the Security Council becomes visible. Although it was the Security Council that responded to the interruption of democracy in Haiti, I submit that it was the values and objectives of the international community that were being defended and promoted. Although the Security Council authorised the restoration of democracy in Haiti, it was the international community that was instrumental to the Security Council's arrival at this decision.

The decision by the Security Council to protect democracy in Haiti was bold and controversial. However, it is open to suggestion that the support of the Security Council for democracy in Haiti may have been *sui generis*, unlikely to be repeated, or at the very least limited to instances of coups against democratically elected governments that emerged under the auspices of UN election monitors. It is in this context that the Security Council's intervention in Sierra Leone becomes significant. The Security Council's intervention in Sierra Leone is so important not just because it represents another example of the Security Council engaging Chapter VII in order to restore a democratic government to power in the event that it had been unlawfully overthrown in a coup d'État, but because of the way in which the Security Council worded the relevant resolution. In May 1997 the recently elected government was overthrown by the Armed Forces Revolutionary Committee. The Security Council's response was to adopt Resolution 1132 on 8 October 1997, declaring that the usurpation of the elected government and the deteriorating humanitarian crisis constituted a threat to international peace and security,[93] demanding that the elected government be returned expeditiously to power.[94]

The importance of the decision by the Security Council in relation to Sierra Leone lies in the bold and unambiguous manner in which Resolution 1132 dismissed the military dictatorship as illegitimate, declared its support for the ousted elected government and authorised

[93] Although do note that the Security Council identified three reasons why the situation in Sierra Leone constituted a threat to international peace and security. First, the failure to restore the democratically elected government to power. Secondly, the deteriorating humanitarian conditions within the country. Thirdly, the consequences of this humanitarian crisis for neighbouring states. However, what is important is that these three reasons were identified *separately and individually* as constituting a threat to international peace and security, as opposed to previous Security Council resolutions, where human rights abuses were relevant only to the extent that they caused refugee flows which negatively impacted upon the integrity of the sovereignty of other states and, for this reason, amounted to a threat to international peace and security.

[94] Indeed, quite extraordinarily, the South Korean ambassador explained that the 'coup had had a destabilizing effect on the whole region by reversing a new wave of democracy which was spreading across the African continent': UN Press Release SC/6425 (8 October 1997) 10.

measures to return the democratic government back to power. The significance of this resolution is accurately captured by Roth. He explains

> [t]hat Sierra Leone is the best evidence yet of a fundamental change in international legal norms pertaining to 'pro-democratic' intervention. The Security Council in this case took authorisation of action against the 'illegitimate' regime beyond the context of United Nations peacekeeping cum electoral 'arbitration', not even bothering to take refuge in assertions of 'extraordinary', 'exceptional', or 'unique' circumstances in invoking Chapter VII. Moreover, its ad hoc ratification of the regional organization's forcible acts neither comported with a literal interpretation of Chapter VIII nor could be rationalised by a threat of imminent humanitarian disaster. The argument can be made, with at least a modicum of plausibility, that coups against elected governments are now, *per se*, violations of international law, and that regional organizations are now licensed to use force to reverse such coups in member states.[95]

As Roth notes, the Security Council's intervention in Sierra Leone was, like in Haiti, in response to a coup d'État against an existing democratic government. The Security Council did not intervene on the basis that there was an absence of democracy per se. In this context the Security Council's response to the civil wars in Kosovo and East Timor is very important. In these instances the Security Council was prepared to engage Chapter VII in order to establish a liberal democratic system of governance even in the absence of a coup against an existing democratic government. The liberal reconstructions in Kosovo and East Timor will be discussed in greater detail in chapter six. This notwithstanding, the Security Council's reactions to the events in Haiti and Sierra Leone nevertheless represent a confident endorsement of democracy as the only legitimate system of political governance.[96] Thus, when the Security Council's responses to the events in Haiti and Sierra Leone are contrasted with the Security Council's indifference to systems of political governance during the Cold War, the influence of the international community over the Security Council becomes apparent.

4. CONCLUSION

In chapter two I suggested that the international community has instituted a form of global governance in its determination to promote respect for liberal democracy to non-liberal states. In this chapter I have argued that the international community has sought to locate this governance (at least in the first instance) within the Security Council. Whilst during the

[95] B Roth, *Governmental Illegitimacy in International Law* (Oxford, Clarendon Press, 1999) 407.
[96] R Rich, 'Bringing Democracy into International Law' (2001) 12 *Journal of Democracy* 20, 31 ff.

Cold War the Security Council was only prepared to declare a threat to international peace and security on the basis that state sovereignty was being threatened or had been violated, in the post-Cold War era the Security Council has proven willing to declare a threat to international peace and security where human rights (including the right to democracy) have been violated, and has taken mandatory enforcement action in order to prevent these violations.[97]

In this chapter I have argued that the extent to which the Security Council is now prepared to engage Chapter VII in order to promote respect for liberal values can be attributed to the international community and its growing influence within the world order.[98] I have suggested that the Security Council is now promoting respect for liberal values because it is dominated by an international community of liberal states that is seeking to defend and expand its zone of liberal peace. Indeed, as the zone of liberal peace expands the international community will become a more powerful international actor. To this end, as the international community's influence grows it is likely to exercise greater control over the decisions taken by the Security Council. It is therefore reasonable to assume that the Security Council is likely to become a more active promoter of liberal values in forthcoming years.

This being said, it is important to realise that whilst the Security Council is now dominated by liberal states, the Security Council has not become a de facto organ of the international community. Although liberal values clearly predominate, the international community is not always capable of manipulating the Security Council unconditionally. First, non-liberal states may simply refuse to acquiesce to a resolution that exhibits an overtly liberal bias irrespective of the pressure placed upon them by the international community. The Security Council's refusal to provide authorisation to intervene in Kosovo is such an example, where members of the international community were forced to act outside of the Security Council in order to achieve their liberal objectives. Alternatively, it maybe that non-liberal states are prepared to allow the Security Council to declare a threat to international peace and security on the basis that human rights are being violated, for example, but nevertheless prevent

[97] See SC Res 1265 (17 September 1999), for example, which neatly captures the Security Council's commitment to promoting the values of human rights, democracy and the rule of law. Although this resolution was not adopted under Chapter VII UN Charter, the Council nevertheless stressed 'the need . . . to enhance the protection of civilians on a long term basis, including the promoting of economic growth, poverty eradication, sustainable development, national reconciliation, good governance, democracy, the rule of law and respect for and protection of human rights'.

[98] 'The reawakening of the Security Council's powers has evoked complaints and criticisms that the Security Council is a tool of the major powers': S Murphy, 'The Security Council, Legitimacy and the Concept of Collective Security after the Cold War' (1994) 32 *Columbia Journal of Transnational Law* 201, 205.

enforcement measures being authorised that will allow for the effective protection of such rights. This is a particularly salient issue in the context of the Security Council's involvement in Darfur. Although the international community has managed to persuade the Security Council to declare that the humanitarian crisis in Darfur constitutes a threat to international peace and security, the international community has not been able to acquire authorisation that would enable them to adequately protect human rights. Despite the crisis being considered to amount to genocide by the US, the Chinese veto is still generally regarded as being the main hurdle to allowing for a more robust response.[99] Thus, considering that non-liberal states continue to occupy permanent seats on the Security Council, the international community's influence over the Security Council will be always substantially restrained. Consequently, if the international community is to effectively protect liberal values, unilateral actions (those not authorised by the Security Council) are likely to continue.

Secondly, the pressure that the international community is able to heap upon non-liberal states to support liberal resolutions is often only partially effective. Often liberally orientated resolutions will have to be tempered by the international community in order for them to achieve the requisite support within the Security Council (or more specifically the support of non-liberal states). For example, in relation to Somalia and Haiti the relevant Security Council resolutions expressly recognised that the decision to engage Article 39 in order to protect human rights and democracy was unique and exceptional, presumably so as to avoid the setting of a precedent.[100] Resolutions may also have to contain token references to Article 2(7), thus maintaining (at least formally) the integrity of the non-intervention principle, even though the resolution clearly impacts upon the organisation of domestic affairs. Such resolutions clearly illustrate the tensions that are currently being experienced within the Security Council. In particular, tension between non-liberal states which require the principles of state sovereignty and non-intervention to be adhered to

[99] In 2004 the US House of Representatives (House Concurrent Resolution 467 (2004)) and the US Senate (Senate Concurrent Resolution 133 (2004)) adopted concurrent resolutions determining that the situation in Somalia constituted genocide. The UN Security Council remains unwilling to use the term genocide, not least because China continues to assert that the crisis is an internal matter and thus the Security Council has no jurisdiction. Chinese President Hu Jintao has explained on numerous occasions that the Security Council must 'respect the sovereignty of Sudan': 'Chinese Leader Boosts Sudan Ties', *BBC News* (2 February 2007), available at: news.bbc.co.uk/1/hi/6323017.stm.

[100] In relation to Somalia, China would have vetoed SC Res 794 (3 December 1992) without the insertion of these terms. Indeed, China further requested that the President of the Council release a statement explaining that 'members of the council have asked me to say that the adoption of this Resolution is warranted by the unique and exceptional situation in Haiti and should not be regarded as constituting a precedent': UN Doc S/PV.3238 (16 June 1993) 9.

and liberal states which seek to promote respect for liberal democratic standards. Again, whilst non-liberal states occupy a seat on the Security Council (and indeed permanent seats), this tension will continue and such ideologically complex resolutions seem inevitable.

Part 2

5

The International Society and Peacekeeping

1. INTRODUCTION

THE ONSET OF the Cold War brought considerable tension to the collective security system established by Chapter VII of the UN Charter, usually preventing the Security Council from taking enforcement action where there had been a violation of state sovereignty. In short, the superpower rivalry between the US and USSR, coupled with their permanent seats on the Security Council, had a debilitating effect on this system of collective security. However, in its determination to protect state sovereignty (and therefore maintain international peace and security) the UN developed the doctrine of peacekeeping which, because of its less intrusive, apolitical and consensual nature, was considered to be a far more agreeable mechanism for protecting state sovereignty.[1] As UN Secretary-General Dag Hammarskjöld explained, although the Cold War prevented the Security Council from pursuing peace enforcement, there was nevertheless still an appetite within the UN for 'preventative diplomacy';[2] peacekeeping became an 'improvisation in the effort of the UN to transcend or bypass the constraints of the Cold War in search of a role in a specific crisis'.[3]

[1] 'The conceptual roots of . . . peacekeeping lie in the Cold War and the UN's attempt to develop a role for itself in the pursuit of international peace and security . . . Superpower rivalry soured the working relations and created a lack of consensus in the Security Council. This meant that the organization was unable to fulfil the collective security function that was initially envisaged for it . . . Within this context the UN was forced to adopt alternative techniques, initially through observer missions but later in the form of traditional peacekeeping': A Bellamy, P Williams and S Griffin, *Understanding Peacekeeping* (Oxford, Polity Press, 2003) 97.

[2] Quoted in B Urquhart, *Hammarskjöld* (New York, WW Norton, 1994) 175.

[3] G Abi-Saab, 'United Nations Peacekeeping Old and New: An Overview of the Issues' in D Warner (ed), *New Dimensions of Peacekeeping* (Dordrecht, Martinus Nijhoff, 1995) 2. 'When the Security Council proved unable to take action in response to breaches of the peace, threats to the peace, and acts of aggression, because its decision-making was obstructed by the divisions between the Western and Eastern blocs, peace-keeping was developed as a partial substitute': C Gray, 'The Use of Force and the International Legal Order' in M Evans (ed), *International Law* (Oxford, Oxford University Press, 2010) 638.

This being said, there is no direct reference to peacekeeping within the UN Charter.[4] However, when faced with the collapse of the collective security system, in its early years the UN developed peacekeeping in order to protect the principles and values of the international society; specifically, the principles of sovereign equality and non-intervention. The UN therefore created peacekeeping in order to encourage the peaceful resolution of conflicts between states by deploying lightly armed military personal under UN command to areas where warring states were in need of a neutral party to encourage, observe and preserve the peace process. 'UN peacekeeping was an improvisation, born out of the need to respond to war between states'.[5] Thus, the objective of peacekeeping was to protect every state's domestic jurisdiction by ensuring that inter-state disputes were resolved peacefully and without recourse to violence. In the event that violence did erupt between states and state sovereignty was violated, peacekeeping forces were deployed along the battle lines in order to prevent fighting and eventually restore state sovereignty.[6] It is worth quoting Durch at length here:

> As a 'neutral' organization, it [the UN] could sometimes help to bring smaller conflicts to an end, keep them from flaring anew, and keep them from leading to a direct and potentially catastrophic clash of US and Soviet arms. Thus, the UN came to be associated over the years with more modest but, under the circumstances, more realistic objectives: the mediation of isolated and idiosyncratic conflicts, the monitoring of cease-fire arrangements and the separation of hostile armed forces.[7]

The deployment of peacekeepers between warring (or potentially warring) member states represents the classic conception of peacekeeping.[8]

[4] In the *Certain Expenses* case the International Court of Justice (ICJ) confirmed the legality of UN peacekeeping operations. In doing so, however, the ICJ refused to identify any particular article within the UN Charter as providing the legal basis for the deployment of peacekeeping forces. This notwithstanding, after reviewing the aims and purposes of the UN the ICJ held that UN organs had an implied power to deploy peacekeeping forces: *Certain Expenses of the United Nations*, Advisory Opinion (1962) ICJ Rep 151 at 159.

[5] A Sens, 'From Peacekeeping to Peacebuilding: The United Nations and the Challenge of Intrastate War' in R Price and M Zacher (eds), *The United Nations and Global Security* (New York, Palgrave, 2004) 142.

[6] 'Traditional peacekeeping activities typically vary from simple observation and fact-finding, to monitoring compliance with the conditions of ceasefires and physical imposition between former belligerents. Peacekeepers monitor borders, patrol buffer zones separating opposing forces, verify the various aspects of demilitarization, including weapons decommissioning and troop withdrawals, and attempt to create a political space that will facilitate a political resolution of the conflict. They do not devise political solutions themselves or enforce agreements between the competing parties': Bellamy et al, *Understanding Peacekeeping* (n 1) at 94.

[7] W Durch, 'Introduction' in W Durch (ed), *The Evolution of Peacekeeping* (New York, St Martin's Press, 1993) 1.

[8] 'Originally peacekeeping forces were confined to inter-state conflicts, where there are clear cease-fire lines to supervise, and a buffer of blue helmets can become the reality': H McCoubrey and ND White, *The Blue Helmets: Legal Regulation of United Nations Military Operations* (Aldershot, Dartmouth, 1998) 26.

However, the UN became quickly aware that violence *within* a state could also threaten state sovereignty because civil unrest can destroy the features of statehood. In particular, where civil unrest leads to a complete breakdown in law and order the government is likely to lose effective physical control over the population. Where this occurs the state becomes vulnerable to losing its status of statehood under international law. As I explained in chapter one, under international law in order for a political community to qualify as a state it must possess a government that is able to exercise effective physical control over the population and territory. Perhaps more importantly, where a political community is denied the status of statehood its sovereignty is also called into question (because for the international society, statehood and sovereignty arise contemporaneously). The significance of this is that if a political community is no longer recognised as a state (and therefore sovereign) it will no longer be part of the institutional grip that the international society seeks to establish; if a political community is denied sovereignty itself, it is unlikely to recognise the sovereignty of other states. Excluding a political community from this regulatory system therefore renders international peace and security vulnerable to violation. In order to be effective, this regulatory framework must be universal in scope. To this end, the UN recognised the importance of protecting and strengthening the legal edifice of statehood. The UN recognised that civil unrest within a state can yield negative consequences for international peace and security and thus began to deploy peacekeepers where a state was experiencing profound civil unrest. The intention of the UN, I argue, was not to eliminate the violence and maintain law and order so as to protect the government from usurpation or to prevent a change in the state's political configuration (which would clearly result in intervention in the state's domestic affairs), but instead to ensure that any changes to the political structure of the state occurred peacefully and without threatening/damaging the legal edifice of statehood. In order to maintain international peace and security, therefore, preventing violence *within* states became just as important as preventing violence *between* states.[9]

With these issues in mind this chapter will proceed as follows. In Section 2 I assess traditional peacekeeping operations deployed during the Cold War and illustrate their determination to protect state sovereignty and the right to non-intervention. In addition, in Section 2 I also analyse the principles of consent, neutrality and the use of force only in self-defence that came to represent the legal framework that would guide peacekeeping operations. Specifically, I argue that this framework was created in order to

[9] As Aksu notes, even within intra-state peacekeeping 'the UN's main objective remained unchanged. Maintenance of international peace and security was the dominant preoccupation': E Aksu, *The United Nations, Intra-State Peacekeeping and Normative Change* (Manchester, Manchester University Press, 2003) 81.

ensure that in their desire to protect state sovereignty and the right to non-intervention, peacekeeping operations did not simultaneously violate these values. The international society's commitment to promoting respect for state sovereignty therefore becomes apparent. In Section 3 I reveal that although the UN began deploying peacekeeping missions within intra-state disputes during the Cold War the UN's overriding objective was nevertheless the protection of state sovereignty and thus the maintenance of international peace and security. That this normative commitment remained constant even within intra-state disputes is illustrated by reference to the UN's deployment of peacekeepers in the Congo and Cyprus.

2. INTER-STATE PEACEKEEPING AND THE TRINITY OF VIRTUES

In its classic conception peacekeeping is defined as 'the peaceful inter-positioning of UN personnel, in response to an invitation of the disputants, to oversee an agreed cease-fire'.[10] This accurately captures the nature of the UN's first peacekeeping mission, which sought to supervise an armistice agreement that had been concluded between warring member states.

In April 1947 Britain terminated its mandate over Palestine. In response, on 14 May 1948 Israel unilaterally declared itself to be an independent sovereign state. This resulted in an outbreak of hostilities between Arab states and Israel. On 29 May 1948 the Security Council adopted Resolution 50, which called upon 'all Governments and authorities concerned to order a cessation of all acts of armed force'. In ordering a ceasefire the UN established the United Nations Truce Supervision Organization (UNTSO), which comprised unarmed military observers that were sent to the region to supervise the armistice agreement that had been negotiated between Israel and its Arab neighbours shortly after the end of the Second World War. Upon a textual interpretation of the resolution, it becomes quite clear that the objective of the Security Council was to prevent these states from using force in order to resolve their dispute. In this sense, UNTSO represented the 'archetypal' peacekeeping mission.[11]

However, this is peacekeeping in its most rudimentary form. As violations of state sovereignty occurred with increasingly frequency the UN sought to expand peacekeeping beyond the mere creation and observation of ceasefire agreements.[12] In 1956 the UN General Assembly, acting

[10] T Franck, *Nation against Nation* (New York, Oxford University Press, 1985) 168.

[11] ND White, 'UN Peacekeeping–Development or Destruction?' (1994) 12 *International Relations* 129, 133.

[12] 1944–1956 is therefore called the 'nascent period' in the UN's history of peacekeeping: I Rikhye, 'Peacekeeping and Peacemaking' in H Wiseman (ed), *Peacekeeping: Appraisals and Proposals* (London, C Hurst & Co, 1983) 1.

under the Uniting for Peace Resolution,[13] established the United Nations Emergency Force (UNEF I) in response to the Suez Canal crisis, where British, French and Israeli troops invaded Egypt in order to ensure continued access to the Suez Canal.[14] When hostilities broke out the UN quickly became aware that it would not be possible to forge a ceasefire immediately. Thus, whilst negotiations were underway the General Assembly took the decision to physically place a peacekeeping force (consisting of several thousand lightly armed military personnel) between the warring states, thereby creating a 'buffer zone' between the belligerents.[15] Thus, '[p]eacekeeping evolved from observation so as to give the United Nations a more active role in the cessation of hostilities'.[16] Indeed, UNEF I was largely successful, preventing the Egyptian and British/French/Israeli forces from engaging in conflict. With hostilities terminated, UNEF I was then able to broker and supervise the withdrawal of the British, French and Israeli troops from Egypt, thereby restoring Egypt's sovereignty and, moreover, international peace and security.[17]

This being said, although UNEF I was initially successful, in October 1973 the UN created UNEF II in response to renewed fighting between Israeli and Egyptian forces. By way of Resolution 338,[18] the Security Council called on all parties to agree a ceasefire and to recognise and respect the sovereignty of other states in the region. It also decided that, concurrently with the ceasefire, negotiations should start between the parties to establish a just and lasting peace in the Middle East. As fighting continued the Security Council demanded in Resolution 340[19] an immediate and complete ceasefire and the return of the parties to the positions they had occupied on 22 October. In addition, the Council decided to establish a new United Nations Emergency Force (UNEF II). The Force, which comprised up to 7,000 military personnel for an initial period of six

[13] GA Res 377 (3 November 1950). It is both important and interesting to note that it was the General Assembly that created and deployed UNEF I. With the Security Council deadlocked by Cold War politics other UN members were unable to tolerate continual violations of state sovereignty. In order to protect the UN's values the General Assembly acted and deployed UNEF I (under the Uniting for Peace Resolution), with the explicit objective of ending the inter-state conflict, restoring state sovereignty and ultimately maintaining international peace and security. This illustrates the determination of the UN to respond to violations of state sovereignty in the event that two of its members (Britain and France), who happened to possess permanent seats on the Security Council, prevented a collective response.

[14] See GA Res 1000 (ES-I) (5 November 1956).

[15] McCoubrey and White, *The Blue Helmets* (n 8) at 24.

[16] ibid. 'The UN was involved because it was viewed as an impartial actor that could serve as a neutral buffer between parties to a conflict': C Stahn, *The Law and Practice of International Territorial Administration: Versailles to Iraq and Beyond* (Cambridge, Cambridge University Press, 2008) 148.

[17] For a comprehensive overview of UNEF I, see R Higgins, *United Nations Peacekeeping, 1946-1967: Documents and Commentary* (London, Oxford University Press, 1969) 355 ff.

[18] SC Res 338 (22 October 1973).

[19] SC Res 340 (25 October 1973).

months, was stationed in the Egyptian-Israeli sector. The dispatch of UNEF II effectively brought the crisis to an end. However, UNEF II's mandate was expanded periodically up until 1979 in order to ensure that violence did not recur.

Importantly, whilst crafting the terms of reference for the UNEF I peacekeeping force, UN Secretary-General Hammarskjöld formulated a 'trinity of virtues'[20] that all peacekeeping forces would be legally required to adhere to in the execution of their mandates. This trinity comprised the principles of consent, neutrality and the use of force only in self-defence.[21] As I shall reveal, this framework was developed in order to ensure that in their attempt to protect state sovereignty peacekeeping forces did not simultaneously violate this norm and, in particular, its corollary of the right to non-intervention in domestic affairs.

2.1 The Trinity of Virtues: Consent, Neutrality and the Use of Force Only in Self-Defence

During the Cold War the requirement that peacekeeping forces be deployed with the consent of the host state became an essential legal prerequisite.[22] That the UN regarded its member states to be sovereign entities that possessed the absolute competence to determine their internal affairs without external intervention demanded that peacekeeping forces be deployed with the consent of the host state. It is important to make clear here that the requirement of consent was a legal necessity rather than simply an issue of operational effectiveness (ie that having the consent of the host state would enhance the effectiveness of the mission). As peacekeeping missions did not qualify as peace enforcement under Chapter VII, Article 2(7) of the UN Charter was operative and thus prohibited non-consensual, external intervention in domestic affairs.[23] As Tsagourias notes,

[20] Report of the Special Committee on Peacekeeping, UN Doc A/56/767 (28 March 2003) para 46.

[21] UN Secretary-General Hammarskjöld, UN Doc A/3943 (9 October 1958). Mark Goulding, former head of the UN Peacekeeping Department, defines peacekeeping as a '[f]ield operation established by the United Nations, with the consent of the parties concerned, to help control and resolve conflicts between them, under United Nations command and control, at the expense collectively of the members, and with military and other personnel and equipment provided voluntarily by them, acting impartially between the parties using force to the minimum extent necessary': M Goulding, 'The Evolution of United Nations Peacekeeping' (1993) 69 *International Affairs* 451, 455.

[22] '[H]ost state consent is a legal prerequisite for the entry and presence of a PKO within a state': N Tsagourias, 'Consent, Neutrality/Impartiality and the Use of Force in Peacekeeping: Their Constitutional Dimension' (2007) 11 *Journal of Conflict and Security Law* 465, 469.

[23] 'The requirement of consent to the deployment of PKOs derives from the principle of state sovereignty and non-intervention, and this is a general principle of international law not specifically attached to peacekeeping': ibid at 478.

> [i]n view of the principles of sovereignty and non-intervention, the emplacement of a PKO [peacekeeping operation] within a state and its continuous presence therein are subject to that state's consent, because otherwise it will violate Article 2(7) UN Charter. This Article exempts peace enforcement measures from the protected sphere of domestic jurisdiction but . . . a PKO is not an enforcement operation.[24]

Generally, the UN sought the consent of all the parties to the conflict. However, this was only a principle of good practice. In legal terms, it was only necessary that the host government provided consent, ie the state into which the peacekeeping force was being deployed and so on whose territory it would be physically present. Without such consent, the deployment of a peacekeeping force would violate the state's sovereignty. Thus, in respect of UNEF I the UN Secretary-General stated that

> [w]hile the General Assembly is enabled to establish the Force with the consent of those parties which contribute units to the Force, it could not request the Force to be stationed or operate on the territory of a given country without the consent of the Government of that country.[25]
>
> [T]he functions of the United Nations Force would be . . . to enter Egyptian territory with the consent of the Egyptian Government . . . and to ensure compliance with the other terms established in the resolution of 2 November 1956. The Force obviously should have no rights other than those necessary for the execution of its function, in cooperation with the local authorities.[26]

It is important to note that the provision of consent by the host state was not considered to be a one-off act. In order for sovereignty to be genuinely respected and preserved consent from the host state had to be continuing.[27] Thus, if consent was revoked then the peacekeeping mission would have to be withdrawn, otherwise the force would be violating the sovereignty of the host state. This was graphically illustrated in May 1967 when UN Secretary-General U Thant ordered the withdrawal of UNEF I from Egyptian territory after President Nasser made it clear that Egypt's consent had been withdrawn. As the UN Secretary-General explained,

> When that consent was withdrawn, the essential part of the basis of UNEF's presence ceased to exist.[28]

[24] ibid at 469.

[25] UN Doc A/3289 (4 November 1956). The UN Secretary-General further explained that '[t]his does not exclude the possibility that the Security Council could use such a Force within the wider margins provided under Chapter VII of the United Nations Charter, [but] I would not for the present consider it necessary to elaborate this point further, since no use of force under Chapter VII . . . has been envisaged'.

[26] Second Report of the UN Secretary-General on the Plan for UNEF, UN Doc A/3302 (6 November 1956) para 9.

[27] M Gagnon, 'Peace Forces and the Veto: The Relevance of Consent' (1967) 21 *International Organization* 812, 814.

[28] United Nations Emergency Force, Special Report of the Secretary-General, UN Doc S/7906 (26 May 1967) in (1967) 6 ILM 575 at 576, para 3.

Neutrality also became a legal principle that sought to regulate the conduct of peacekeepers during the Cold War.[29] This principle required that peacekeeping forces should be disinterested and unbiased, in the sense that they should not become partisan, helping one side or hindering another. Neutrality required that peacekeepers be indifferent to the political dispute and

> d[id] not brand one side or another responsible for the military conflict . . . [and did not] overtly favour one side or the other. At the very least, they [were] not designed to provide a military advantage . . . to either side.[30]

Quite overtly, this principle can be seen as a derivative of the principle of non-intervention in domestic affairs.[31] Neutrality meant that the peacekeeping forces could not pronounce upon who was in the right and who was in the wrong of a particular conflict.[32] Instead, the objective was to ensure that an environment was created whereby political disputes could be resolved without state sovereignty being violated. Thus, when UNEF I was deployed UN Secretary-General Hammarskjöld emphasised that the UN did not intend to 'influence the military balance in the conflict and, thereby, the political balance affecting efforts to settle the conflict'.[33]

Related to this notion of neutrality was the additional legal requirement that peacekeepers were only permitted to use force in self-defence.[34] This was based upon the principle of non-aggression that derives from the principle of sovereignty equality,[35] and had become firmly entrenched within the UN's legal framework.[36] As I explained, as a neutral military deployment peacekeepers were not intended to have any role in resolving the dispute, but instead were mandated to facilitate the resolution of the conflict and restore state sovereignty. Thus, peacekeepers were not per-

[29] The terms neutrality and impartiality were used interchangeably by the UN during the Cold War era: see D Donald, 'Neutral is Not Impartial: The Confusing Legacy of Traditional Peace Operations Thinking' (2003) 29 *Armed Forces and Society* 415, 423.

[30] P Diehl, *International Peacekeeping* (Baltimore MD, Johns Hopkins University Press, 1994) 7–8.

[31] '[U]tmost emphasis [was] placed on protecting the sovereignty of the state parties to the conflict. At the same time, the UN was required to respect fully state sovereignty, that is, uphold the principle of non-intervention . . . the importance of protecting and respecting state sovereignty was not open to question': Aksu, *The United Nations, Intra-State Peacekeeping and Normative Change* (n 9) at 78–79.

[32] Neutrality means 'that the PKO should hold no prejudices towards the participants in a conflict and should not influence the course of the events': Tsagourias, 'Consent, Neutrality/Impartiality and the Use of Force in Peacekeeping' (n 22) at 478.

[33] UN Doc A/3302 (6 November 1956) para 8. More generally, 'the Force should not be used to enforce any political solution of pending problems or to influence the political balance decisive to such a solution': UN Doc A/3943 (9 October 1958) para 166.

[34] 'This limitation in the use of force is an important corollary to the requirement of impartiality': S Vohra, 'Impartiality in UN Peacekeeping' (1996) 9 *Leiden Journal of International Law* 63, 66.

[35] S Ratner, *The New UN Peacekeeping: Building Peace in Lands of Conflict after the Cold War* (Basingstoke, Macmillan, 1995) 32 ff.

[36] GA Res 3314 (14 December 1974).

mitted to use force against a particular party as this could be perceived as UN intervention and political favouritism: 'peacekeeping troops have neither an offensive military mission nor the capability to carry one out. Peacekeeping troops are not designed to alter the prevailing distribution of power in the area of deployment'.[37]

3. INTRA-STATE PEACEKEEPING

Although peacekeeping operations were conventionally deployed in order to help formulate or observe ceasefires or to create a buffer zone between warring states, in its determination to protect state sovereignty and thus maintain international peace and security the UN recognised the utility of peacekeeping in instances where states were experiencing *intra*-state conflict. Where a state was experiencing violent civil unrest, the UN sought to deploy a peacekeeping force in order to eradicate violence and create conditions where the parties contributing to the violence could resolve their political disputes peacefully.

Significantly, even within intra-state disputes the legal principles of consent, neutrality and the use of force only in self-defence were still operative. The peacekeeping force could only operate within the territory providing the government gave its consent to the mission. The sovereignty of the state was thereby preserved. Moreover, when deployed the peacekeeping force would not favour any party to the dispute. The peacekeeping force was required to remain neutral vis-à-vis the parties, being concerned exclusively with preventing violence and creating an environment conducive to the peaceful resolution of political disputes. In this sense, in its endeavour to preserve the features of statehood and thus maintain international peace and security, the peacekeeping force would nevertheless demonstrate respect for the principle of non-intervention in domestic affairs. In addition, peacekeepers were required to abstain from using force except in the narrow instance of self-defence, which again provided a further check that would prevent peacekeepers from becoming embroiled in domestic disputes.

The UN's willingness to deploy peacekeepers within states that were experiencing internal violence is vividly illustrated by the deployment of peacekeepers in the Congo and Cyprus. Indeed, the UN's response to the crisis in the Congo deserves special attention because it is often considered to be an aberration within the UN's Cold War peacekeeping practice. In particular, it is argued that the Security Council established a peacekeeping mission with a mandate that deviated from the principles of consent, neutrality and the non-use of force except in self-defence. Instead, a

[37] Diehl, *International Peacekeeping* (n 30) at 7.

peacekeeping mission was deployed that indicated a turn '[t]owards UN intervention in "domestic" affairs'.[38] In essence, the claim is that the UN's response to the Congo crisis cannot be regarded as an expression of the international society.

In the following section I reject this interpretation of the UN's response to the Congo crisis. I argue that it is extremely important to deconstruct the Security Council's response and assess each resolution adopted individually. As I illustrate, once this is undertaken it becomes apparent that in the majority of resolutions taken by the Security Council in relation to the Congo crisis the Council remained loyal to the principles of consent, neutrality and the non-use of force except in self-defence. True, aspects of Security Council Resolution 161 are in particular difficult to reconcile with these principles. This notwithstanding, I will show that the objectives of the Security Council nevertheless remained consistent with the objectives of the international society: namely, that in adopting Resolution 161 the Security Council was seeking to end the political violence and widespread civil unrest in the Congo and thus strengthen the features of statehood. The intention was to ensure that the Congo retained its title of statehood and thus remained a member of the international society's regulatory framework. To this end, the overriding objective of Resolution 161 was to maintain international peace and security.

Notwithstanding the fact that the primary objective of Resolution 161 was to maintain international peace and security, the Security Council's slight deviation from the trinity of virtues proved extremely controversial.[39] It is therefore not surprising that, when confronted with the civil unrest in Cyprus in the same year that the Congo mission was drawing to a close (1964), the Security Council crafted a mandate for a peacekeeping force there that was to be deployed in response to an intra-state dispute that adhered strictly to the principles of consent, neutrality and the use of force only in self-defence. In the context of Cold War peacekeeping, then, the Cyprus operation is important because it illustrates the determination of the UN unambiguously to respect the trinity of virtues and, in turn, the principles of state sovereignty and non-intervention. In light of the Cyprus operation, therefore, 'ONUC [can] be regarded as an isolated phenomenon. The Congo mission did not usher in a new "phase". There was nothing quite like it either immediately before or immediately after, or indeed for some time to come'.[40]

[38] Aksu (n 9) at 109.

[39] Aksu explains that the Congo peacekeeping force was 'one of the most controversial peacekeeping operations in its [the UN's] history': ibid at 100.

[40] ibid at 212.

3.1 Congo: ONUC

With its vast natural mineral resources in its southern region of Katanga the Congo was attractive to foreign powers and was colonised by Belgium in the 1880s. In January 1960 Belgium, under UN pressure for decolonisation, reluctantly agreed to the Congo's demand for independence. On 30 June 1960 Congo became an independent sovereign state.[41] Significantly, Belgian companies possessed exclusive mining rights in Katanga, enjoying long contracts that were not due to expire until 1999.[42] Thus, although Belgium was prepared to grant the Congo its independence it was concerned to maintain its mining rights in Katanga. For this reason Belgium was slow to remove its forces regardless of the immediate demands for withdrawal from the new Congolese government. As Belgian withdrawal stagnated the local Congolese population began committing violent attacks against remaining Belgians. In response, Belgium used military force to (re)enter the Congo, justifying the intervention on the basis of humanitarian intervention.[43]

Within days the Congolese government sought assistance from the UN, requesting a peacekeeping mission to be deployed in response to what it determined to be 'external aggression' from Belgium and 'not to restore an internal situation'.[44] On 14 July 1960 the UN passed Resolution 143 authorising the deployment of a United Nations Force in Congo (ONUC).[45] In line with the demands from the Congolese government, this resolution regarded the events in Congo as an exclusively *inter*-state dispute and called for the immediate withdrawal of Belgian military personnel from the territory.[46] The second operative paragraph of this resolution explained that the Security Council

> [d]ecides to authorize the Secretary-General to take necessary steps, in consultation with the Government of the Republic of the Congo, to provide the Government with such military assistance as may be necessary until, through the efforts of the Congolese Government with the technical assistance of the United Nations, the national security forces may be able, in the opinion of the Government, to meet fully their tasks.

41 Upon independence the Congo would quickly become a member of the UN: see SC Res 152 (23 August 1960).

42 For an overview of Belgium's economic interests in the Congo see J Gordon, *The United Nations in the Congo: A Quest for Peace* (New York, Carnegie Endowment for International Peace, 1962).

43 See generally S Weissman, *American Foreign Policy in the Congo 1960-1964* (London, Cornell University Press, 1974).

44 UN Doc S/4382 (13 July 1960).

45 SC Res 143 (14 July 1960). ONUC is derived from the French '*Organisation des Nations Unies au Congo*'.

46 'Calls upon the Government of Belgium to withdraw its troops from the territory of the Republic of the Congo': ibid.

From the outset the deployment of peacekeeping forces in the Congo was therefore with the consent and agreement of the Congolese government.[47] It was not designed to intervene in the political dispute, but instead to facilitate Belgium's withdrawal from the sovereign state of the Congo, which was considered to be a threat to international peace and security.[48]

Belgium failed to respond to the Security Council's demands in Resolution 143. Ten days after Resolution 143, the Security Council passed a second resolution.[49] This resolution also focused upon the external dimensions of the crisis. The first operative paragraph repeated what was called for in Resolution 143, namely the complete withdrawal of Belgian military personnel from the Congo. However, the significance of this second resolution (Resolution 145) lies in its second operative paragraph. This paragraph explains that the Security Council

> [r]equests all States to refrain from any action which might tend to impede the restoration of law and order and the exercise by the Government of the Congo of its authority and also to refrain from any action which might undermine the territorial integrity and the political independence of the Republic of Congo.

Thus, for the first time the Security Council referred to domestic matters within the Congo – namely the restoration of law and order – something that was manifestly absent from Resolution 143. However, this notwithstanding, from a textual interpretation of Resolution 145 it is nevertheless clear that these words were not intended to address the internal aspects of the conflict per se. Rather, the extent to which the Security Council was concerned with the internal situation could be attributed to the external intervention by Belgian forces, which was preventing the government from exercising effective control over the territory. As Aksu notes, '[b]y putting the emphasis on the Congo's territorial integrity and political independence, the paragraph unambiguously conveyed the UN's primary normative objective, namely the protection of the Congo's (external) sovereignty'.[50] To this end, the Security Council still clearly regarded the matter as an *inter*-state dispute. As the fifth (introductory) paragraph of Resolution 145 states, 'the complete restoration of law and order in the Republic of the Congo would effectively contribute to the maintenance of international peace and security'.

[47] UN Secretary-General Hammarskjöld continually repeated that the consent of the Congolese government was the legal basis for the peacekeeping operation. For a review of the Secretary-General's role in the Congo see T Franck and J Carey, 'The Role of the United Nations in the Congo – a Retrospective Perspective' in L Tondel Jr (ed), *The Legal Aspects of the United Nations Action in the Congo* (New York, Oceana Publications, 1963) 16.

[48] 'Initially the threat to international peace and security was seen as resulting from the Belgian intervention in the Congo and, more indirectly, from the possibility that other states might intervene also': D Bowett, *United Nations Forces* (London, David Davies Memorial Institute, 1964) 186.

[49] SC Res 145 (22 July 1960).

[50] Aksu (n 9) at 104.

In the face of these two resolutions, Belgium began formally to withdraw its military presence from the Congo. This being said, Belgium did (somewhat surreptitiously) retain a military presence within the region of Katanga in order to protect its economic interests there. Furthermore, Belgium expressed its support for the governor of Katanga (Moise Tshombe), who had previously declared Katanga to be an independent state that had seceded from the Congo. The Belgian government considered that it had found a friendly governor in Tshombe who, unlike the central Congolese government, would not interfere with Belgium's mining rights in Katanga. In August 1960 Tshombe (with the support and encouragement of Belgium) made it quite clear that ONUC would not be permitted entry to Katanga, regardless of ONUC's Security Council mandate to maintain law and order throughout the Congo. The Security Council responded by passing Resolution 146.[51] The wording of Resolution 146 is important and requires deliberation.

Like previous resolutions, this resolution again repeated the demand that Belgium remove its forces from the Congo (and in particular from Katanga) and required the establishment of effective governance throughout the state. The gist of the resolution was thus the removal of external intervention from the domestic political dispute that had emerged between Katanga and the central Congolese government. The UN made it quite clear that its role was not to take sides between Katanga and the central government. Indeed, Resolution 146 clearly stated that ONUC would 'not be a party to or in any way interfere in or be used to influence the outcome of any internal conflict, constitutional or otherwise'.[52] Instead, the sole concern for the UN was the removal of external (Belgian) intervention in this domestic political dispute. This was clearly spelt out by Secretary-General Hammarskjöld. Commenting upon Resolution 146 he explained:

> The United Nations is directly concerned with the attitude taken by the province of Katanga to the extent that it may be based on the presence of Belgian troops . . . [Resolution 146], which reaffirmed the principle of non-intervention, put the main emphasis on the withdrawal of Belgian troops. Therefore . . . if the Belgian troops were withdrawn . . . the question between the provincial government and the central government would be one in which the United Nations would in no sense be a party and on which it could in no sense exert an influence. It might be held that the United Nations is bound to uphold Fundamental Law as the legal constitution and, therefore, should assist the central government in exercising its powers in Katanga. However, the United Nations has to observe that, de facto, the provincial government is in active opposition – once a Belgian assurance on non-intervention and withdrawal has been given – using only its own military means in order to achieve political aims.[53]

[51] SC Res 146 (9 August 1960).
[52] ibid at para 4.
[53] UN Doc S/4417/Add.6 (12 August 1960) para 6.

Thus, this statement clearly reveals that the UN Secretary-General adamantly refused to favour either the provincial or central government, considering both parties equally legitimate in what was a dispute of an essentially internal nature and therefore beyond the purview of the UN. In legal terms, the only role the UN could perform was to ensure the expeditious withdrawal of Belgian troops and the elimination of foreign intervention in the domestic dispute. Secretary-General Hammarskjöld therefore considered that the external and internal dimensions surrounding the Congo could be clearly demarcated and that the UN's role should be focused on the external dimension, ie the removal of Belgian intervention.

The crisis in the Congo changed drastically in September 1960 when senior members within the central Congolese government fell into dispute over how the problems in Katanga should be addressed. Indeed, tensions escalated when Prime Minister Patrice Lumumba was kidnapped and murdered. Joseph Mobutu subsequently led a coup d'État against the central government, dismissing the existing administration. The response of the Security Council to this series of events was both ground-breaking and highly controversial. The Security Council responded by adopting Resolution 161 on 21 February 1961, which conferred additional functions on ONUC. In particular, operative paragraph 1 of Resolution 161 authorised ONUC to make arrangements for a ceasefire; the halting of all military operations; and the prevention of violent clashes. The authorisation to use force was given in the event that it was considered necessary to attain these objectives. In addition, ONUC was required to evacuate all non-UN foreign military personnel from the Congo; to undertake an immediate and impartial investigation into Lumumba's killing; to ensure punishment of those responsible for his death; to take proactive measures to enable the reconvening of the Congolese Parliament; and to make arrangements to ensure that Congolese armed units and personnel were reorganised and brought under control.[54]

Resolution 161 was so controversial because it clearly deviated from the trinity of virtues that had provided the legal framework for peacekeeping operations since UNEF I. First, when the Security Council adopted Resolution 161 there was no government in the Congo that was capable of providing consent to the intervention. Although consent was given when ONUC was originally deployed, given that any governmental structure had ceased to exist by the time Resolution 161 was adopted, the presumption that governmental consent was being continually conferred is difficult to sustain. Secondly, it is very difficult to see how ONUC could be regarded as being neutral to the disputing parties, not least because ONUC was charged with the responsibility of identifying and punishing

[54] See paras 2 and 4 of Part A and paras 1–2 of Part B of Resolution 161 (21 February 1961) UN Doc S/4741.

the murderers of Prime Minister Lumumba. In essence, ONUC was required to tell 'right' from 'wrong' and apportion criminal liability. Moreover, it would appear that that the Security Council authorised ONUC to interfere in the domestic political affairs of the Congo in so far as it was required to reconvene Parliament and therefore formally reactivate the democratic process. Thirdly, ONUC was expressly conferred the authority to use military force in the last resort in order to discharge its functions and secure these objectives. As Bowett explains, 'it is difficult to avoid the conclusion that the Security Council by this Resolution [Resolution 161] abandoned a strict reliance on the principle of self-defence'.[55] Consequently,

> [i]t is very difficult to see ONUC as a true peacekeeping operation, in that it was authorised to use force beyond that necessary for strict self-defence, it was not impartial in the conflict, it received little cooperation, and although it did have formal consent of the central government, the fact was that for a period until August 1961 there was no real government in the Congo.[56]

Incontrovertibly, Resolution 161 conferred upon ONUC functions that deviated from the trinity of virtues. This being said, however, it is extremely important to appreciate that notwithstanding this deviation the Security Council's overriding objectives in relation to the Congo remained consistent with the objectives of the UN and, more generally, the international society. From a textual interpretation of Resolution 161 it is apparent that the objective of the Security Council was to prevent civil war rather than to intervene in a domestic political dispute and to impose an externally defined (UN) solution. The intention of the Security Council was to preserve the features of statehood (effective governance) and thus the Congo's sovereign status. Indeed, the prevention of civil war was clearly given pride of place within Resolution 161. As the preamble to Resolution 161 explained, the Security Council's involvement was motivated because of 'the danger of a widespread civil war and bloodshed in the Congo'. The Security Council proceeded to authorise ONUC to take 'all appropriate measures to prevent occurrence of civil war in the Congo'. As Aksu notes,

> [t]he Security Council, no longer able to ignore the internal tensions in the Congo, made prevention of civil war the main mandate for ONUC. The whole preamble and first operative paragraph of Part A were devoted to the issue of civil war.[57]

All the functions conferred upon ONUC were thus pursuant to the objective of avoiding civil war and to creating a political environment that was

[55] Bowett, *United Nations Forces* (n 48) at 201–2.
[56] White, *UN Peacekeeping – Development or Destruction?* (n 11) at 150.
[57] Aksu (n 9) at 116.

conducive to the peaceful resolution of political disputes. For example, in conferring on ONUC the function of investigating Prime Minister Lumumba's death and punishing those found to be responsible, the Security Council explained that it was concerned about the 'grave repercussions of these crimes'. Indeed, in the same sentence the Council proceeded to express its determination to avoid civil war and further bloodshed in the Congo. Thus, the grave repercussions of these crimes (the murder of the Prime Minister) were clearly linked to the concern that it would fuel disorder, bloodshed and potentially civil war. ONUC was authorised to investigate the murder and punish those responsible because by dispensing justice the supporters of the Prime Minister would be less likely to cause civil unrest. Furthermore, Resolution 161 authorised ONUC to reconvene Parliament. Significantly, however, ONUC was authorised to reconvene *existing* Parliamentary institutions. Thus, the intention was not to create any new political institutions but instead to rehabilitate pre-existing ones, which could then be used as a peaceful forum where the parties could initiate dialogue and resolve their political differences through mediation: 'the purpose [of Resolution 161] was to bring the parties, which were in a formal sense equally respected, to the negotiation table'.[58] Indeed, that the real objective of Resolution 161 was to protect the sovereignty of the Congo and not to intervene in its domestic political affairs is illustrated by the demands of the British Ambassador to the UN. The British Ambassador warned Secretary-General Hammarskjöld that Britain would veto Resolution 161 unless he assured the Security Council that the resolution would not extend ONUC's mandate to any other objective than the prevention of civil war. Consequently, Secretary-General Hammarskjöld informed the Security Council that Resolution 161 could not be used to impose any political solution on the parties.[59]

Finally, the Security Council was required to deal more directly with Katanga and its unilateral declaration of independence. In Resolution 169 the Security Council 'completely rejected the claim that Katanga was a sovereign independent nation'.[60] Again, from Resolution 169 it would appear that the UN had become embroiled in a domestic political matter. In particular, that the UN was interfering in domestic politics, supporting the central government and rejecting the secessionist claims of the provincial government:

> [O]n the basis of this resolution [Resolution 169] UN forces took military action in Katanga that contributed decisively to ending its secession and that could be

[58] ibid at 116.

[59] The dialogue between the British Ambassador and the Secretary-General is examined in E Lefever, *Crisis in the Congo: A United Nations Force in Action* (Washington DC, Brookings Institution, 1965) 55 ff.

[60] SC Res 169 (24 November 1961).

> seen as at odds with the principle . . . that the UN force could not be used to enforce any specific political solution.[61]

The conclusion is that this represented a significant normative shift in the UN's approach to peacekeeping and another departure from the trinity of virtues, particularly the principle of neutrality. I reject this interpretation of Resolution 169. As the fifth (introductory) paragraph of Resolution 169 explained, the UN's rejection of Katanga's declaration of independence was based upon 'secessionist activities and armed action being carried out by the provincial administration of Katanga *with the aid of external resources and foreign mercenaries*' (emphasis added). Thus, the UN rejected Katanga's declaration of independence because the secession was encouraged by external influences (notably Belgium) which wanted to retain control over the mineral-rich region. In this sense, the dispute was not wholly domestic in nature. As Bowett notes, 'many Member States did not regard the secessionist movements as a purely internal matter, since the evidence of external support for them was overwhelming'.[62] Consequently, the UN's refusal to allow secession was motivated by a 'preoccupation with the protection of the Congo's sovereignty against 'externally manipulated' secessionist activities';[63] specifically, that the UN perceived Belgium to be engaging in a de facto (re)colonisation of the resource-rich province of Katanga.

All in all, although initially the UN's involvement in the Congo was in response to a classic inter-state dispute, eventually the UN became embroiled in what was an essentially intra-state dispute. As I suggested, in light of Resolution 161 it became very difficult for the Security Council to maintain that it was strictly adhering to the legal principles of consent, neutrality and the use of force only in self-defence. However, notwithstanding the fact that the Security Council did inevitably deviate from a strict understanding of the trinity of virtues it is extremely important to realise that Resolution 161 was ultimately concerned with avoiding civil war in the Congo, preserving its features of statehood and therefore maintaining international peace and security. Moreover, when all resolutions relating to the Congo are taken together, it becomes quite apparent that the Security Council's response to the Congo crisis

> did not entail a change in objectives. Maintenance of *international* peace and security was the main preoccupation of the international community throughout the ONUC episode – even when ONUC was required to maintain domestic law and order. While international actors remained largely silent on human rights during the Congo operation, the principle of state sovereignty, perceived in its 'external'

[61] J Sutterlin, *The UN and the Maintenance of International Security: A Challenge to be Met* (Westport CT, Praeger, 2003) 32.
[62] Bowett (n 48) at 197.
[63] Aksu (n 9) at 81.

dimension and with the emphasis very much on territorial integrity and political independence, informed international normative expectations of the UN.[64]

3.2 Cyprus: UNFICYP

The Cyprus conflict also emerged out of the colonial context. Cyprus came under British rule in 1878 and it was not until 1960 that Britain, under international pressure to relinquish its colonies, created an independent Republic of Cyprus. Upon decolonisation the constitution of Cyprus provided for strict power sharing between the Greek and Turkish communities. In 1963 the Greek Cypriot President sought to amend the constitution in order to ensure that the Greek Cypriot majority retained control over the Republic of Cyprus. This was rejected by the Turkish Cypriot minority and violence soon erupted, resulting in a complete breakdown of law and order within the state.

In response to the civil strife the Cypriot government called for UN assistance, not least because it feared a Turkish intervention.[65] The Security Council was presented with two different accounts of the history of Cyprus and the relationship between the two opposing communities. However, in responding to the civil conflict the Security Council refused to determine which community was in the right or in the wrong and thus chose to ignore the substance of the dispute. The Security Council did not seek to resolve the root causes of the conflict but instead focused upon avoiding renewed violence. Thus, on 4 March 1964 the Security Council deployed the United Nations Peacekeeping Force in Cyprus (UNFICYP) under Resolution 186, explaining in paragraph 5 of this resolution that

> the function of the Force should be in the interest of preserving international peace and security, to use it best efforts to prevent recurrence of fighting and, as necessary, to contribute to the maintenance and restoration of law and order and a return to normal conditions.

This resolution clearly stated that the objective of the force was to prevent the Greek and Turkish communities from fighting and to restore law and order.[66] Quite demonstrably, UNFICYP was not to take sides in this domestic political dispute.[67] In the words of the Norwegian Ambassador to the Security Council:

[64] ibid at 122.

[65] UN Doc S/5508 (1964).

[66] 'The mandate given to UNFICYP was to use its best efforts to prevent recurrence of fighting; to contribute to the maintenance and restoration of law and order; and to promote a return to normal conditions': Rikhye, *The Theory and Practice of Peacekeeping* (n 12) at 92.

[67] Security Council Resolution 186 (4 March 1964), also established a UN Mediator and authorised him to 'use his best endeavours . . . for the purposes of promoting a peaceful solution and an agreed settlement of the problem confronting Cyprus . . . having in mind the well-being of the people of Cyprus as a whole and the preservation of international peace and

> There is no merit in the Council discussing whether these treaties and the Constitution that was adopted was good or bad. It is the view of my Government that it is not for the Security Council to pronounce upon the Constitution of a Member State, nor to pass judgement on a set of treaties which were negotiated as a an integral part of the whole process of granting independence to that State.[68]

Rather, the objective of the mission was to create an environment where the opposing communities could resolve their political disputes peacefully and without recourse to violence. The objective was to preserve the features of statehood and therefore ensure that Cyprus retained its sovereign status. In turn, this would contribute to the maintenance of international peace and security by locking Cyprus within the institutional grip that the principle of sovereign equality engenders.

The role and objectives of UNFICYP were made abundantly clear by the Secretary-General in a significant aide-memoire.[69] This document laid down the principles that would guide the mission. Indeed, it is clear that these principles were consistent with the trinity of virtues (consent, neutrality and the use of force only in self-defence). The importance of the aide-memoire, therefore, resides in the Secretary-General's determination that, unlike the peacekeeping mission in the Congo, there would be no deviation from the trinity of virtues. In particular, the aide-memoire stated that UNFICYP's legal basis in Cyprus was dependent upon the consent of the Cypriot government (although UNFICYP often pushed hard to acquire the consent of the Turkish community as well).[70] Moreover, in line

security'. The Mediator thus had long-term objectives of helping to establish an open dialogue between the conflicting parties so that their differences could be resolved. But it is important to recognise that the Mediator possessed a very minimal role and certainly did not favour either party to the dispute. Moreover, the extent to which the Mediator mediated between the parties was driven by a desire to end the politically motivated violence, protect the features of statehood and thus maintain international peace and security.

[68] Norwegian statement before the Security Council, UN Doc S/PV.1097 (1964) 22. See also the statement of the Czechoslovakian representative to the Security Council, who explained that '[o]ur understanding follows from the fundamental principles of the Charter. We are convinced that the Security Council, proceeding from these principles, must deal with the solution of the question before us unequivocally from the point of view of safeguarding the security, independence, sovereignty and territorial integrity of Cyprus . . . All other interests must be subjected to this primary objective': UN Doc S/PV.1097 (1964) 38–40. Indeed, the General Assembly also stressed the 'sovereignty, unity, independence and territorial integrity of the republic of Cyprus' and 'the fact that . . . Cyprus . . . should enjoy full sovereignty and complete independence without any foreign intervention or interference': GA Res 2077 (18 December 1965).

[69] UN Doc S/5653 (11 April 1964).

[70] The USSR representative to the Security Council made it quite clear that the consent of the Cypriot government was imperative in order for their agreement to the deployment of a peacekeeping force: 'Only the people of Cyprus have the right on decide upon their domestic affairs . . . The Soviet Union in principle is negatively disposed toward the dispatch to Cyprus of any foreign military forces including United Nations forces . . . In order to meet the wishes of the Government of Cyprus, the Soviet delegation is prepared not to hamper the adoption of this draft resolution': UN Doc S/PV.1102 (4 March 1964).

with the principle of neutrality the Secretary-General stated that the peacekeeping force must avoid any action 'designed to influence the political situation in Cyprus except through contributing to a restoration of quiet and through creating an improved climate in which political solutions may be sought'.[71] Thus, UNFICYP was to concentrate its efforts upon restoring order and creating an environment where the disputing parties could resolve their political disputes peacefully and without recourse to violence. UNFICYP therefore remained firmly indifferent to the underlying political dispute.[72] Indeed, the Secretary-General's aide-memoire stated that the use of armed force was only permissible in self-defence, and that the principle of minimum force should be applied.[73] As a general rule, UNFICYP was allowed to use force only when all peaceful means of persuasion had been exhausted.[74] This being said, as the mission progressed authorisation to use force was extended, but only 'where specific arrangements accepted by both communities [had] been, or in the opinion of the commander on the spot [were] about to be, violated[,] thus risking recurrence of fighting or endangering law and order'.[75] Consequently, '[i]n general, the UN's authority in Cyprus was defined within the parameters of the Hammarskjöldian formula. UNFICYP was expected to use force only in self-defence, and most importantly, to remain "neutral"'.[76] Furthermore, although the UN had intervened in an intra-state dispute the objective was to preserve Cyprus's statehood (and therefore its sovereignty), which was in turn motivated by a desire to maintain international peace and security.[77] As Aksu records, 'the UN's involvement in the Cyprus conflict reflected a dominant preoccupation with the maintenance of regional stability, and in that sense *international* peace and security'.[78]

[71] UN Doc S/5653 (11 April 1964).

[72] For example, in November 1967 Greek Cypriots engaged in a violent offensive against the Turkish community (the notorious Kophinou incident). Although the UNFICYP sought to prevent and eliminate the violence it adamantly refused to take sides or apportion blame.

[73] UN Doc S/5653 (11 April 1964).

[74] ibid at para 18.

[75] ibid at para 17.

[76] Aksu (n 9) at 149.

[77] The UN was again required to intervene in Cyprus in 1974 when the Greek Cypriots announced their desire for an early *enosis* (unification with Greece), provoking widespread civil unrest and eventual external intervention by Turkey. In response, the Security Council gave UNFICYP a fresh mandate, requiring it to establish and observe a security zone between the Turkish community in the north of Cyprus and the Greek community in south. Again, the objective of the UN was clear. There was no intention to become involved in what was considered an essentially domestic political dispute. For the UN, the only appropriate role it could assume was to attempt to prevent violence between the two communities, providing a peaceful environment in which dialogue and communication could be established: see SC Res 355 (1 August 1974).

[78] Aksu (n 9) at 148.

4. CONCLUSION

It has not been the objective of this chapter to provide a comprehensive review of peacekeeping missions undertaken during the Cold War. Rather, the objective has been to illustrate that during the Cold War the UN developed the doctrine of peacekeeping in order to protect state sovereignty and thus maintain international peace and security. Initially, peacekeeping missions were designed to respond to warring states, preventing them from using force against each other in order to resolve their disputes. Once deployed, in order to respect the international society's core principles of state sovereignty and non-intervention, peacekeeping missions were required to operate with the consent of the state in which they were physically present, to be neutral vis-à-vis the political preferences of the disputing parties and not to use force unless in self-defence. Thus, '[f]undamentally, peace-keeping was about maintaining a peace between states, and the political and operational parameters of peace-keeping were firmly consistent with the Westphalian principles of state sovereignty and territorial integrity'.[79] In this sense, traditional peacekeeping can be perceived as a manifestation of the international society and an attempt to protect its core principles (state sovereignty, non-intervention) and thus realise its overriding objective (the maintenance of international peace and security).

In addition, I have suggested that in order to fully preserve international peace and security the UN began deploying peacekeeping forces within states that were experiencing internal conflict, particularly after decolonisation. The intention was that peacekeeping forces would help eradicate violence and restore law and order. In this way, the features of statehood could be preserved and state sovereignty maintained. To this end, the regulatory framework represented by the international society would remain universal in scope and therefore at its most effective. From the perspective of the international society, this would enable international peace and security to be maintained. Thus, as Aksu records, 'the maintenance of *international* peace and security emerged as the UN's main objective, even in intra-state peacekeeping environments'.[80] Importantly, even when deployed in intra-state disputes, peacekeeping forces were still required to adhere to the trinity of virtues. In particular, the UN's mission in the Congo has been discussed at length because certain aspects of this mission (notably Resolution 161) resulted in deviation from this legal framework. Notwithstanding this deviation, however, I have suggested

[79] Sens, 'From Peacekeeping to Peacebuilding: The United Nations and the Challenge of Intrastate War' in Price and Zacher (eds), *The United Nations and Global Security* (n 5) at 142.
[80] Aksu (n 9) at 81.

that ultimately the functions conferred upon ONUC by Resolution 161 had as their overriding objective the prevention of civil war, the restoration of law and order and the creation of conditions under which the disputing parties could resolve their differences without recourse to force. In no way did Resolution 161 seek to impose an external solution to the underlying internal political dispute.

The mission in Cyprus was discussed as well because it was the first major peacekeeping mission since ONUC's mission in the Congo. As I have revealed, both the Security Council and the Secretary-General were adamant that the trinity of virtues would be strictly adhered to. The legal basis of the UNFICYP was dependent upon the consent of the Cypriot government. The peacekeeping force was required to remain strictly neutral between the disputing internal parties. The use of force was limited to self-defence. In this sense, the peacekeeping force in Cyprus can be seen as an important corrective to the mission creep that did inevitably occur in the Congo and a restatement that, at least during the Cold War, peacekeeping missions would, in their determination to protect state sovereignty and thus maintain international peace and security, ardently respect the principles of consent, neutrality and the use of force only in self-defence. To this end, my claim in this chapter has been that peacekeeping missions deployed during the Cold War, even in response to intra-state disputes, can be seen as expression of the international society and an attempt to protect its values and secure its objectives.

6

The International Community and Peacebuilding

1. INTRODUCTION

SINCE THE END of the Cold War and the emergence of the international community there has been a substantial shift in the normative basis of UN peacekeeping. With the growing influence of the international community over the UN (and particularly the international community's growing influence over the Security Council) peacekeeping forces are now being increasingly deployed with overt political objectives. Specifically, peacekeeping missions are now being deployed by the UN in order to promote respect for democracy, human rights and the rule of law. This fundamental transformation in the UN's approach is most vividly captured by the former Secretary-General Boutros-Ghali's change in language from peacekeeping to *peacebuilding*.[1] For the Secretary-General, the UN should become actively involved in peacebuilding, which includes

> disarming the previously warring parties, the restoration of order, the custody and possible destruction of weapons, repatriating refugees, advisory and training support for security personnel, monitoring elections, advancing efforts to protect human rights, reforming or strengthening governmental institutions and promoting formal and informal processes of political participation.[2]

[1] Tansey argues that peacebuilding has become a euphemism for 'democratic regime-building': O Tansey, 'The Concept and Practice of Democratic Regime-Building' (2007) 14 *International Peacekeeping* 633,

[2] Report of the Secretary-General, 'An Agenda for Peace-Preventive Diplomacy, Peacemaking and Peacekeeping' UN Doc A/47/277 – S/24111 (17 June 1992) 55. See also the statement by the President of the Security Council: 'peace-building is aimed at preventing the outbreak, the recurrence or continuation of armed conflict and therefore encompasses a wide range of political, development, humanitarian and human rights programmes and mechanisms. This requires short and long term actions tailored to address the particular needs of societies sliding into conflict or emerging from it. These actions should focus on fostering sustainable institutions and processes in areas such as sustainable development, the eradication of poverty and inequalities, transparent and accountable governance, the promotion of democracy, respect for human rights and the rule of law and the promotion of a culture of peace and non-violence': Statement by the President of the Security Council, 'Peacebuilding: towards a comprehensive approach', UN Doc S/PRST/2001/5 (20 February 2001).

This is not to say, however, that in the post-Cold War era peacekeeping missions have disappeared. On the contrary, peacekeeping missions are still being deployed in order to establish and observe ceasefires, create a *cordon sanitaire* between warring (or potentially warring) states and to maintain law and order within states that are experiencing profound civil unrest.[3] In these circumstances, the trinity of virtues that guided peacekeeping operations during the Cold War continue to apply, and provide the 'constitutional'[4] framework for peacekeeping missions. However, my argument in this chapter is that since the end of the Cold War *peacekeeping* missions have been increasingly replaced by *peacebuilding* missions that seek to reconstruct states emerging from conflict upon a liberal basis.

> This suggests that the end of the Cold War did not inspire a sudden and dramatic about-turn in international perceptions of the role of peacekeeping in global politics. Instead, there was a handful of large missions supported by Western states that embarked upon a new form of 'wider', more complex, better resourced and much more ambitious peacekeeping [ie peacebuilding].[5]

Although these peacebuilding missions may initially contain peacekeeping features (such as the removal of violence and the creation of a peaceful environment), they are often supplemented with additional functions, specifically the promotion of human rights and democratic processes. Thus, whereas during the Cold War the UN was adamant that peacekeeping missions would not become involved in domestic political matters, in the post-Cold War era the UN's political bias in favour of liberal democracy has become overt. Significantly, this has resulted in the abandonment of the trinity of virtues. Although the UN has repeatedly affirmed that the principles of consent, impartiality and the use of force only in self-defence continue to apply to peacebuilding operations,[6] this

[3] In 1991, for example, the UN reiterated the importance of peacekeeping missions, defining them as an 'operation involving military personnel, but without enforcement powers, undertaken by the United Nations to help maintain or restore international peace and security in areas of conflict. These operations are voluntary and are based on consent and co-operation': United Nations, 'The Blue Helmets: A Review of United Nations Peacekeeping' (New York, United Nations Department of Information, 1990) 4. See generally the Special Committee on Peacekeeping, 'Comprehensive Review of the Whole Question of Peacekeeping Operations in all their Aspects', UN Doc A/56/767 (28 March 2003) para 46.

[4] N Tsagourias, 'Consent, Neutrality/Impartiality and the Use of Force in Peacekeeping: Their Constitutional Dimension' (2006) 11 *Journal of Conflict and Security Law* 465.

[5] A Bellamy, P Williams and S Griffin, *Understanding Peacekeeping* (Cambridge, Polity Press, 2004) 76.

[6] '[T]he last few years have confirmed that respect for certain basic principles of peacekeeping are essential to its success. Three particularly important principles are the consent of the parties, impartiality and the non-use of force except in self-defence': UN Secretary-General Boutros Boutros-Ghali, 'Supplement to an Agenda for Peace', UN Doc A/50/60 – S/1995/1 (3 January 1995) para 33. In 2000 the Brahimi Report stated that 'consent of the local parties, impartiality and the use of force only in self-defence should remain the bedrock principles of peacekeeping': L Brahimi, Report of the Panel on United Nations Peace Operations, UN Doc A/55/305 – S/2000/809 (21 August 2000) para 48. Most recently (2008), the UN reaffirmed that the trinity of virtues continue to 'provide a navigation aid, or compass' for all peace opera-

has clearly become a 'legal fiction'.[7] Peacebuilding missions often do not operate with the consent of the host, not least because in many post-conflict societies no central authority is capable of giving consent. Although the UN will often try to acquire consent of the parties to the conflict, this is out of political prudence rather than legal necessity. Since the deployment of the peacebuilding mission in Somalia, Chapter VII has generally provided the legal basis for such politically orientated operations. As I have already suggested, peacebuilding missions can in no way be regarded as politically neutral. They exhibit a profound bias in favour of promoting respect for liberal democratic standards, although they do seek to realise these liberal objectives impartially, without favour or prejudice to any party that is privy to the dispute. The objective is to treat all parties even-handedly against the mission's mandate, which is to promote respect for liberal values. Moreover, peacebuilding forces are now authorised to use force in order to defend their (liberal) mandate, rather than merely in defence of the safety of UN personnel, as was the case during the Cold War.[8]

In light of this, the central argument of this chapter is that this shift from peacekeeping to peacebuilding is a product of the international community and its desire to promote liberal democracy (which is perceived as a 'superior' form of governance)[9] to non-liberal states. The willingness of the UN to deploy peacebuilding missions as opposed to peacekeeping missions can be seen as an expression of the international community's desire to protect and expand its zone of liberal peace. 'In its attempt to construct a zone of "stable peace", the theory and practice of peace[building] is informed by a commitment to the liberal peace'.[10] Whereas peacekeeping was designed to respond to a 'sovereignty problem' (protecting and preserving state sovereignty), in the post-Cold War era the peacekeeping tool has been appropriated by an increasingly powerful international community and employed

tions, ie both peacekeeping and peacebuilding missions: 'United Nations Peacekeeping Operations: Principles and Guidelines' (2008), available at: pbpu.unlb.org/PBPS/Library/Capstone_Doctrine_ENG.pdf (referred to as the Capstone Document).

[7] Tsagourias, 'Consent, Neutrality/Impartiality and the Use of Force in Peacekeeping' (n 4) at 481.

[8] It should be noted that in the Capstone Document the UN recognised that the use of force should be generally considered to be authorised in order to defend the mandate rather than merely in self-defence: Capstone Document (n 6) 34.

[9] 'Although modern peacebuilders have largely abandoned the archaic language of civilised versus uncivilised, they nevertheless appear to act upon the belief that one model of governance – liberal market democracy – is superior to all others': R Paris, 'International Peacebuilding and the "*Mission Civilisatrice*"' (2002) 28 *Review of International Studies* 637, 638.

[10] Bellamy, Williams and Griffin, *Understanding Peacekeeping* (n 5) 26. See generally D Chandler, *International Statebuilding: the Rise of Post-Liberal Governance* (London, Routledge, 2010) ch 2 ('The "liberal peace" critique of international intervention').

to respond to a 'governance problem',[11] ie a lack of respect for liberal democracy.[12] The purpose of this chapter is therefore to examine peacebuilding missions since the end of the Cold War and illustrate their contribution to the promotion of liberal values to non-liberal states. It should be pointed out, however, that in this chapter I do not attempt to provide a comprehensive review of all peacebuilding operations since the end of the Cold War. Rather, my intention is to examine specific peacebuilding missions so that the normative preferences of the UN (or more accurately the international community acting through the UN) can be observed. This will contribute to my thesis that an international community of liberal states has formed within the international society that now commands a powerful presence within the world order (and particularly within the Security Council) and is determined to promulgate its liberal values to non-liberal states.[13] In this sense, the doctrine of peacebuilding can be situated within and explained by the international community's commitment to building a durable liberal peace.

The chapter will therefore proceed as follows. In Section 2 I examine (chronologically) the peacebuilding missions in Namibia, Cambodia and Somalia in order to illustrate the increasing normative commitment of the UN to the promotion of liberal values since the end of the Cold War. In particular, I dedicate much attention to examining the UN's role in Kosovo and East Timor because the UN's contribution to promoting respect for liberal democracy in these territories represents an example of peacebuilding par excellence. A detailed analysis of these territorial administrations will clearly illustrate the strength of the normative commitment of the UN to promoting respect for liberal values and a correlative weakening of its concern for respecting state sovereignty and, in particular, respecting the right to non-intervention in domestic political affairs.[14] In Section 3 my focus will turn to the reconstruction of Afghanistan. Afghanistan is singled out for special consideration because, in dramatic

[11] The terms 'sovereignty problem' and 'governance problem' are borrowed from Wilde: R Wilde, 'From Danzig to East Timor and Beyond: The Role of the United Nations Missions in Kosovo and East Timor' (2001) 95 *American Journal of International Law* 46, 46.

[12] 'While traditional peacekeeping strove primarily to sustain cease-fires or peace agreements between two states by providing a "cordon sanitaire", post-conflict peace-building (PCPB) was designed to transform intra-state conflicts through free and fair elections, and the introduction of liberal-market reforms': M Kartas, 'Post-Conflict Peacebuilding – Is the Hegemony of the 'Good Governance' Discourse Depoliticising the Local?' (2007) Paper for the Annual Conference of the Nordic International Studies Association 1, 1.

[13] 'Without exception, peacebuilding missions in the post-Cold War period have attempted to 'transplant' the values of institutions of the liberal democratic core into the domestic affairs of peripheral host states': Paris, 'International Peacebuilding' (n 9) at 638.

[14] 'While the underlying principles are firmly recognised in article 2 of the UN Charter, both the world community's understanding and practice have increasingly departed from these principles in favour of global interests and stronger human rights': O Korhonen, J Gras and K Creutz, *International Post-Conflict Situations: New Challenges for Co-Operative Governance* (Helsinki, Erik Castrén Institute Research Reports 18/2006) 3.

contrast to the complete takeover of the administration of Kosovo and East Timor, the UN decided to adopt a 'light footprint' approach in Afghanistan. This raises important questions over the international community's commitment to promoting liberal democracy in Afghanistan. Why didn't the international community, acting through the UN, take over and reconstruct Afghanistan as it did in Kosovo and East Timor? Is it because the international community's commitment to promoting liberal values has waned in recent years, perhaps seeking other objectives, such as creating a strong stable state (even if non-liberal) so that it can more effectively combat international terrorists that operate within its borders? In Section 3 I assess the role of the international community in post-conflict Afghanistan and argue that whilst the UN failed to adopt a similar approach to that in Kosovo and East Timor this certainly does not illustrate that the international community lacks commitment to reconstructing Afghanistan upon a liberal basis. On the contrary, I argue that the international community has remained committed to promoting liberal democracy in Afghanistan, but has done so without the complete takeover of governance of the territory. In this sense, the international community's role in Afghanistan represents a change of strategy rather than a change in normative commitment. As I illustrate, the international community's substantial involvement in Afghanistan demonstrates that it remains very much committed to its liberal campaign.

2. THE UN AND PEACEBUILDING

During the Cold War concern over the protection of human rights and the promotion of democracy was largely absent from the conceptual framework of UN peacekeeping. 'Although international actors sporadically expressed regret about violation of human rights and lack of humanitarian assistance, these considerations were only marginally attached to prescriptions for UN conduct in peacekeeping environments'.[15] With the end of the Cold War and the emergence of the international community, however, the protection of fundamental human rights has featured far more prominently in the mandates of peacekeeping (or rather peacebuilding) missions.

It is important to note that peacebuilding missions that sought to transplant liberal democracy into non-liberal post-conflict societies did not emerge immediately after the end of the Cold War. Instead, the transition

[15] E Aksu, *The United Nations, Intra-State Peacekeeping and Normative Change* (Manchester, Manchester University Press, 2003) 83. For example, in the Dominican Republic although human rights and humanitarian concerns were at the forefront of UN discussions, they did not figure in the Security Council resolution that deployed the peacekeeping force: SC Res 203 (14 May 1965).

from peacekeeping to peacebuilding mandates was rather more gradual. As the international community gathered momentum in the years following the end of the Cold War (as more states underwent liberal reformation) it began to enjoy greater influence over the UN (and particularly the Security Council). With this growing influence, the promotion of liberal values has featured with increasing frequency and intensity in Security Council resolutions: each peacebuilding mission has become 'more "daring" than the missions that came before'.[16]

The first peacebuilding mission after the end of the Cold War was the UN Transitional Assistance Group (UNTAG).[17] On the face of it, this mission resembled a traditional peacekeeping mission. UNTAG was deployed with the consent of the parties (South Africa and Namibia)[18] in order to facilitate and oversee the process of decolonisation and ensure a peaceful transfer of power from South African authorities to Namibian authorities, creating an independent sovereign state in its wake. Significantly, however, the UN did not merely oversee the peaceful transfer of power from South African to Namibian authorities. Rather, UNTAG was mandated to ensure that power was transferred to authorities that were chosen by the people through democratic elections. Thus, UNTAG's 'central purpose was political; namely, to establish conditions for the holding of free, universal elections in Namibia and to ensure that they were carried out in acceptable fashion. All of its responsibilities related to this central objective'.[19] Clearly, UNTAG represents an important symbolic moment in the transition from peacekeeping missions that sought to protect state sovereignty and the right to non-intervention to peacebuilding missions that are determined to foster respect for democratic practices.[20]

This being said, it needs to be pointed out that UNTAG possessed a quite limited role in the organisation of elections. UNTAG merely provided advice to the South African administrator so that a political environment could be created that was conducive to the holding of free and fair elections. Significantly, in Cambodia the UN played a far greater role in the organisation and coordination of elections. Although at first the UN's Transitional Authority in Cambodia (UNTAC)'s role resembled traditional peacekeeping insofar as it was mandated to secure and monitor a

[16] Aksu, ibid at 7.

[17] Although UNTAG was the first post-Cold War peacebuilding mission, it was established by SC Res 435 on 29 September 1978. However, only with the end of the Cold War was the political environment conducive to the deployment of a UN force of this nature.

[18] In other words, UNTAG was not authorised under Chapter VII UN Charter. The legal basis of this mission was located in the consent of the host state.

[19] J Sutterlin, *The UN and the Maintenance of International Security* (Westport CT, Greenwood, 2003) 41.

[20] '[T]he mission became the experiment of a new school of peacekeeping; expanding the role of the UN from traditional military and security functions to electoral matters': C Stahn, *The Law and Practice of International Territorial Administration* (Cambridge, Cambridge University Press, 2008) 220.

ceasefire between Vietnam and Cambodia and operated consistently with the principles of consent, neutrality and the use of force only in self-defence,[21] the cessation of hostilities marked the beginning of UNTAC's involvement in Cambodia rather than the end. Once security conditions were satisfactory UNTAC's mission was to enter its electoral phase.[22] Importantly, the UN became co-administrator in the territory, possessing the power to take direct governmental action in organising the elections.[23] Although UNTAC still operated with the consent of the Cambodian authorities, any notion of neutrality was completely lost. Instead, the UN clearly expressed its preference for Cambodia to emerge as a state that derived its authority (even sovereignty) from the will of the people as expressed through free, fair and impartial elections. To this end, UNTAC used its powers widely, taking responsibility for a whole array of tasks which included verifying the impartiality of the electoral authorities; ensuring freedom of organisation, movement, assembly and expression for political parties; monitoring fair access by all political parties to state radio and television; monitoring the registration of electors; determining electoral law; electoral processes; electoral codes of conduct; civic education and training; and overseeing polling on election day, including the counting and verification of votes cast.[24]

Significantly, for the first time a UN mission was conferred the explicit power to promote human rights.[25] In particular, UNTAC was required to 'foster . . . an environment in which respect for human rights will be ensured', including 'the investigation of human rights complaints' and 'general human rights oversight during the transitional period'.[26] As Ratner explains, 'the goals were both immediate and long range: to prevent a climate of fear from tarnishing the election, and to create a long-term consciousness among Cambodians about universally accepted human rights'.[27] Thus, 'UNTAC was given the most comprehensive human rights mandate ever entrusted to a United Nations peace keeping

[21] SC Res 745 (28 February 1992) para 8.

[22] In Resolution 745 the Security Council explained that it was deploying UNTAC with the objective of 'contribut[ing] to the restoration and maintenance of peace in Cambodia, to the promotion of national reconciliation, to the protection of human rights and to the assurance of the right of self-determination of the Cambodian people through free and fair elections': SC Res 745 (28 February 1992).

[23] ibid at paras 1–3.

[24] See generally S Ratner, *The New UN Peacekeeping: Building Peace in Lands of Conflict after the Cold War* (Basingstoke, Palgrave, 1995) ch 6.

[25] For an overview of UNTAC's contribution in this context see E de Wet, 'The Direct Administration of Territories by the United Nations and its Member States in the Post-Cold War Era: Legal Bases and the Implications for National Law' (2004) 8 *Max Planck UNYB* 291, 296.

[26] Section E of Annex 2 to the Agreement on the Political Settlement of the Cambodian Conflict.

[27] Ratner, *The New UN Peacekeeping* (n 24) at 152.

operation',[28] possessing the power to initiate investigations into human rights violations and, with the conclusion of the investigation, pass a binding decision. In the context of promoting human rights and, in particular, the right to democratic governance, UNTAC was therefore extremely significant in relation to the development of peacebuilding as a UN doctrine. This does not mean, however, that in deploying UNTAC the UN was not concerned with international peace and security. Although the Security Council stated in Resolution 745 (1992) that by establishing a liberal system of governance in Cambodia a domestic peace could be achieved (in the sense of ensuring the individual protection of human rights), the Council also explicitly stated that the promotion of liberal democracy would contribute to achieving an *international* peace. The Security Council explained that it was '*[c]onvinced* that free and fair elections are essential to produce a just and durable settlement to the Cambodia conflict, thereby contributing to regional and international peace and security'. By steering Cambodia towards liberal statehood the maintenance of international and security would be enhanced. This, I submit, is an explicit endorsement of the perceived inextricable link between the promotion of liberal values and the maintenance of international peace and security. Moreover, I suggest that the Security Council's identification of the link between respect for liberal democracy and international peace can be attributed to the influence that the international community was able to bring to bear over the Security Council at that particular time.

Notably, however, UNTAC's presence in Cambodia and the powers it possessed were nevertheless subject to the continuing consent of the Cambodian authorities (specifically the Supreme National Council, which was considered to embody the sovereignty of Cambodia). UNTAC was not deployed under Chapter VII of the UN Charter, but instead operated with the consent of the sovereign authority in Cambodia.

At least initially, this was the position adopted in relation to the humanitarian crisis in Somalia in 1992. The UN deployed a traditional, consensual (ie not Chapter VII based) peacekeeping mission into Somalia to oversee a cease-fire and facilitate the delivery of humanitarian assistance.[29] However, as Murphy notes, 'this was a failed state and the application of conventional thinking and methods was inappropriate'.[30] To this end, after the brief deployment of a peace enforcement mission in order to establish an environment in Somalia that was more conducive to a robust

[28] N de Rham-Azimi, *The United Nations Transitional Authority in Cambodia (UNTAC): Debriefing and Lessons: Report and Recommendations of the International Conference* (Singapore, Institute of Policy Studies, 1994) 23.

[29] SC Res 746 (3 December 1992).

[30] R Murphy, *UN Peacekeeping in Lebanon, Somalia and Kosovo: Legal and Operational Issues in Practice* (Cambridge, Cambridge University Press, 2007) 51.

peacebuilding mission,[31] the Security Council deployed a muscular peacebuilding mission under Chapter VII of the UN Charter (referred to as UNOSOM II).[32] In expressing its regret at the 'violence in Somalia', the Council reaffirmed 'the need for . . . representative democratic institutions', 'economic rehabilitation' and the urgent provision of 'humanitarian assistance'.[33] Accordingly, UNOSOM II was mandated to provide 'humanitarian relief to all in need throughout the country' and to assist Somali authorities in the 'reorganization of the Somali police and judicial system' and 'the ongoing political process in Somalia, which should culminate in the installation of a democratically elected government'.[34] Since Cambodia an expansive mandate of this nature was nothing new. What was 'remarkable',[35] however, and indeed important, was that unlike any peacebuilding (and to that extent peacekeeping) operation before it, UNOSOM II was authorised to carry out its peacebuilding activities under Chapter VII of the UN Charter.[36] The consequence of this was that the peacebuilding force could pursue its stipulated objectives regardless of whether domestic (Somali) authorities consented to the mission. This would prevent 'spoilers'[37] from disrupting the promotion of human rights and the democratisation programme. That the Security Council was prepared to deploy these forces under Chapter VII, and thus depart from the principle of consent that had historically constituted the legal basis of peacekeeping missions, illustrates an important development in the UN's commitment to promoting human rights and democratic governance.[38] Moreover, UNOSOM II was authorised to use force in order to realise its mission objectives. The use of force was authorised to defend the mandate (defined as the alleviation of an humanitarian crisis and thus the protection of human rights), rather than the safety of UN personnel.

Notwithstanding these important developments in Cambodia and Somalia, the Security Council's reaction to the civil unrest in Kosovo and

[31] This peace enforcement mission was known as UNITAF and is discussed in detail in chapter 4 of this volume.

[32] SC Res 814 (26 March 1993).

[33] ibid.

[34] SC Res 897 (4 February 1994). Although UNITAF's mandate was adopted under Chapter VII UN Charter this is better characterised as a Security Council enforcement mission by a coalition of the willing rather than a peacebuilding mission.

[35] S Chesterman, *You, The People: The United Nations, Transitional Administration and State-Building* (Oxford, Oxford University Press, 2004) 107.

[36] SC Res 814 (26 March 1993).

[37] 'Spoilers' are defined as 'factions who see a peace agreement as inimical to their interests, power or ideology, [and] use violence to undermine or overthrow settlements': Report of the High Level Panel on Threats, Challenges and Change, 'A More Secure World: Our Shared Responsibility' UN High Level Panel Report, UN Doc A/59/565 (2 December 2004) 222.

[38] Although it should be noted that with the shooting down of two US Black Hawk helicopters in Mogadishu and the death of many US troops in October 1993, the Security Council restricted the activities of UNOSOM II to a consensual peacekeeping mission that sought cooperative disarmament of the warring factions: SC Res 897 (4 February 1994).

East Timor occupies a fundamentally important position within the history of UN peacebuilding. This is because in these instances the Security Council deployed territorial administrations under Chapter VII but, unlike in Cambodia and Somalia, these missions did not merely possess co-administrative powers. Instead, they enjoyed *full sovereign powers of administration* over the territory with the explicit objective of rebuilding these states upon a liberal basis.[39] For this reason the peacebuilding missions in Kosovo and East Timor will be discussed at length.

2.1 Kosovo and East Timor: Historical Background

In 1999 NATO forces engaged in an 11-week bombing campaign against the Former Republic of Yugoslavia (FRY) in order to force Serbian forces out of Kosovo and halt their violent repression of Kosovar Albanians.[40] The intervention was considered successful and the Serbian military was expelled from Kosovo. However, as the Serbian army retreated it became clear that Kosovo's governmental, administrative and judicial infrastructure had been destroyed. Moreover, the long campaign of ethnic cleansing perpetrated by the Serbs against the Kosovar Albanians had left a civil society vanquished and rife with ethnic tensions.

The UN Kosovo Force (KFOR) was initially deployed in order to quell any outbreaks of violence and was mandated to bring peace and stability to the territory.[41] Only once KFOR had created stable and relatively peaceful conditions within Kosovo could the international community, acting through the United Nations Security Council, start the process of peacebuilding.[42] The Security Council deployed the United Nations Mission in Kosovo (UNMIK) and Security Council Resolution 1244 provided its mandate. Resolution 1244 established UNMIK

[39] It should be recorded here that territorial administrations are not a new phenomenon. Historically, the UN had been prepared to deploy territorial administrations that exercised governmental powers. Significantly, however, these administrations were deployed not to make political changes to the territory but were intended to facilitate the process of de-colonisation. Such administrations were designed to ensure that when the coloniser left the territory, these territories exhibited the necessary characteristics of statehood so that it became a sovereign state and thus a member of the international society: Stahn, *International Territorial Administration* (n 20) at 212 ff. In relation to the de-colonisation of Libya (from Italian control), for example, Pelt notes that the UN had good reasons 'to be satisfied with its achievement in creating the independent and sovereign State of Libya' as it had helped the 'Libyan people to freely determine its future form of government' and by 'assisting and advising it in the process of decolonisation and the creation of an independent State': A Pelt, *Libyan Independence and the United Nations: A Case of Planned Decolonization* (Yale CT, Yale University Press, 1970) xxiv.

[40] See A Roberts, 'NATO's "Humanitarian War" over Kosovo' (1999) 41 *Survival* 102.

[41] SC Res 1244 (10 June 1999).

[42] As Marsden explains, '[s]ecurity is regarded by all as the absolute prerequisite for a successful reconstruction process': P Marsden, 'Afghanistan: the Reconstruction Process' (2003) 79 *International Affairs* 91, 103.

in order to provide an interim administration for Kosovo under which the people of Kosovo can enjoy substantial autonomy within the Federal Republic of Yugoslavia, and which will provide transitional administration and overseeing the development of provisional democratic self-governing institutions to ensure conditions for a peaceful and normal life.

In essence, Resolution 1244 conferred a mandate to rebuild Kosovo upon a liberal basis. As the UN Secretary-General explained, UNMIK would concern itself with 'promoting democracy, good governance and the respect for human rights'.[43] Evidently, however, UNMIK was not mandated to build an independent liberal state. Although Resolution 1244 mandated UNMIK to reconstruct Kosovo upon a liberal basis, UNMIK was not authorised to grant Kosovo independence.[44] Instead, the status of Kosovo was to be determined at a later date once the political objectives stipulated in Resolution 1244 had been realised.[45]

In order to achieve the objectives stipulated by Resolution 1244 UNMIK was split into four pillars. Each pillar was placed under the general authority of the Special Representative of the Secretary-General and under the direct control of a Deputy Special Representative of the Secretary-General: Pillar I (humanitarian affairs) was the responsibility of the United Nations High Commissioner for Refugees (UNHCR); Pillar II (Civil Administration) was run by the UN; Pillar III (Democratisation and Institution Building) was undertaken by the Organization for Security and Co-Operation in Europe (OSCE) mission in Kosovo; and Pillar IV (Economic Reconstruction) was run by the European Union (EU). Significantly, the Special Representative of the Secretary-General was conferred all necessary powers to pursue the objectives outlined in Resolution 1244. In Regulation 1000/1 of 25 July 1999 the Secretary-General stated that

[t]he Security Council, in its Resolution 1244 (1999), has vested in the interim civil administration authority over the territory and the people of Kosovo. All legislative and executive powers, including the administration of the judiciary, will, therefore, be vested in UNMIK.[46]

[43] Report of the Secretary-General on the UN Interim Administration of Kosovo, UN Doc 2/1999/1259 (23 December 1999) para 79. See also the Statement of the President of the Security Council: 'The Security Council reaffirms its commitment to the objective of a multi-ethnic and democratic Kosovo and calls upon all communities to work towards this goal and actively participate in the public institutions as well as the decision-making process, and integrate into society': Statement by the President of the Security Council, UN Doc S/PRST/2003/1 (6 February 2003).

[44] However, Resolution 1244 did entrust UNMIK with the task of facilitating a 'political process designed to determine Kosovo's future status'. However, 'standards before status' was a recurrent theme in the UNMIK administration. Kosovo's future status would not be open to discussion until liberal standards of government had been attained. This issue of standards before status will be discussed in greater detail below.

[45] I revisit the issue of Kosovo's final status later in this chapter.

[46] Report of the Secretary-General on the UN Interim Administration of Kosovo, UN Doc S/1999/779 (12 July 1999) para 3.

The effect was that UNMIK became the only legitimate authority in Kosovo and for all intents and purposes exercised sovereignty over the territory and its population.[47]

After four centuries of Portuguese colonial rule and 24 years of brutal occupation by Indonesia,[48] the UN finally brokered negotiations between Portugal and Indonesia to allow for popular consultation over whether East Timor should become independent or remain under Indonesian rule.[49] On 30 August 1999 a referendum was held and, despite violence from pro-Indonesian militia, over 78.5 per cent of Timorese voted for independence.[50] In the wake of the referendum, militia engaged in a 'scorched earth' campaign in which an estimated 2,000 East Timorese were killed, 230,000 forcibly deported to refugee camps in West Timor and over 700,000 were internally displaced.[51] Under international pressure, Indonesia consented to an Australian-led International Force for East Timor (INTERFET), which was successful in suppressing the violence.[52] INTERFET played a similar role to that of KFOR in Kosovo, seeking to maintain security by demilitarising the warring factions and creating a buffer zone between them.[53] With a force comprising 11,500 military personnel, INTERFET was successful in ending the violence. On 25 October 1999 the Security Council mandated a UN mission to take over the responsibility of administering East Timor.[54] This mission was named the United Nations Territorial Administration in East Timor (UNTAET).

Resolution 1272 mandated UNTAET to 'assist in the development of civil and social services; to ensure the coordination and delivery of humanitarian assistance, rehabilitation and development assistance; to support capacity building for self-government; [and] to assist in the establishment of conditions for sustainable development'.[55] To achieve these objectives the Special Representative of the Secretary-General was 'endowed with overall responsibility for the administration of East Timor'.[56] Resolution 1272 therefore provided UNTAET with the express power to construct an independent and self-sustaining state, being consti-

[47] ibid at para 35.

[48] For a good account of East Timor's turbulent (and colonial) history see T Hohe, 'The Clash of Paradigms: International Administration and Local Political Legitimacy in East Timor' (2002) 24 *Contemporary Southeast Asia* 569.

[49] SC Res 1246 (11 June 1999).

[50] For an account of the referendum see I Martin, *Self-Determination in East Timor: the United Nations and International Intervention* (Boulder CO, Lynne Rienner, 2001) 3 ff.

[51] J Taylor, *East Timor: The Price of Freedom* (London, Zed Books, 1999) xvi–xxix.

[52] SC Res 1264 (15 September 1999).

[53] This being said, INTERFET differed from KFOR in so far as INTERFET operated within (rather than alongside) the territorial administration. Thus, INTERFET's mandate to maintain security and prevent violence was also contained within SC Res 1272 (25 October 1999).

[54] ibid.

[55] ibid at para 2(e).

[56] UNTAET/REG/1999/1 (27 November 1999).

tuted by liberal principles.[57] Whilst the Security Council was responsible for 'inventing' this state,[58] UNTAET was to play 'midwife' to it.[59]

With these issues in mind, my intention is to look more closely at how UNMIK and UNTAET implemented these mandates. In particular, I look to the contribution that these territorial administrations made to promoting respect for democracy, human rights and the rule of law.

2.1.1 Democracy

Both UNMIK and UNTAET were mandated by the Security Council to provide Kosovo and East Timor with effective democratic institutions. However, the process of democracy-building (democratisation) is not just about holding elections. Before elections can be contemplated important decisions have to be taken about how to organise and conduct the elections, including educational initiatives so that individuals can appreciate the importance of their role in democratic government, providing advice and support to nascent political parties, creating a system for voter registration, deciding on appropriate electoral systems and constructing electoral management bodies. Physical infrastructure has to be established so that authorities, once elected, can govern effectively.

Thus local elections, and a fortiori national elections, cannot be considered in the immediate aftermath of conflict.[60] Elections must instead come to represent the end point of the process of democratisation. Clearly, in post-conflict societies this process can take many years. However, during this time many decisions will need to be taken and many tasks will need to be performed in order to bring a modicum of normality back to the lives of the population. This will include the provision of humanitarian relief, establishing law and order, devising and creating political institutions, organising civil society and re-structuring the justice system.

[57] As the Special Representative of the Secretary-General to East Timor explained, the objective of Resolution 1272 was to encourage a 'political transition to independence, culminating in the adoption of a constitution and democratic elections;' to create 'an East Timor administration that is financially sustainable . . . [and with] a credible system of justice in which fundamental human rights are respected': Special Representative of the Secretary-General Sergio Vieira de Mello, Address to the First CNRT Congress (21 August 2000). In addition, the Secretary-General explained that UNTAET's objective was 'to ensure the establishment and maintenance of the rule of law and to promote and protect human rights': Report of the Secretary-General on the United Nations Mission in East Timor, UN Doc S/1999/1024 (4 October 1999).

[58] J Traub, 'Inventing East Timor' (2000) 79 *Foreign Affairs* 74.

[59] M Benzing, 'Midwifing a New State: The United Nations in East Timor' (2005) 9 *Max Planck UNYB* 295, 297.

[60] '[M]ost war torn societies lack the political climate, social and economic stability, institutional infrastructure, and even political will to mount successful elections': K Kumar, 'Post-Conflict Elections and International Assistance' in K Kumar (ed), *Post-Conflict Elections, Democratization and International Assistance* (Boulder CO, Lynne Rienner, 1998) 7.

In Kosovo and East Timor both UNMIK and UNTAET were authorised to perform such tasks. However, it was considered vital that indigenous representatives be incorporated into this process. In terms of effectiveness, the incorporation of the local population into the process allows cultural peculiarities to be taken into account and, more generally, enables the population to feel a sense of ownership over the system that is emerging around them. Perhaps more significantly, at least in the context of fostering democratic traditions, by being incorporated into the administrative structure local representatives are able to experience and learn about the importance of mediation and compromise in the context of policy formation. That these individuals are representative of all elements of society will allow the population to feel part of this conciliatory form of decision-making and be gradually introduced to the system of democratic governance.

This being said, at the start of the administrations in Kosovo and East Timor local participation was low. However, this is understandable given that decisions needed to be taken quickly in order to ensure public safety and provide emergency humanitarian relief. Once security and humanitarian concerns were alleviated, though, and the reconstruction process could begin, it was considered imperative to bring local representatives into the administration.

In Kosovo, from July 1999 to January 2000, UNMIK established the Kosovo Transitional Council (KTC) in order to integrate domestic actors into the decision-making process. The KTC was widely representative of the ethnic and political mix in Kosovo and was empowered to make legislative recommendations to UNMIK.[61] In addition UNMIK established a Joint Advisory Council (JAC), composed of 20 members, who were national and international legal experts, which commented and reviewed draft legislation proposed by UNMIK. Through the establishment of the KTC and the JAC the population was provided with a channel for direct input into UNMIK's decision-making process. As the UN Secretary-General noted, enhanced local participation in UNMIK's decisions 'thereby creat[e] a climate where participation in democratic processes is the norm'.[62]

With the security environment improving and the decisions taken by UNMIK becoming increasingly significant (the drafting and implementation of human rights legislation, for example, or the shaping of political institutions), greater local involvement was considered necessary. Security concerns could no longer justify the lack of effective local participation

[61] '[The KTC] gives the main political parties and ethnic groups – including the Kosovo Democratic League, the Kosovo Liberation Army, members of the Serb, Bosniac and Turkish communities, independents and other Kosovo representatives – an opportunity to have a direct input into UNMIK's decision-making process. It is also a forum for achieving a consensus on a broad range of issues related to civil administration, institution-building and essential services': B Kouchner, 'The Challenge of Rebuilding Kosovo' (1999) 3 *NATO Review* 1, 2.

[62] Report of the Secretary-General on the UN Interim Administration of Kosovo, UN Doc S/1999/987 (16 September 1999).

within the administration. To this end, in January 2000 the Joint Interim Administrative Structure (JIAS) was established.[63] This marked a shift in UNMIK policy from mere consultation with local actors to a system of co-governance. Membership of the KTC was enlarged to better reflect the pluralist configuration of Kosovo. The KTC's powers were extended to include proposing legislation and to suggest amendments to the applicable law.[64] These proposals and amendments would then be submitted to UNMIK who would accept the proposals or provide 'reasons for differing decisions'.[65] In addition, UNMIK established an eight-member Interim Administrative Council (IAC), comprising three Kosovar Albanians, one Serb and the four Deputy Special Representatives of the Secretary-General. The IAC dealt with mainly procedural and administrative issues at first (in contrast to the KTC's generic function), but later addressed more substantive issues, such as management of the 'Mitrovica problem', a Northern city divided between Serbs and Albanians, and preparation for municipal elections in October 2000. When creating the JIAS the Special Representative of the Secretary-General (SRSG) explained,

> I wanted to implicate the Kosovars, all the ethnic groups – Albanians and Serbs, Bosniacs and Roma, Ashkali, Turks and the others – in the ensemble of decisions that concerned them or that had a bearing on the future of Kosovo . . . The sharing of competences would allow them to become players but also responsible actors – that is, equally accountable with the international community: partners in success as well as failure. Another advantage of this co-piloting was to permit the Kosovars to familiarise themselves with the administrative responsibilities from which they had been distanced for ten years during Milosevic's reign. From the perspective of the 'substantial autonomy' anticipated by Resolution 1244, this apprenticeship was indispensable.[66]

The third stage of development, moving from co-government to self-government, started in Kosovo with UNMIK's elections for municipal assemblies in October 2000.[67] 'The transfer of authority to the Municipal Assemblies was the first real step of UNMIK in establishing provisional institutions of self-government and in transferring power'.[68] Albeit at the local level, for the first time UNMIK's governing powers were transferred

[63] UNMIK/REG/2000/1 (14 January 2000).
[64] ibid at section 2.
[65] ibid at section 6(2).
[66] B Kouchner, *Les Guerriers de la Paix* (Paris, Grasset & Fasquelle, 2004) 326–27. Although Chesterman is critical of the JIAS on the basis that '[n]o one was under the illusion that these bodies [KTC and IAC] wielded any actual power': S Chesterman, 'Building Democracy through Benevolent Autocracy: Consultation and Accountability in UN Transitional Administrations' in E Newman and R Rich (eds), *The UN Role in Promoting Democracy: Between Ideals and Reality* (Tokyo, UN University Press, 2004) 91.
[67] Report of the Secretary-General on the UN Interim Administration of Kosovo, UN Doc S/2000/196 (March 2000).
[68] J Friedrich, 'UNMIK in Kosovo: Struggling with Uncertainty' (2005) 9 *Max Planck UNYB* 227, 257.

to locally, democratically elected leaders. However, it is important to point out here that despite the existence of democratically elected representatives the Special Representative nevertheless retained the exclusive right to administer and veto all decisions.[69] Hysa notes '[t]hat the SRSG could have the final word in decision-making did not sit comfortably with the need to develop democracy in Kosovo'.[70] This notwithstanding, the creation of municipal assemblies did enable local leaders to become heavily involved in the regulation of local issues and be responsible and accountable to the people for the effectiveness of this regulation. Indeed, the importance of these municipal elections was that they precipitated the transfer of power at the central level. Consequently UNMIK, in consultation with local leaders, began devising the institutions for provisional self-government in Kosovo. This was articulated in UNMIK's promulgation of the Constitutional Framework for Provisional Self Government on 15 May 2001.[71] This anticipated the transfer of authority to provisional institutions in the executive, legislative and judicial fields that were to be established following elections to a Kosovo-wide Assembly. Importantly, this Constitutional Framework unambiguously committed these legislative organs to a democratic future.[72] The preamble, for example, stipulates that the Provisional Institutions of Self-government 'shall be established through the participation of the people of Kosovo in free and fair elections'.

Elections to the Kosovo Assembly were held on 17 November 2001 and were considered a success, despite a poor Serb turnout, and the people of Kosovo played a key role in helping UNMIK organise the elections and conducting them to a free and fair standard.[73] The Assembly, comprising 120 seats, was the main organ of the provisional institutions of self-government. Importantly, 20 of the 120 seats were reserved for individuals from minority communities.[74] It exercised all legislative power over Kosovo, except for responsibility for the Kosovo Protection Corps, monetary policy, customs, international relations, property administration and coordination with KFOR.[75] The Assembly then elected a President and a government with a Prime Minister.[76]

[69] M Brand, 'The Development of Kosovo Institutions and the Transition of Authority from UNMIK to Local Self-Government', Centre for Applied Studies in International Negotiations (January 2003) 3.

[70] Y Hysa, 'Kosovo: A Permanent International Protectorate?' in Newman and Rich (eds), *The UN Role in Promoting Democracy* (n 66) at 297

[71] UNMIK/REG/2001/9 (15 May 2001).

[72] Section 1.4 explains that 'Kosovo shall be governed democratically through legislative, executive, and judicial bodies and institutions'.

[73] Report of the Secretary-General on the UN Interim Administration of Kosovo, UN Doc S/2002/62 (15 January 2002) paras 3-4.

[74] UNMIK/REG (n 71).

[75] ibid at ch 8.

[76] Elections to the Kosovo Assembly were subsequently held in October 2004, November 2007 and again in December 2010.

The UN adopted a similar approach to introducing a democratic culture and democratic institutions to East Timor.[77] However, unlike in Kosovo, Resolution 1272 expressly required that UNTAET establish close cooperation with the Timorese during the period of administration:

> [The Council] stresses the need for UNTAET to consult and cooperate closely with the East Timor people in order to carry out its mandate effectively with a view to the development of local democratic institutions including an East Timorese human rights institution, and the transfer to these institutions of its administrative and public service functions.[78]

Like in Kosovo, in the initial stages of administration such was the urgent need to provide humanitarian aid that local inclusion in decision-making was low, amounting to merely non-committal consultation. Thus, in the initial stages 'UNTAET's anti-democratic features [could] be defended by comparison with the operational difficulties inherent in a more democratic model'.[79] However, as humanitarian and security conditions improved and long-term reconstruction efforts were being implemented, local participation was intensified so that decisions were taken cooperatively between local institutions and UNTAET (what was known as the co-decision format) until power could be completely devolved to East Timorese institutions.[80] By incorporating local representatives into their decision-making structure, the local population gained experience of participatory politics (enabling them to engage in democratic dialogue) and was given a sense of ownership over the emerging system.[81]

The first formal East Timorese institution was developed approximately two months after UNTAET was established. The National Consultative Council (NCC)[82] comprised 15 non-elected members, who were representative of all aspects of East Timorese society. Seven members came from the CNRT (the only coherent political party in East Timor), three from other various political groups, and one from the Catholic Church. Other members included the Transitional Administrator and three UNTAET members. The

[77] See M Cogen and E de Brabandere, 'Democratic Governance and Post-Conflict Reconstruction' (2007) 20 *Leiden Journal of International Law* 669.

[78] SC Res 1272 (25 October 1999).

[79] T Hohe, 'Delivering Feudal Democracy in East Timor' in Newman and Rich (eds) (n 66) at 315.

[80] The operating principle was a 'progressive delegation of authority until authority is finally transferred to the government of the independent state': Report of the Secretary-General on the UN Mission in East Timor, UN Doc S/2001/42 (16 January 2001).

[81] 'The effectiveness of UNTAET will rest in its ability to perform its duties in close consultation and cooperation with the people of East Timor, as it will have to exercise its authority on their behalf. In this context, the establishment of a permanent dialogue with representatives of the East Timorese people will be essential. Pending the holding of elections, the Special Representative will establish advisory bodies at all levels to ensure the participation of East Timorese in the governance and administration of the territory': Report of the Secretary-General on the UN Mission in East Timor, UN Doc S/1999/1024 (1999) at para 30.

[82] UNTAET/REG/1999/2 (2 December 1999).

NCC was, however, a purely consultative body, advising UNTAET 'on all matters related to the exercise of the Transitional Administrator's executive and legislative functions'.[83] This being said, the NCC nevertheless provided a 'mechanism through which the representatives of the people of East Timor [could] actively participate in the decision making process . . . and through which the views, concerns, traditions and interests of the East Timorese people [could] be represented'.[84] Even mere consultation was considered essential, as it allowed knowledge of participatory politics to be experienced, learnt and disseminated. As the CNRT President Xanana Gusmao explained, '[w]e are concerned about a lack of political knowledge . . . [of] democracy, human rights, justice . . . our concern is to put together knowledge to create a civil society'.[85] The creation of the NCC sought to address this concern.

Pursuant to this objective, in the summer of 2000, with the security situation improving and an environment conducive to political and legal change established, UNTAET initiated the move from local consultation to co-government. On 14 July 2000 UNTAET issued a regulation officially replacing the NCC with an East Timorese National Council (NC) and a Cabinet.[86] Together, these were referred to as the First Transitional Government, and accordingly the first state institutions were created.[87] The NC was a non-elected advisory council, with its 36 members being appointed by the SRSG on the basis of popular nomination, but being representative of political parties, the Catholic Church, organisations for women and the youth, NGOs, professional and labour organisations, the farming and business community, and East Timor's 13 districts.[88] To this end, the NC was a type of 'proto-parliament', authorised 'to initiate, to modify, and to recommend draft regulations . . . [and] to amend regulations' subject to approval by the Transitional Administrator.[89] Unlike the NCC the NC was not chaired by the Transitional Administrator and its membership was exclusively East Timorese. The creation of the NC yielded two important consequences. First, it resulted in a change in the scope of participation. Rather than the narrow factional (political party) representation in the NCC, the NC exhibited greater representation, including political parties from across the

[83] ibid at para 1.1.
[84] ibid at para 1.2.
[85] Quoted in H Strohmeyer, 'Building a new Judiciary for East Timor: Challenges of a Fledgling Nation' (2000) 11 *Criminal Law Forum* 259. Xanana further added that 'East Timor will be democratic. This means real democracy, not a one-party democracy, not a rigged democracy, but a multi-party democracy. Underlying this democracy, and essential to it, will be a judicial system which is independent of government'.
[86] UNTAET/REG/2000/24 (14 July 2000).
[87] S Ingram, 'Mission Implementation: Developing Institutional Capacities' in N Azimi and C Ling (eds), *The United Nations Transition Administration in East Timor (UNTAET): Debriefing and Lessons – Report of the 2002 Tokyo Conference* (Leiden, Martinus Nijhoff, 2003) 86.
[88] UNTAET/REG/2000/24 (14 July 2000) para 3.2.
[89] ibid at para 2.1.

spectrum and individuals coming from different geographic units and civil society sectors. Secondly, there was a change in the nature of participation. Whilst the NCC was only empowered to draft regulations that were then subject to UNTAET approval, the NC generated legislation and policy proposals. 'This shift was significant in that it gave the East Timorese members greater control over the early stages of the policy process, including problem-definition, issue prioritization, and formulation of options'.[90] 'By giving local stakeholders a voice in decision-making, the transitional administration teaches by example, fosters pluralism, encourages local engagement with the political process, and aids the development of civil society'.[91] This in turn 'fosters both short term legitimacy and long term democratization by making the scope of participation more inclusive and by shifting the nature of participation away from mere consultation and towards policy formation'.[92]

The Cabinet contained both East Timorese leaders and international experts and was designed to take over UNTAET's responsibility for governance and public administration.[93] The Cabinet was thus entrusted with executive tasks (whereas the NC only performed legislative tasks). The 10 members of the Cabinet had different portfolios: five portfolios (international affairs, internal administration, infrastructure, economic affairs and social affairs) were entrusted to East Timorese members and four portfolios (police and emergency services, political affairs, justice and finance) to international experts. The Transitional Administrator served as chair. Each member could make decisions relevant to his area, although major decisions were taken collectively.

In September 2001 the NC and Cabinet were supplanted by a Second Transitional Government,[94] consisting of a Council of Ministers and an elected Constituent Assembly. The Council of Ministers headed public administration and could recommend draft regulations and directives to UNTAET. However, they were appointed by the Transitional Administrator and were not elected. This is where an elected Constituent Assembly was important. Its task was to draft a constitution for East Timor. Elections were held on 30 August 2001[95] and certified as free and fair by international observers.[96] The Assembly, enjoying a democratic mandate, then

[90] J Beauvais, 'Benevolent Despotism: A Critique of U.N. State-Building in East Timor' (2000) 33 *NYU Journal of International Law and Politics* 1101, 1129.

[91] ibid at 1118.

[92] ibid at 1135.

[93] UNTAET/REG/2000/23 (14 July 2000).

[94] UNTAET/REG/2001/28 (19 September 2001).

[95] UNTAET/REG/2001/2 (16 March 2001).

[96] European Union Election Observations Mission, *Final Report of the EU Election Observations Mission in East Timor* (14 April 2001). The President of the Security Council explained that '[t]he Security Council warmly welcomes the successful staging on 30 August 2001 of the elections for East Timor's first Constituent Assembly, in particular the orderly and peaceful conduct of the elections and the very high voter turnout, which demonstrated

proceeded to draft a constitution to articulate the political principles upon which East Timor would be grounded. Importantly, the constitution committed East Timor to a democratic future, explaining that East Timor is a 'democratic, sovereign and unitary state' whose fundamental objective is, inter alia, 'to defend and guarantee political democracy and participation of the people in the resolution of national problems'.[97]

The constitution was approved by the Assembly on 22 March 2002 and provided for the direct election of a President and National Parliament. Presidential elections were held soon after, on 14 April, with Xanana Gusmao emerging as the clear winner, capturing 82.7 per cent of the popular vote. The election was certified as free and fair by international observers.[98] East Timor became a sovereign state with functioning national and local democratic institutions one month later on 20 May 2002.[99]

2.1.2 Human Rights

In both Kosovo and East Timor the legislative system had been previously employed by Serbia and Indonesia respectively to discriminate against and repress the indigenous populations, providing for arbitrary restrictions upon fundamental freedoms and inadequate mechanisms through which to challenge actions of the state. Consequently, in order to achieve their liberal objectives and secure the protection of fundamental human rights, both UNMIK and UNTAET prioritised revision of the existing legislative frameworks in Kosovo and East Timor.

Indeed, Resolution 1244 explicitly mandated UNMIK to 'protect and promote human rights in Kosovo'.[100] Thus,

> [i]n assuming its responsibilities, UNMIK will be guided by internationally recognised standards of human rights as the basis for the exercise of its authority in

the wish of the East Timorese people to establish a full participatory democracy': UN Doc S/PRST/2001/23 (10 September 2001).

[97] Constitution of East Timor (in force 20 May 2002), Preamble and Section 6(c) respectively. In addition, section 7(1) provides that '[t]he people shall exercise the political power through universal, free, equal, direct, secret and periodic suffrage'. More generally, but equally as important, the Preamble states that elected representatives of East Timor '[s]olemnly reaffirm their determination to fight all forms of tyranny, oppression, social, cultural or religious domination and segregation, to defend national independence, to respect and guarantee human rights and the fundamental rights of the citizen, to ensure the principle of the separation of powers in the organization of the State, and to establish the essential rules of multi-party democracy, with a view to building a just and prosperous nation and developing a society of solidarity and fraternity'.

[98] European Union Election Observations Mission, (n 96).

[99] East Timor has since held presidential and parliamentary elections in 2007 and 2012. These elections have been considered a success and have been regarded as free and fair by the international community: see M Berry, 'Observing Democracy Blossom in East Timor', *The Australian* (10 August 2012), available at: www.theaustralian.com.au/opinion/world-commentary/observing-democracy-blossom-in-east-timor/story-e6frg6ux-1226446951132.

[100] SC Res 1244, para 11(j).

> Kosovo. UNMIK will embed a culture of human rights in all areas of activity, and will adopt human rights policies in respect of its administrative functions.[101]

This paragraph was strengthened by Regulation No 1/1999, which was promulgated by the Special Representative of the Secretary-General. Section 2 provided that

> [i]n exercising their functions, all persons undertaking public duties or holding public office in Kosovo shall observe internationally recognized human rights standards and shall not discriminate against any person on any ground such as sex, race, colour, language, political or other opinion, national, ethnic or social origin, association with a national community, property, birth or other status.[102]

Regulation No 1999/24 (section 1(3)) gave greater clarification as to what internationally recognised standards of human rights meant.[103]

> [i]n exercising their functions, all persons undertaking public duties or holding public office in Kosovo shall observe internationally recognized human rights standards, as reflected in particular in:
>
> (a) The Universal Declaration of Human Rights
> (b) The European Convention of Human Rights . . . and the Protocols . . .
> (c) International Covenant on Civil and Political Rights . . .
> (d) The International Covenant on Economic, Social and Cultural Rights . . .
> (e) The Convention on all forms of Racial Discrimination . . .
> (f) The Convention on the elimination of all forms of Discrimination against Women . . .
> (g) The Convention against Torture or Other Cruel, Inhumane or Degrading Treatment or Punishment . . .
> (h) The International Convention on the Rights of the Child.

With this mandate to protect human rights, UNMIK sought to radically transform the legal and institutional framework of Kosovo. In order to achieve this objective, UNMIK was conferred wide legislative powers. The Special Representative was empowered 'to change, repeal or suspend existing laws to the extent necessary for the carrying out of his functions, or where existing laws are incompatible with the mandate, aims and

[101] OSCE, Permanent Council, Decision No 306, PC.DEC/306 (1 July 1999) para 42. UNMIK entrusted the OSCE with the responsibility of performing this task.

[102] In order to make this obligation comprehensive, in Regulation 45/2000 on Self-Government of Municipalities in Kosovo UNMIK expressly stated that municipal authorities were also bound by international human rights standards. This regulation required that 'law and justice shall bind the administration of the municipality, and in particular the human rights and fundamental freedoms contained in the ECHR and the Protocols thereto shall be observed. All administrative actors shall comply with the applicable law': section 33. In addition, the Security Council 'called on the leaders of the Provisional Institution of Self-Government actively to demonstrate their commitment and support efforts to promote security, returns, human rights, economic development, and a multi-ethnic and fair society with peaceful co-existence and freedom of movement for all the population of Kosovo': UN Doc S/PRST/2002/11 (24 April 2002).

[103] UNMIK/REG/1999/24 (12 December 1999).

purposes of the interim civil administration' and 'to issue legislative acts in the forms of regulations'.[104] At the outset, UNMIK explained that the law in Kosovo would be as it had been before 1989, which was considered to mark the start of Serbian oppression. Laws after that date were invalid.[105] The role of UNMIK was to take this pre-1989 law and ensure it that it complied with international human rights norms. Indeed, any laws that did not comply with internationally recognised human rights were also void.[106]

Not only was UNMIK required to create a legal system dedicated to the protection of human rights but it was also required to comply with these human rights norms in its temporary administration of the territory. As the Ombudsman for Kosovo explained, however, UNMIK demonstrated a poor record of complying with human rights, especially in its pursuit of civil order.[107] In particular, the Ombudsman criticised UNMIK's practice of holding arrested individuals in detention for extended periods of time before bringing them before a judicial authority, and of extended detention prior to trial. Moreover, individuals had been held in detention even where a judicial authority (comprising international and national judges) demanded their release. UNMIK justified these transgressions from accepted international standards on the basis that despite being two years into the mission Kosovo still qualified as an 'internationally-recognized emergency'. For this reason,

> international human rights standards accept the need for special measures that, in the wider interests of security, and under prescribed legal conditions, allow authorities to respond to the finding of intelligence that are not able to be presented to the court system.[108]

Thus, although UNMIK clearly had as its focus the desire to create a legal system that could adequately protect human rights, the appearance at least was that UNMIK, because of the state of emergency existing within Kosovo, felt able to derogate from this legal framework. In essence, the argument was that the ends (to create a legal framework orientated by the desire to protect human rights) justified the means (the occasional viola-

[104] Report of the Secretary-General on the UN Interim Administration of Kosovo, UN Doc 1999/779 (12 July 1999) paras 39 and 41.

[105] UNMIK/REG/1999/24 (12 December 1999).

[106] OSCE, 'Report on the Criminal Justice System' (2000) at section 3.

[107] The Kosovo Ombudsman, established by the Organization for Security and Cooperation in Europe (OSCE) to monitor, protect and promote human rights in Kosovo, found that 'UNMIK . . . does not respect important international human rights norms. The people of Kosovo are therefore deprived of protection of their basic rights and freedoms three years after the end of the conflict by the very entity set up to guarantee them': Ombudsman Institution in Kosovo, Second Annual Report 2001–2002 (2002).

[108] 'UNMIK Refutes Allegations of Judicial Bias and Lack of Strategy', *UNMIK News* (25 June 2001).

tion of human rights in order to maintain security). In the words of Chesterman, the objective of UNMIK was to deliver 'democracy through benevolent autocracy'.[109]

As the administration progressed and national institutions were created in order to allow for Kosovo to enjoy 'substantial autonomy', UNMIK established a Constitutional Framework which would serve as a constitutional document that would guide the activities of the provisional institutions for self-government that UNMIK had established until Kosovo's ubiquitous 'final status' could be determined. This Constitutional Framework also afforded particular prominence to the protection of human rights. Chapter 2(b) of this Constitutional Framework required that these institutions '[p]romote and fully respect the rule of law, human rights and freedoms, democratic principles and reconciliation'. Chapter 3(1) explained that '[a]ll persons in Kosovo shall enjoy, without discrimination on any ground and in full equality, human rights and fundamental freedoms'. Chapter 3(2) provided that the provisional institutions of self-government 'shall observe and ensure internationally recognised human rights and fundamental freedoms'.[110] The consequence was that 'the provisions on rights and freedoms set forth in these instruments shall be directly applicable in Kosovo as part of this Constitutional Framework'.[111]

In contrast to Resolution 1244, in East Timor Resolution 1272 did not explicitly require that UNTAET promote and protect human rights.[112] However, '[n]otwithstanding the absence of a more generalised human rights reference in its mandate, UNTAET clearly saw itself as having a human rights role'.[113]

In addition, section 2 of UNTAET Regulation 1999/1 required that '[i]n exercising their functions, all persons undertaking public duties or holding public office in East Timor shall observe internationally recognized

[109] S Chesterman, 'Building Democracy through Benevolent Autocracy' (n 66).

[110] The Constitutional Framework explained that this included the UN Charter, the Universal Declaration of Human Rights (1948), the International Covenant on Civil and Political Rights (1966) and its Protocols, the Convention on the Elimination of all forms of Racial Discrimination, the Convention on the Elimination of all forms of Discrimination against Women, the Convention on the Rights of the Child, the European Convention on Human Rights and its Protocols, the European Charter for Regional or Minority Languages, the Council of Europe's Framework Convention for the Protection of National Minorities and other relevant principles reflected in internationally recognised legal instruments.

[111] Chapter 3(3) of the Constitutional Framework.

[112] This being said, Resolution 1272 did require 'steps to be taken' to address past human rights violations. Also, UNTAET was required to work towards the establishment of an independent East Timorese human rights institution, in cooperation with the East Timorese.

[113] A Devereux, 'Searching for Clarity: a Case Study of UNTAET's application of International Human Rights Norms' in ND White and D Klassen (eds), *The UN, Human Rights and Post-Conflict Situations* (Manchester, Manchester University Press, 2005) 299. For evidence that the promotion of human rights was an overriding objective for UNTAET see the Report of the Secretary-General on the UN Mission in East Timor, UN Doc S/1999/1024 (4 October 1999).

human rights standards'.[114] Internationally recognised human rights expressly included those rights protected by

- Universal Declaration of Human Rights
- International Covenant on Civil and Political Rights;
- International Covenant on Economic, Social and Cultural Rights;
- The Convention on the Elimination of all forms of Racial Discrimination;
- The Convention on the Elimination of all forms of Discrimination against Women;
- The Convention against Torture or Other Cruel, Inhumane or Degrading Treatment or Punishment;
- The International Convention on the Rights of the Child.

Moreover, section 2 explained that all persons undertaking public duties or holding public office in East Timor 'shall not discriminate against any person on any ground such as sex, race, colour, language, religion, political or other opinion, national, ethnic or social origin, association with a national community, property, birth or all other status'. Consequently, despite the absence of a human rights provision in the enabling resolution, UNTAET was clearly determined to protect and promote human rights.

Pursuant to this, UNTAET declared that the applicable law in East Timor would be that which existed prior to 25 October 1999, except for those laws that conflicted with international human rights standards.[115] However, certain laws were immediately abolished because of their incompatibility with human rights standards. In particular, the regulation declared the Indonesian Law on Anti-Subversion (used in the past to prosecute resistance), the Law on Social Organisations (forbidding certain organisations), the Law on National Security, the Law of Mobilization and Demobilization, and the Law on Defence and Security inapplicable. Section 3 thus had the important effect of immediately abolishing some of East Timor's most egregious laws and offering the promise of a future where discriminatory legislation would not be applied.

The constitution, which effectively granted East Timor its independence, provides that East Timor is based on 'the respect for the dignity of the human person'.[116] Section 6(b) provides that the fundamental objectives of the state are, inter alia, '[t]o guarantee and promote fundamental rights and freedoms of the citizens'. These include, amongst others, freedom of speech and information, freedom to assemble and demonstrate and the right to political participation.[117] The importance of this was that '[t]he validity of laws and other actions of the State and local Government

[114] UNTAET/REG/1999/1 (27 November 1999).
[115] ibid.
[116] UNTAET/REG/1999/1 section 1.
[117] Title II, Personal Rights, Liberties and Guarantees.

depends upon their compliance with the Constitution'.[118] Indeed, such was the determination of the government of East Timor to comply with international human rights standards that Xanana Gusmao, the first democratically elected President of East Timor, explained 'we [East Timor] will prove that respect for human rights is not a western concept that is foreign to Asian Societies. There will be no democracy without respect for human rights'.[119]

2.1.3 Rule of law

Human rights can be only protected where there are effective judicial mechanisms to enforce them.[120] Legislative (even constitutional) protection is not enough. Indeed, although conventional courts are essential to this process of enforcement, wider judicial systems are also necessary in order to impartially monitor compliance with human rights, make authoritative determinations of whether or not human rights standards have been transgressed and, where suitable, provide an adequate remedy. To this end, establishing the rule of law became both UMIK's and UNTAET's principal objective.[121] As the Security Council explained in relation to Kosovo, it 'reaffirms the fundamental importance of the rule of law in Kosovo's political development and condemns any attempt to undermine it'.[122]

In Kosovo, any semblance of an independent effective court system had been destroyed. Law and order had completely collapsed. Qualified legal personnel were scarce. Of those remaining most were insufficiently qualified because of the restrictions on Albanian lawyers under the judicial rules imposed by Serbia.[123] UNMIK was therefore required to rebuild the justice system, introducing legal personnel that could independently and impartially arbitrate disputes on the basis of the rule of law rather than in accordance with ethnic loyalties.[124]

[118] Section 2(2).

[119] Quoted in Strohmeyer, 'Building a new Judiciary for East Timor' (n 85) at 271.

[120] Barnes defines the rule of law as 'independent and effective judicial systems that can force officials to act within their legal authority': S Barnes, 'The Contribution of Democracy to Rebuilding Post-Conflict Societies' (2001) 95 *American Journal of International Law* 86, 89.

[121] 'Apart from weaving human rights commitments into the founding legal texts forming the basis for UNMIK's interim administration, UNMIK has also created a number of bodies and institutions whose specific role is the protection, promotion and monitoring of human rights in Kosovo': M Brand, 'Institution-Building and Human Rights Protection in Kosovo in the Light of UNMIK Legislation' (2001) 70 *Nordic Journal of International Law* 461, 479.

[122] Statement by the President of the Security Council, UN Doc S/PRST/2002/4 (13 February 2002).

[123] See generally C Stahn, 'The United Nations Transitional Administration in Kosovo and East Timor: A First Analysis' (2001) 5 *Max Planck UNYB* 105, 174–75.

[124] The Secretary-General explained that an important component of UNMIK's administration was the 'immediate re-establishment of an independent, impartial and multi-ethnic judiciary': Report of the Secretary-General on the UN Interim Administration of Kosovo, UN Doc S/1999/779 (12 July 1999) para 66.

On 28 June 1999, 15 days after his arrival in Kosovo, Special Representative Sergio Vieira de Mello established a Joint Advisory Council on Provisional Judicial Appointments comprising two Kosovar Albanians, one Muslim Slav, one Serb and three UNMIK representatives. This Council was empowered to appoint (ultimately subject to UNMIK's approval) judges and prosecutors that were suitably qualified to perform these roles, subject to the caveat that all appointments were representative of the ethnic mix in Kosovo. This notwithstanding, UNMIK decided to employ international judges alongside domestic ones and, in December 2000, authorised panels with a majority of international judges. This was because 'it [was] very difficult for a Serb to get a fair trial in Kosovo without the participation of international jurists':[125]

> a long and continuing climate of ethnic conflict has severely impacted upon the objective impartiality of the courts and raises concerns as to actual bias on the part of certain judging panels. One response has been to appoint international judges and prosecutors to deal particularly with those serious criminal trials involving defendants from minority groups. This initiative is to be supported and should be pursued, even though, in the light of the majority voting system in the panels, the influence of the international judges over deliberations is restricted.[126]

In addition, mixed panels not only ensured impartial decisions but also proved a useful educational tool, allowing national judges to benefit from the experience of international experts (both in practical terms of achieving due process and also in interpreting and implementing international human rights norms).

UNMIK also established the Ombudsman institution in order to complement the emerging court system in Kosovo.[127] The mandate of the Ombudsman was to 'promote and protect the rights and freedoms of individuals and legal entities and ensure that all persons in Kosovo are able to exercise effectively the human rights and fundamental freedoms safeguarded by international human rights standards'.[128] Pursuant to this objective, the Ombudsman was required to 'provide accessible and timely mechanisms for the review and redress of actions constituting an abuse of authority by the interim civil administration or any emerging central or local institution'.[129] The Ombudsman could 'receive complaints, monitor, investigate, offer good offices, take preventative steps, make recommendations and advise on matters'.[130] If the Ombudsman determined that a

[125] W O'Neil, *Kosovo: An Unfinished Peace* (Boulder CO, Lynne Rienner, 2002) 84.

[126] OSCE, 'Review 1 – The Criminal Justice System in Kosovo' (February–July 2000)', 10 August 2000.

[127] UNMIK/REG/2000/38 (30 June 2000).

[128] ibid at section 1.1.

[129] ibid at section 1.2.

[130] ibid at section 4.1.

violation of human rights or an abuse of authority had been committed, he was empowered to make a public statement outlining the violation and draw the Special Representative's attention to it.[131] This institution was designed to receive complaints from individuals who believed they had been subject to an abuse of authority. Crucially, this also exists in relation to the judiciary, and so helps maintain their independence and impartiality. 'Despite the fact that it cannot directly prevent human rights violations occurring, it does represent an important safeguard against impunity and against future repetitions of violations'.[132]

Like in Kosovo, the conflict in East Timor destroyed any semblance of an effective justice system. Not only had all the qualified legal personnel fled East Timor with the outbreak of violence but the militia had also physically destroyed the court houses, burning them down, along with all the necessary legal materials. Thus, in East Timor establishing an effective justice system was not just a matter of recruiting and training competent legal personnel (itself a huge task) but in addition physically reconstructing judicial institutions. Given the importance of an effective impartial justice system to the protection of human rights, UNTAET prioritised the creation of 'a credible judiciary system that respects human rights and that can appropriately maintain law and order'.[133]

At the outset, UNTAET established a Transitional Judicial Service Commission, comprising three East Timorese members and two international experts,[134] to create an independent judiciary, draft codes of ethics for judges and prosecutors and to act as a disciplinary body to hear complaints about members of the judiciary.[135] Despite the dearth of legal personnel in East Timor, the Commission sought to ensure that East Timorese nationals were appointed as judges and prosecutors to allow for a vigorous expression of national identity and 'to mark an immediate commitment to domestic democratic institution-building, especially in the legal sector'.[136] In view of their relative legal inexperience (in terms of both substantive legal knowledge and experience of how to conduct a court) the Commission initiated intensive training programmes, with particular focus upon how to maintain impartiality and how to protect

[131] ibid at section 4.11.

[132] R Opie, 'International Human Rights Promotion and Protection' (2002) 7 *International Peacekeeping* 100, 135.

[133] UN Doc S/PV 4165 (2000).

[134] UNTAET/REG/1999/3 (3 December 1999).

[135] See generally H Strohmeyer, 'Making Multilateral Interventions Work: The UN and the Creation of Transitional Justice Systems in Kosovo and East Timor' (2001) 25 *Fletcher Forum of World Affairs* 107.

[136] Strohmeyer (n 85) at 264 ('Hopes for self-determination and self-government meant that the possible appointment of East Timorese judges – an unprecedented move that was unknown even under Portuguese colonial rule – took on a massive symbolic importance').

internationally recognised human rights.[137] This training involved mandatory 'quick impact' sessions, on-going training exercises and mentoring schemes where national judges were shadowed by experienced international legal practitioners. In addition, cases were often heard by a judicial panel comprising national judges and international experts.[138]

Unlike UNMIK, UNTAET did not establish an Ombudsman Institution. However, it did create a Commission for Reception, Truth and Reconciliation that was designed to initiate a cathartic process that engendered community reconciliation.[139] Its objective was 'to promote national reconciliation and healing following the years of political conflict in East Timor, and in particular, following the atrocities committed in 1999 . . . [by] establishing the truth regarding the commission of human rights violations'.[140] An individual responsible for committing criminal or non-criminal acts could contact the Commission,[141] outline the facts, admit responsibility and, following a public hearing, the Commission would agree an 'act of reconciliation' that the petitioner would be bound to accept and carry out.[142] It is important to realise that this Commission did not pose a challenge to the emerging judicial system. On the contrary, it was a realisation of the fragile state of the judicial system and the fact that it could not deal with the magnitude of minor crimes that had been committed during the conflict. The Commission therefore attempted to ease the pressure on the conventional criminal justice system (giving it time and space to develop) whilst also providing justice for minor crimes committed during the conflict and encouraging community reconciliation.

2.2 Independence, Declarations of Independence and Beyond

UNMIK was never intended to administer Kosovo indefinitely. The administration was always envisaged to be temporary. However, Kosovo's final political settlement was a highly contentious matter that was always going to be difficult to resolve. Whilst Resolution 1244 was unambiguous in its requirement that Kosovo be reconstructed upon a liberal basis and enjoy substantial autonomy within the greater Serbia, Resolution 1244 nevertheless reaffirmed Serbia's territorial integrity. In short, Resolution

[137] 'In a society that has never before experienced respect for the rule of law and in which the law was widely perceived as being yet another instrument for the exercise of power and control over the individual, a fundamental understanding of the meaning of independence and impartiality of the judiciary must gradually be developed': ibid at 271.

[138] UNTAET/REG/2000/11 (6 March 2000).

[139] UNTAET/REG/2001/10 (13 July 2001).

[140] ibid at section 3.1.

[141] Where the act was criminal, this process was only available in relation to 'non-serious' criminal acts, such as theft, minor assault, arson or property damage: ibid at section 1(m).

[142] UNTAET/REG (n 139) at section 27(7).

1244 did not provide the legal basis for creating an independent state. This notwithstanding, as the political reconstruction gathered pace in Kosovo, Kosovo's elected institutions began to demand that Kosovo secede from Serbia and be recognised as an independent sovereign state. Serbia vehemently rejected any such secession and declared that any attempted secession would violate Resolution 1244. For a substantial period of time, UNMIK avoided this issue, reaffirming that Kosovo had to demonstrate 'standards before status': Kosovo had to meet the high liberal benchmarks stipulated by Resolution 1244 before any discussion over political settlement could begin. In particular, UNMIK identified eight standards that must be achieved: 'functioning democratic institutions; rule of law; freedom of movement; returns and reintegration; economy; property rights; dialogue with Belgrade; and the Kosovo Protection Corps'.[143] In effect, Kosovo had to 'earn'[144] its right to begin negotiations over its final political status.

Kosovo's insistence that it had attained these standards was seriously undermined by the violent uprisings on 17 March 2004. In particular, there were reports of intimidation of Serb youths, resulting in the (alleged) drowning of three Kosovar Albanian children by Serbs. This prompted large-scale riots and attacks against Serb areas throughout Kosovo, with 19 people killed, thousands injured, nearly 400 internally displaced persons and 35 Serbian Orthodox Churches destroyed.[145]

> Although lasting only two days, the violence raised serious questions about the commitment within the Albanian community to the goals of a democratic and multi-ethnic Kosovo, combining as it did widespread violence against Serbs, disregard for UNMIK and the NATO security force (KFOR), and lack of moderating leadership from elected officials and the media.[146]

At least from the perspective of UNMIK, Kosovo (and in particular its elected leaders, who remained somewhat apathetic throughout the incident) had yet to genuinely embrace liberal norms and accept the requirement that internal disputes must be resolved peacefully through mediation rather than violence. 'The March violence . . . indicat[ed] that Kosovo was still a great distance from fully embracing democratic norms

[143] This became known as the 'standards before status' approach: UNMIK/PR/1078 (10 Dec ember 2003). See the Statement by the President of the Security Council, which endorsed these standards: UN Doc S/PRST/2003/26 (12 December 2003).

[144] P Williams and F Pecci, 'Earned Sovereignty: Bridging the Gap between Sovereignty and Self-Determination' (2004) 39 *Stanford Journal of International Law* 347.

[145] UNMIK described the violence as a 'targeted effort to drive out Kosovo Serbs, as well as members of the Roma and Ashkali communities, and to destroy the social fabric of their existence in Kosovo': Report of the Secretary-General on the UN Interim Administration of Kosovo, UN Doc S/2004/348 (30 April 2004).

[146] Tansey, 'The Concept and Practice of Democratic Regime-Building' (n 1) at 642. See generally International Crisis Group (ICG), 'Collapse in Kosovo': ICG Europe Report No 115 (22 April 2004).

and practices'.[147] In order to protect the (albeit uneasy) transition to genuine liberal democracy and prevent the recurrence of violence, UNMIK maintained its presence in Kosovo. In particular, UNMIK responded to the violence of March 2004 by encouraging greater decentralisation, allowing decisions on key issues (such as policing, education, justice) to be taken locally, as this was regarded as affording more effective guarantees for minority communities.[148]

By February 2008 Kosovo determined that it had made sufficient progress and had attained the standards that UNMIK had previously stipulated. Kosovo considered that it had constituted itself upon a liberal democratic basis and had thus earned independent sovereign statehood. On 17 February the Constituent Assembly unilaterally declared Kosovo's independence from Serbia.[149] Significantly, many members of the international community quickly acknowledged that Kosovo had attained the requisite liberal standard and thus formally recognised Kosovo's independence.[150] Other states, such as Russia, China and Serbia, have determined that Kosovo's declaration of independence and its subsequent recognition by other states is unlawful, being contrary to Security Council Resolution 1244, which explicitly required that Serbia's territorial integrity had to be respected at all times.[151] Indeed, Serbia successfully lobbied the General Assembly to request an Advisory Opinion on the legality of Kosovo's unilateral declaration of independence. On 22 July 2010 the International Court of Justice (ICJ) determined that Kosovo's unilateral declaration of independence was *not* unlawful under international law.[152]

In relation to East Timor, 'the international community paraded its newest state in May 2002'.[153] Albeit in rudimentary form, East Timor displayed a democratic system of governance whose power was located in the will of the people, an inherently liberal constitution dedicated to

[147] Tansey, ibid at 642. In October 2005 the Secretary-General explained that the standards had not been attained and so the issue of independence was off the agenda: Report of the Secretary-General on the UN Interim Administration of Kosovo, UN Doc S/2005/335 (23 May 2005).

[148] See Working Group on Local Government, Framework for the Reform of Local Self-Government in Kosovo (19 July 2004).

[149] 'We, the leaders of our people, democratically elected, through this declaration proclaim Kosovo an independent and sovereign state': Kosovar Prime Minister Hashim Thaci, quoted in *The New York Times* (18 February 2008), available at: www.nytimes.com/2008/02/18/world/europe/18kosovo.html?pagewanted=all&_r=0.

[150] For a list of the states that have recognised Kosovo's statehood see: www.president-ksgov.net/?page=2,54.

[151] See 'Kosovo Independence move not Illegal, says UN Court', *BBC News* (22 July 2010), available at: www.bbc.co.uk/news/world-europe-10730573.

[152] *Accordance with International Law of Unilateral Declaration of Independence of Kosovo*, Advisory Opinion (2010) ICJ Rep 403. For a critique of this Advisory Opinion see E Cirkovic, 'An Analysis of the ICJ Advisory Opinion on Kosovo's Unilateral Declaration of Independence' (2010) 11 *German Law Journal* 895.

[153] O Richmond and J Franks, 'Liberal Peacebuilding in Timor Leste: The Emperor's New Clothes' (2008) 15 *International Peacekeeping* 187, 109.

protecting individual liberty and an ever-strengthening impartial and independent judicial system. However, despite the progress of these liberal reforms, East Timor's liberal features remained very fragile. For this reason, despite the declaration of independence the UN maintained a presence in East Timor (UNMISET)[154] in order to consolidate its gradual transition to a fully-fledged liberal democracy. In particular, UNMISET's mandate was to 'provide assistance to core administrative structures critical to the vitality and political stability of East Timor', assisting East Timor in realising 'stability, democracy and justice'.[155] As Resolution 1410 explained,

> the emerging institutions in East Timor remain fragile and that in the period immediately after independence assistance will be required to ensure sustained momentum in the development and strengthening of East Timor's infrastructure, public administration, law enforcement and defence capabilities.

With political progress being made, in 2005 UNMISET was replaced by a smaller mission: the UN Office in Timor Leste (UNOTIL).[156] Its mandate, however, remained the same: to assist in the development of critical state institutions and the police, as well as to provide training in the observance of democratic governance and human rights.[157]

Despite these political gains and the waning presence of the UN in East Timor, just before the expiration of UNOTIL's mandate in May 2006 violence broke out in the capital, Dili. Gang violence erupted leaving 20 dead, hundreds of homes burnt and tens of thousands internally displaced. As Richmond and Franks note, '[t]he outbreak of violence was a threat to the stability of the new liberal state'.[158] Indeed, this was recognised by the Special Representative for UNOTIL, Sukehiro Hasegawa, who explained that '[t]he latest developments have reminded us that not only is democracy in Timor-Leste still fragile, but also the internal security is easily assailable'.[159] In response, UNOTIL's presence was substantially bolstered in order to provide security and ensure the integrity of the liberal state. As the UN Secretary-General explained, 'the building of institutions on the basis of fundamental principles of democracy and the rule of law is not a simple process that can be completed within a few short years'.[160] Of

[154] SC Res 1410 (17 May 2002). UNMISET was initially deployed for 12 months but its mandate was extended for two more years: see SC Res 1480 (19 May 2003), SC Res 1543 (14 May 2004) and SC Res 1573 (16 November 2004). The mandate was concluded on 20 May 2005.

[155] See UNMISET's website, available at: www.un.org/Depts/dpko/missions/unmiset/mandate.

[156] SC Res 1599 (28 April 2005).

[157] ibid at para 2 (i)–(iii).

[158] Richmond and Franks, 'Liberal Peacebuilding in Timor Leste' (n 153) at 185.

[159] UNOTIL Press Release 5 May 2006.

[160] UNOTIL Press Release, 'Timor-Leste: Annan Appeals to Security Council for Renewed UN Action' (13 June 2006).

course this is true, but what is interesting (and indeed significant) is that the UN reacted to this violence, recognising the threat that it posed to the liberal reforms that had been achieved. I suggest that this clearly exemplifies the UN's commitment to entrenching liberal values in East Timor and its determination to create a liberal state.

3. AFGHANISTAN AND THE 'LIGHT FOOTPRINT' APPROACH

In 2001 the United States (US) invaded Afghanistan in response to the terrorist attacks of 9/11. The intervention was justified on the basis of self-defence.[161] The initial intention was to topple the Taliban from power and substantially weaken (if not destroy) the Al Qaeda terrorist organisation and thus prevent Afghanistan from being used to harbour international terrorists. According to the liberal peace thesis, however, in order to completely remove the threat that Afghanistan posed to the international community (and specifically the US), removing the Taliban from power and weakening Al Qaeda's network was insufficient. In order to fully avert the threat that Afghanistan posed, the liberal peace thesis required that Afghanistan be reconstructed upon a liberal basis.[162]

With the (relative) success of the liberal reconstructions in Kosovo and East Timor,[163] one would have expected the international community, acting through the UN, to deploy a territorial administration comparable to those in Kosovo and East Timor.

Significantly, the UN did not deploy a territorial administration. The UN did have a civilian presence in Afghanistan, the UN Assistance Mission in Afghanistan (UNAMA).[164] However, the UNAMA was merely an advisory body, mandated to provide the Afghan authorities, who represented the sovereign authority in Afghanistan, with advice and support in their reconstruction efforts. In addition, the UN deployed the International Security Assistance Force (ISAF) under Chapter VII of the UN Charter, but its mandate was limited to providing security. Initially, this role was limited to Afghanistan's capital, Kabul.[165] In 2003, however, this role was

[161] See SC Res 1378 (14 November 2001).

[162] Indeed, this was no easy task because the situation in Afghanistan was at crisis point; 'a quarter-century of warfare had pounded nearly every bit of the country's already-uneven physical infrastructure to rubble, created the world's largest refugee population (as gauged from 1981 to 1997), and wrecked or gravely distorted most social, economic, and political institutions as well': L Goodson, 'Bullets, Ballots, and Poppies in Afghanistan' (2005) 16 *Journal of Democracy* 24, 27–28.

[163] These missions were generally regarded as a success: see Chesterman, *You, The People* (n 35) at 174.

[164] SC Res 1401 (28 March 2002).

[165] SC Res 1386 (20 December 2001). US forces pursued similar security objectives outside of the capital. These forces formed part of Operation Enduring Freedom (OED), discussed below.

extended to the whole country.[166] The UN's role in Afghanistan is thus characterised by Brahimi's metaphor of a 'light expatriate footprint'.[167] The essence of this approach is that in organising and conducting the reconstruction the Afghans would be allowed 'do it themselves'.

Evidently, this light footprint approach is in sharp contrast to the highly intrusive role that the UN possessed in Kosovo and East Timor: '[t]his choice is a reversal of the increasingly intrusive trend in transitional administration, from the international exercise of executive and legislative powers in Eastern Slovenia, Brčko and Kosovo to global sovereignty in East Timor'.[168] Inevitably, this light footprint approach raises important questions over the UN's (or more specifically the international community's) commitment to promoting liberal democracy in Afghanistan. Does this light footprint approach illustrate a waning in the normative commitment of the international community to the promotion of liberal values? If so, the doctrine of the international community that has been presented in this book is substantially weakened.

I strongly disagree with the contention that the international community has not demonstrated a sustained commitment to promoting liberal democracy in Afghanistan. That they did not impose a territorial administration under Chapter VII does not indicate a weakening of normative commitment. Rather, I suggest, it is illustrative of a change in *strategy*. It must be remembered that the international community has at its core the idea that liberal democracy represents a universally desired system of governance.[169] Thus, promoting liberal democracy to non-liberal states is not to be regarded as imposing liberal democracy on an unwilling population that resists these reforms. Instead, the international community regards its promotion of liberal values as an exercise in releasing and realising the population's universal desire for liberal governance. This transition to liberalism is something the population welcomes, encourages and contributes towards, although of course there will be always those that are determined to (violently if necessary) derail this process. However, the process of democratisation is a complicated and costly task and thus the population requires substantial and sustained assistance from international actors. This is where the international community considers its role to lie: in assisting, supporting, encouraging and guiding the liberal transition.

In Kosovo and East Timor the assistance provided by the international community was considerable. The international community was principally responsible for establishing the liberal system of governance. This

[166] SC Res 1510 (13 October 2003).

[167] Report of the Secretary-General on the Situation in Afghanistan and Its Implications for International Peace and Security, UN Doc A/56/875 – S/2002/278 (18 March 2002).

[168] A Their and J Chopra, 'The Road Ahead: Political and Institutional Reconstruction in Afghanistan (2002) 23 *Third World Quarterly* 893, 894.

[169] See chapter 3 of this volume.

degree of assistance, albeit considered largely successful in Kosovo and East Timor, was considered 'not necessary and not possible' in Afghanistan.[170] Not possible insofar as Afghanistan was a huge territory and thus an international territorial administration was inconceivable.[171] Not necessary insofar as it was considered that liberal reforms could nevertheless be achieved through the provision of advice and support but without needing to assume governmental control.[172] Moreover, Afghanistan has a troubled history of intervention in its internal affairs and so is sensitive to external interference. Consequently, the perception of the international community was that the Afghans would prefer to take the reins in relation to the liberal reconstruction, albeit with considerable assistance from external actors. This would allow them to craft a liberal system of governance to emerge that embraces local traditions.[173]

Consequently, the international community adopted a light footprint approach towards the reconstruction of Afghanistan. The international community preferred an Afghan authority to spearhead the liberal reconstruction and thus be ultimately responsible for the reforms introduced. As I illustrate below, the international community remained committed to promoting liberal democracy in Afghanistan.[174] Three forms of assistance are identified: i) the UN's instrumental role in the formulation of the Bonn Agreement, ii) the role of the UNAMA in ensuring the implementation of this Agreement, and iii) providing funding specifically designed to promote liberal values. Moreover, I demonstrate that the vast resources the international community has contributed towards the liberal reconstruc-

[170] Statement by Special Representative Brahimi, quoted in Chesterman (n 35) at 90. 'An armed UN peacekeeping force is not recommended. The Secretary-General would require several months to obtain from Member States sufficient numbers of troops to pose a credible military deterrence, and to subsequently deploy them. Furthermore, UN peacekeepers have proven successful when deployed to implement an existing political settlement among willing parties – not to serve as a substitute for one': L Brahimi, 'Special Representative of the Secretary-General for Afghanistan, Briefing to the Security Council' (13 November 2001).

[171] This is because '[t]he broad administrations of Kosovo and East Timor with fewer than one million inhabitants each in small territories were the exceptions rather than the rule, nothing that could be repeated in Afghanistan with 25 million inhabitants': Korhonen, Gras and Creutz, *International Post-Conflict Situations* (n 14) at 64.

[172] 'What Afghanistan needs above all is assistance in building a state': B Rubin, 'Statement to Implementation Group' 2002, quoted in E Afsah and A Guhr, 'Afghanistan: Building a State to Keep the Peace' (2005) 9 *Max Planck UNYB* 373, 392.

[173] 'A too intrusive international effort would have been perceived as foreign domination, and could have triggered the kind of violent resistance that Afghans have shown throughout their history towards external interference. The respect shown by the international community towards the Afghan political process is in part a result of that history. It is therefore arguable that the United Nations had little choice but to stay consciously out of the limelight, whatever the conceptual lessons learned from the past': Afsah and Guhr, 'Afghanistan: Building a State' (n 172) at 381.

[174] 'The international community as a whole provides vital support as Afghans rebuild their country': Statement by President of the Security Council, UN Doc S/PRST/2002/25 (11 September 2002).

tion of Afghanistan have been (and currently are) justified on the basis that a liberal Afghanistan is necessary to preserve the security of the international community and thus dilate the scope of the liberal peace:

> [t]he externally led democratization process in Afghanistan is part of a consensus among international organizations to foster a 'liberal peace', which, since the mid-1990s, has been based on the Kantian call for the simultaneous opening up of political and economic systems and the interaction between economic interdependence and political democracy as a fundamental instrument for promoting international peace.[175]

3.1 The Bonn Agreement[176]

In the context of the liberal reconstruction of Afghanistan the Bonn Agreement is vitally important because it delineates the road map for political reform.[177] Significantly, this conference was conducted under the auspices of the UN, where the Special Representative to the Secretary-General, Lakhdar Brahimi, was the 'architect' of the Bonn process and 'instrumental' in the formulation of the Bonn Agreement.[178]

> Brahimi's role in selecting these groups and persuading them to join forces together, as well as enlisting the German government to host their meeting in Bonn, and in chairing the meeting for nearly two weeks from late November, cannot be overstressed.[179]

The UN invited four Afghan political parties to the conference. However, their invitation was dependent upon their accepting the principles that Brahimi insisted must be adhered to in framing any agreement concerning the reconstruction of Afghanistan. The most important of these principles was that there be agreement on 'the need for a broad-based, multi-ethnic, politically balanced, freely chosen government enjoying both domestic and international legitimacy'.[180]

[175] S Tadjbakhsh and M Schoiswohl, 'Playing with Fire? The International Community's Democratization Experiment in Afghanistan' (2008) 15 *International Peacekeeping* 252, 253.

[176] For a detailed discussion of the formulation of the Bonn Agreement and its implementation see R Ponzio, *Democratic Peacebuilding: Aiding Afghanistan and other Fragile States* (New York, Oxford University Press, 2011) especially chs 3 and 4.

[177] The agreement, signed on 5 December 2001, was termed 'Agreement on Provisional Arrangements in Afghanistan Pending the Re-establishment of Permanent Government Institutions'. In SC Res 1383 (6 December 2001), this Agreement was endorsed by the Security Council: '*Reiterating* its endorsement of the Agreement on provisional arrangements in Afghanistan pending the re-establishment of permanent government institutions, signed in Bonn on 5 December 2001' (preamble). It is important to note, however, that this resolution was not taken under Chapter VII. Again, the light footprint approach is evident.

[178] Chesterman (n 35) at 89, 92.

[179] A Saikal, 'The United Nations and Democratization in Afghanistan' in Newman and Rich (eds) (n 68) at 325.

[180] L Brahimi, 'Briefing to the Security Council' (n 170).

The negotiations in Bonn resulted in the signing of the Bonn Agreement on 5 December 2001. In conformity with Brahimi's guidelines the agreement unambiguously envisioned a political process that would eventually result in parliamentary and presidential elections. That Afghanistan would be democratic was made clear by the preamble to the Bonn Agreement.[181] The preamble explained that Afghanistan's political future would be based upon 'the right of the people of Afghanistan to freely determine their own political future' and that by creating the Bonn Agreement the 'first step toward the establishment of a broad-based, gender-sensitive, multi-ethnic and fully representative government' had been taken.

However, given the destruction and humanitarian crisis in Afghanistan, Afghanistan lacked both the capacity and political will to mount national elections immediately. In the interim, therefore, the Bonn Agreement explained that Afghan authorities would possess sovereignty over the territory until conditions were conducive for legitimately elected representatives to be chosen.

In the first instance, the representatives at Bonn invested authority in the Interim Authority. This Authority was convened on 22 December 2001 and charged with 'the day-to-day conduct of the affairs of the state'.[182] Although the members of this Authority were not elected, its 30 members were carefully selected by the representatives at Bonn on the basis of their 'professional competence and personal integrity . . . with due regard to the ethnic, geographic and religious composition of Afghanistan and to the importance of women'.[183]

The Interim Authority was always intended to be temporary and was given a mandate of six months, during which an emergency *loya jirga* (great council) would be convened in order to select a more representative government until national democratic elections could be held.[184] The emergency *loya* comprised 1,051 delegates. These delegates were elected nationwide by 15,000 electoral persons, who were themselves elected within their discrete districts. In addition, pursuant to the Bonn Agreement's requirement that 'the participation of women as well as the equitable representation of all ethnic and religious communities in the . . . Emergency Loya Jirga',[185] this delegation of 1,051 members was supple-

[181] The Bonn Agreement created 'an overall framework to guide Afghanistan's ongoing journey from failed statehood under the brutal misrule of extreme Islamists and their terrorist allies to moderate and functional democratic government': L Goodson, 'The Lessons of National-Building in Afghanistan' in F Fukuyama (ed), *Nation-Building: Beyond Afghanistan and Iraq* (Baltimore MD, The Johns Hopkins University Press, 2006) 146.

[182] Chapter III, Part C, s 1 of the Bonn Agreement.

[183] ibid at Chapter III, Part A, s 3.

[184] A *loya jirga* is a form of great assembly or council and refers to a century old forum in which tribal elders gathered together to consult and decide upon important issues.

[185] Chapter V, s 4 of the Bonn Agreement. '[P]opular support for a democratic political process in Afghanistan is steadily being broadened, with the traditional system of consensus-

mented by 550 delegates appointed by the Interim Authority to ensure representation of minority groups, women, handicapped persons and refugees.[186] Once convened, the emergency *loya* elected a Transitional Government and a temporary Head of State in June 2002. Upon its creation the Interim Authority ceased to exist.

In addition, the Bonn Agreement required that once the Transitional Government was established, full, free, fair competitive elections would be held within two years of the convening of the emergency *loya*.[187] During this period the government was required to draft a constitution for Afghanistan, which had to be approved by a constitutional *loya*. The constitution was duly created and approved by the *loya* and on 9 October 2004 full presidential elections were held. This election drew a 70 per cent turnout, with over 8 million voters taking part in the election.[188] Elections for the National (legislative) Assembly and local Provincial Councils were held in September 2005. Under the close observation of the international community, both were held to be free and fair.[189]

It is apparent that the Bonn Agreement heavily influenced Afghanistan's transition to liberal democracy. Thus, it has been argued that 'the Bonn negotiations resulted in very few *substantive* issues being settled, but rather concentrated on laying down the time-table and the overall framework in which to proceed'.[190] To a certain extent this is true. However, the Agreement did address other issues: specifically, the legal framework that would apply in Afghanistan and the need to protect human rights. The Agreement provided that the Constitution of 1964 would represent the applicable law, although only to the extent that its incumbent rules and regulations were 'not inconsistent with . . . international legal obligations

building (*loya jirga*) being used as a vehicle': K Komano, 'The Role of Elections in the Peace-Building and Reconstruction of Afghanistan' (2005) 12 *Asia-Pacific Review* 1, 5. That any interim arrangements, ie before free and fair elections establish a democratic government, should be as representative as possible was a requirement at Bonn: '*Recognizing* the need to ensure broad representation in these interim arrangements of all segments of the Afghan population' (preamble).

186 See generally Human Rights Watch, 'Afghanistan: Return of the Warlords' Briefing Paper (June 2002) 10, available at: dspace.cigilibrary.org/jspui/bitstream/123456789/17775/1/Afghanistan%20Return%20of%20the%20Warlords.pdf?1.

187 The Bonn Agreement was keen to ensure 'that these interim arrangements are intended as a first step toward the establishment of a broad-based, gender-sensitive, multi-ethnic and fully representative government, and are not intended to remain in place beyond the specified period of time' (preamble).

188 'The principal reasons why this was so [a success] were probably the enthusiasm for the election of the Afghan people themselves, their participation in its planning, and the concerted support of the international community': Islamic Republic of Afghanistan, 'Afghanistan National Development Strategy, An Interim Strategy for Security, Governance, Economic Growth and Poverty Reduction' (2006) 11.

189 US State Department, Press Statement (3 November 2004), available at: www.state.gov/r/pa/prs/20004/27760.htm.

190 Afsah and Guhr (n 172) at 383.

to which Afghanistan is a party'.[191] In addition, it required that all authorities in Afghanistan must 'act in accordance with basic principles and provisions contained in international instruments on human rights and international humanitarian law to which Afghanistan is a party'.[192]

3.2 The Implementation of Bonn and the United Nations Assistance Mission in Afghanistan (UNAMA)

The UN is physically present in Afghanistan through UNAMA, which provides an integrated structure for the UN's assistance (and its specialised agencies[193]) for the reconstruction of Afghanistan.[194] The mandate of this mission is provided for by the Bonn Agreement, which confers upon UNAMA a general role to oversee the implementation of the Bonn Agreement,[195] to investigate violations of human rights and, where found, to recommend corrective measures.[196] In particular, UNAMA possesses three main functions:

i) Fulfilling the tasks and responsibilities, including those related to human rights, the rule of law and gender issues, entrusted to the United Nations in the Bonn Agreement;
ii) Promoting national reconciliation and rapprochement throughout the country, through the good offices of the Special Representative;

[191] Chapter II, s 1 (ii) Bonn Agreement.

[192] ibid at Chapter V, s 2 Bonn Agreement. Moreover, the Bonn Agreement required that the Interim Authority establish an independent human rights commission that would monitor human rights protection, investigate alleged violations of human rights and develop effective domestic human rights institutions: Chapter III, Part C, s 6.

[193] UNICEF, UNDP and UNHRC have all been active in Afghanistan. These agencies, however, are part of UNAMA's structure and are subordinated to the authority of the Special Representative.

[194] SC Res 1401 (28 March 2002). UNAMA's mandate has been extended on various occasions. Most recently see SC Res 2041 (22 March 2012).

[195] '[UNAMA's] overall objective [is] to provide support for the implementation of the Bonn Agreement . . . while recognizing that the responsibility for the Agreement's implementation ultimately rests with the Afghans themselves': Report of the Secretary-General on the Situation in Afghanistan and its Implications for International Peace and Security, UN Doc A/56/875 – S/2002/278 (18 March 2002).

[196] The Bonn Agreement provides UNAMA with a particularly prominent role in the area of monitoring and investigating alleged violations of human rights: 'The United Nations shall have the right to investigate human rights violations and, where necessary, recommend corrective action. It will also be responsible for the development and implementation of a programme of human rights education to promote respect for and understanding of human rights': Bonn Agreement, annex II, section 6. As the Secretary-General explains, 'UNAMA continues to monitor and investigate human rights violations, to ensure that human rights fundamentals are incorporated in the process of institution-building and to support the Afghan Independent Human Rights Commission as the primary national institution responsible for protecting and promoting human rights': Report of the Secretary-General on the Situation in Afghanistan and its Implications for International Peace and Security, UN Doc S/2003/1212 (30 December 2003) para 44.

iii) Managing all the United Nations humanitarian relief, recovery and reconstruction activities in Afghanistan, under the overall authority of the Special Representative and in coordination with the Interim Authority and the successor administrations of Afghanistan.[197]

UNAMA's role is clarified further by various Security Council resolutions, especially by Resolution 1806 (2008)[198] and Resolution 1868 (2009).[199] Collectively, these resolutions provide that, with the consent of the Afghan authorities, UNAMA will actively promote political outreach in Afghanistan, support Afghan reconciliation programmes, promote peace and help coordinate humanitarian assistance, help realise the protection of fundamental rights and freedoms, support the Afghan Independent Electoral Commission and, more generally, provide support for a stable and prosperous Afghanistan.

In actuality, therefore, it appears that UNAMA is competent to advise Afghan authorities on all matters relating to its liberal reconstruction. Albeit in an advisory role, UNAMA nevertheless plays a 'central role . . . in promoting peace and stability in Afghanistan'.[200] Although the consensual nature of UNAMA's presence in Afghanistan has resulted in it being characterised as a 'light footprint' mission, 'in practice there has been an extremely heavy footprint'.[201] In essence, although it is Afghan authorities that have spearheaded the programme for liberal reform, drafting and establishing a whole series of laws and institutions in order to protect human rights and instal democracy at the national and local levels, these authorities have operated under the considerable influence of UNAMA.

Most significantly, UNAMA has assisted the Transitional Administration in drafting a constitution for Afghanistan. In particular, UNAMA created the Constitutional Commission Support Unit, which provided technical support and financial assistance to the Constitutional Review Commission, the body established by the Transitional Authority to draft the constitution. The constitution was adopted on 4 January 2004 by a constitutional *loya* and commits Afghanistan to a future firmly based upon the protection of individual liberty. The preamble to the constitution provides, for example, that Afghanistan will be 'an order based on the peoples' will and democracy' and 'void of oppression, atrocity, discrimination as well as violence, based on the rule of law, social justice, protecting integrity and

[197] Report of the Secretary-General on the Situation in Afghanistan (n 195) at para 97.
[198] SC Res 1806 (20 March 2008).
[199] SC Res 1868 (23 March 2009).
[200] SC Res 1776 (19 September 2007).
[201] J Goodhand, 'From War Economy to Peace Economy? Reconstruction and State Building in Afghanistan' (2004) 58 *Journal of International Affairs* 155, 169.

human rights, and attaining peoples' freedoms and fundamental rights'.[202] In addition, the constitution imposes an obligation upon the state to 'create a prosperous and progressive society based on social justice, preservation of human dignity, protection of human rights, realization of democracy, attainment of national unity as well as equality between all peoples and tribes'.[203]Article 7 requires that the state respect the major international human rights instruments, including the Universal Declaration of Human Rights. Gender equality finds particular support within the constitution. Article 22 provides for the legal equality of men and women: '[a]ny kind of discrimination and distinction between citizens of Afghanistan shall be forbidden. The citizens of Afghanistan – whether women or men – have equal rights and duties before the law'. Article 24 provides that

> liberty is the natural right of human beings. This right has no limit unless affecting others' freedoms as well as the public interest, which shall be regulated by law. Liberty and human dignity are inviolable. The state shall respect and protect liberty as well as human dignity.[204]

3.3 Operation Enduring Freedom, ISAF and Provincial Reconstruction Teams

In addition to the work being carried out by UNAMA two other international community-sponsored missions are operating in Afghanistan: Operation Enduring Freedom (OEF) and the International Security Assistance Force (ISAF). OEF is under US control (as opposed to that of the UN) and is a remnant of the initial military intervention. This force has been supplemented by the International Security Assistance Force (ISAF), which is a NATO-led mission and operates separately and under a different legal basis than OEF.[205] It does, however, perform a similar role, albeit in a different geographical area. Whilst OEF is charged with providing security outside of Kabul (the Afghan capital), ISAF was initially respon-

[202] Preamble to the Constitution. Article 3 firmly locates sovereignty within the will of the people: 'National sovereignty in Afghanistan shall belong to the nation, manifested directly and through its elected representatives'.

[203] Article 6 of the Constitution.

[204] Zalmay Khalilzad, US Ambassador to Afghanistan, declared that the new constitution was 'one of the most enlightened Constitutions in the Islamic world' and represents 'a milestone on the Afghan people's path to democracy': Z Khalilzad, 'Afghanistan's Milestone', *The Washington Post* (6 January 2004), available at: 2001–2009.state.gov/p/sca/rls/rm/27702.htm. 'The final text of the constitution is a modern constitution that is in conformity with international human rights standards and which provides a legal structure that will aid the reconstruction process in Afghanistan': Afsah and Guhr (n 172) at 433.

[205] ISAF was authorised by the Security Council under Chapter VII UN Charter: see SC Res 1386 (20 December 2001).

sible for ensuring security in Kabul. This being said, ISAF's role has been extended across Afghanistan, operating alongside (albeit distinct from) OEF. [206]

Initially both missions possessed a limited role: as counter-insurgency forces intended to enhance security so that the Bonn Agreement could be implemented as effectively as possible and political reforms undertaken. However, eventually the mandate of OEF, and later ISAF,[207] was extended from a principally security-based role to a mission that actively assists in the implementation of the Bonn Agreement and its liberal vision. This new role has manifested itself most clearly through the development of Provincial Reconstruction Teams (PRTs). PRTs are principally civil missions that are designed to facilitate reconstruction. However, in order to ensure their effectiveness, they are accompanied by military personnel in order to provide secure conditions.[208] Typically, a PRT comprises 60–100 soldiers, Afghan advisors and representatives from civilian agencies like the US State Department, the US Agency for International Development and the US Department for Agriculture. Ultimately, the purpose of PRTs is to extend the authority of the Afghan government, improve security and promote civil reconstruction. Thus,

> [t]here is a common misconception that the PRT is all about the physical reconstruction of Afghanistan. This is not the way we do business. Our concept of operations and development priorities are primarily concerned with: a) government institution building and b) security sector reform.[209]

Indeed, PRTs were regarded as indispensable in mobilising Afghans to participate in selecting representatives for the *loyas* and in the elections. This included educational programmes that disseminated important information about the role of individual participation in democratic politics, the role and function of the Legislative Assembly, how delegates of this Assembly are selected and the importance of widespread participation in elections and the need for broad representation (and for the representation of women in particular). In the presidential election of October 2004 PRTs provided security and advice in contested/hostile regions, guarding polling stations, securing ballot boxes and providing advice to election workers. Indeed, the success of these elections was generally

[206] SC Res 1510 (13 October 2003).

[207] SC Res 1623 (13 September 2005) expressly authorised ISAF to establish Provincial Reconstruction Teams and encourages these PRTs to contribute to the holding of elections in Afghanistan and to its reconstruction more generally. Again, this resolution was taken under Chapter VII UN Charter.

[208] For an outline and the role and functions of PRTs see the Report of the Secretary-General to the General Assembly, UN Doc A/58/616 (3 December 2003) para 34 ff.

[209] NATO, 'Provincial Reconstruction Team North (West)', available at: www.hrf.tu.nato.int/isaf/public/prtl.php?prt=north.

attributed to the advice and support provided by the PRTs.[210] In addition, PRTs contributed to the establishment of schools, clinics, wells, roads, bridges and the construction of public facilities, including police stations, courthouses and civil administration buildings. To this end, PRTs have achieved 'great success' and 'played important roles in everything from election support to school-building to disbarment to mediating factional conflicts'.[211] All these activities, I suggest, are pursuant to the wider objective of reconstructing Afghanistan upon a liberal basis.

3.4 Funding

In order to rebuild a state devastated by war, famine and mismanagement, finance is obviously of crucial significance.[212] On their own, the Afghan authorities do not possess the necessary material resources to radically reconstruct Afghanistan's political and legal system. In its determination to encourage the liberal reconstruction, the international community has provided not just advice and assistance but also substantial funding. Significantly, this funding has always been linked to political objectives: the international community has provided funding on the basis that Afghanistan continues to take steps towards liberalisation and that any funding is used to help realise this liberal objective. Since 2002, the international community has held a number of 'donor conferences' in order to rally funding. Several of these conferences have particular significance in the context of steering Afghanistan towards liberal democracy. For example,

> [a]n international conference on Afghanistan was convened in London in January 2006, where the international community pledged continued assistance to the country in exchange for the realization of concrete goals within the areas of security, counter-narcotics, social and economic development, governance, rule of law, and human rights.[213]

In light of the demands made at this conference, the government of Afghanistan produced the Interim-Afghanistan National Development

[210] 'PRTs played a similarly important role during parliamentary elections in September 2005': R Perito, 'The US Experience with Provisional Reconstruction Teams in Afghanistan: Lessons Identified' United States Institute of Peace Special Report Number 152 (October 2005). PRTs again adopted this role in relation to the presidential elections in 2009 and the parliamentary elections in 2010.

[211] M McNerney, 'Stabilization and Reconstruction in Afghanistan: Are PRTs a Model or a Muddle? (2005–06) *Parameters, US Army War College Quarterly* 32, 32.

[212] '[T]he reconstruction process that is currently being coordinated by UNAMA will require the continued assistance of the international community, not least in financial terms': Afsah and Guhr (n 172) at 438.

[213] B Rubin and H Hamidzada, 'From Bonn to London: Governance Challenges and the Future of Statebuilding in Afghanistan' (2007) 14 *International Peacekeeping* 8, 12.

Strategy (I-ANDS) which prioritised these (overtly liberal) objectives.[214] In particular, I-ANDS explains that 'democratic governance and the protection of human rights constitute the cornerstone of sustainable political progress in Afghanistan'.[215] With this in mind, I-ANDS provides that

> [b]y 2020 we envisage a state in which institutions are more accountable and responsive to poor people, strengthening their participation in the political process and in local decision-making regardless of gender or social status. We will continue to mature as a stable Islamic constitutional democracy with regular national and provincial elections that are peaceful and fair.[216]

In Rome 2007 another international donor conference was held. Donations were made in order to consolidate and enhance the rule of law in Afghanistan.[217] 2008 witnessed a similar donor conference (held in Paris) where international actors reaffirmed their commitment to a liberal democratic Afghanistan. Over US$20 billion was pledged, with this money being used to support the objectives outlined in the Afghanistan National Development Strategy (ANDS), which was formulated in Paris by the Afghan authorities in conjunction with members of the international community. ANDS provided the roadmap for political development over the next five years. In a similar vein to the previous interim development strategy, these objectives include a) security (nationwide stabilisation, strengthened law enforcement and improved personal security for every Afghan); b) governance, the rule of law and human rights (strengthening democratic practice and institutions, human rights, the rule of law, delivery of public services and Government accountability); and c) economic and social development (poverty reduction, sustainable development).[218] In addition, this funding was pledged on the basis that Afghan authorities continue to work closely with international actors (principally UNAMA) in realising these stipulated liberal objectives. The most recent conference, held in Tokyo in 2012, provided huge sums of money in order facilitate Afghanistan's liberal reconstruction. International actors donated US$16 billion dollars to Afghanistan, although crucially the provision of this aid was dependent upon Afghanistan meeting a number of clearly defined objectives. These included organising free and fair presidential and

[214] 'The London conference concluded with an apparent renewal of the commitment of the international community to Afghanistan for at least the next five years to see through the implementation of the Afghan National Development Strategy': ibid at 10.

[215] The Afghanistan Compact (February 2006) 3, available at: unama.unmissions.org/Portals/UNAMA/Documents/AfghanistanCompact-English.pdf.

[216] Islamic Republic of Afghanistan, 'Afghanistan National Development Strategy: An Interim Strategy for Security, Governance, Economic Growth and Poverty Reduction' (2006) 15.

[217] The Rome Agreement is available at: www.diplomatie.gouv.fr/fr/IMG/pdf/Romejointrecommandations.pdf.

[218] The Afghanistan National Development Strategy is available at: www.undp.org.af/publications/KeyDocuments/ANDS_Full_Eng.pdf.

parliamentary elections in 2014 and 2015, improving controls on financial markets, tackling corruption and implementing laws condemning violence against women.[219]

4. CONCLUSION

Since the end of the Cold War the transition from peacekeeping to peacebuilding has become stark. In this chapter I have argued that the international community has developed peacebuilding as a tool to assist post-conflict states in reconstructing themselves upon a liberal basis, and thereby enhancing the scope of the liberal peace. Whereas historically peacekeeping was indifferent to the political nature of a dispute, peacebuilding exhibits a profound liberal bias. This is most evident from the territorial administrations in Kosovo and East Timor where the international community, operating through the UN, systematically rebuilt these territories upon a liberal basis. Significantly, in Afghanistan there was a change of strategy. The international community did not take over administration of the state but allowed domestic authorities to be the figurehead for the liberal reconstruction, albeit with considerable support, encouragement and guidance from the international community. I have suggested that the international community's determination to reconstruct Afghanistan upon a liberal basis is comparable to its determination to reconstruct Kosovo and East Timor upon a liberal basis. Although there was a change in approach/strategy by the international community, their normative commitment held firm.

In 2000 Lakhdar Brahimi produced an influential report that criticised the UN for deploying peacebuilding missions with the explicit (and ambitious) mandate of promoting respect for human rights but failing to adequately resource these missions. Brahimi stated that 'if an operation is given a mandate to protect civilians . . . it also must be given the specific resources needed to carry out that mandate'.[220] In order to better resource peacebuilding missions the UN established the Peacebuilding Commission (PBC) in 2005.[221] In '*recognizing* that development, peace and security and human rights are interlinked and mutually reinforcing',[222] the General Assembly and Security Council created this Commission in order to pro-

[219] The Declaration of the Tokyo Conference is available at: unama.unmissions.org/LinkClick.aspx?fileticket=gbuRF5l17C8%3d&tabid=12254&language=en-US.

[220] UN Doc A/55/505 – S/2000/809 (Brahimi Report) 21 August 2000. As White explains, 'poor resourcing of peacebuilding mandates has resulted in there being "form over substance"'; ND White, 'Empowering Peace Operations to protect Civilians: Form over Substance' (2009) 13 *International Peacekeeping* 327.

[221] GA Res 60/180 (30 December 2005) and SC Res 1645 (20 December 2005).

[222] SC Res 1645 (20 December 2005) preamble.

vide peacebuilding missions with greater coherence and better resources. As the UN explains,

> the Peacebuilding Commission plays a unique role in (1) bringing together all of the relevant actors, including international donors, the international financial institutions, national governments, troop contributing countries; (2) marshalling resources and (3) advising on and proposing integrated strategies for post-conflict peacebuilding and recovery and where appropriate, highlighting any gaps that threaten to undermine peace.[223]

Indeed, the PBC has recently played an important role in coordinating the UN's response to the civil unrest in Burundi. After gaining its independence Burundi experienced a number of violent conflicts which led to the breakdown of law and order, resulting in serious and widespread human rights abuses. In its determination to end the conflict and restore law and order the Burundi government requested assistance from the PBC. In response, the PBC played an important role in organising international aid and providing advice and support to the government so that democratic processes could be strengthened and human rights protected.[224] In its attempt to enhance the capacity of peacebuilding missions the creation of the PBC therefore exemplifies the commitment of the UN (under the influence of the international community) to promoting respect for liberal democracy in states emerging from conflict.[225]

[223] See www.un.org/peace/peacebuilding/. In addition, the General Assembly and Security Council resolutions that established the PBC also established the Peacebuilding Fund and Peacebuilding Support Office, which are designed to enhance the capacity of peacebuilding missions.

[224] The following objectives were stipulated: a) promoting good governance, b) strengthening the rule of law within the security services, c) strengthening justice, promotion of human rights, reconciliation and action to combat impunity, d) the land issue, with particular reference to the reintegration of affected populations, and community-based recovery particularly targeting women, young people and affected populations: PBC/1/BD1/4 (22 June 2007). The PBC is performing a similar role in Sierra Leone. After a request from the government the PBC is assisting in justice sector reforms, consolidating democracy and promoting good governance. For an overview of the PCB's priorities in Sierra Leone and the initiatives it has implemented see PBC/2/SLE/1 (3 December 2007). For a discussion of the PBC see C Stahn, 'Institutionalising Brahimi's "Light Footprint": A Comment on the Role and Mandate of the Peacebuilding Commission' (2005) 2 *International Organizations Law Review* 403.

[225] For a good discussion of the PBC's contribution to the dissemination of liberal democratic standards to post conflict societies see R Jenkins, 'The UN Peacebuilding Commission and the Dissemination of International Norms' (June 2008) Working Paper 38, Regional and Global Axes of Conflict.

7

The International Community and the Occupation of Iraq

1. INTRODUCTION

NOTWITHSTANDING THE 'LIGHT footprint' approach to the reconstruction of Afghanistan, the peacebuilding operations in Kosovo and East Timor indicated that the future format for the reconstruction of post-conflict societies would be not just inherently liberal in design but also UN led: the UN would utilise its Chapter VII powers in order to reconstruct post-conflict societies upon a liberal basis.

At least in terms of conditions on the ground, the situation in Iraq after the 2003 invasion was very similar to that in Kosovo and East Timor. All were post-conflict societies exhibiting similar pernicious features; serious abuses of fundamental human rights; profound internal security concerns; the disintegration of institutions of government; and the breakdown of the rule of law. Like in post-conflict Kosovo and East Timor, the international community was heavily involved in the reconstruction of Iraq, undertaking a substantial programme for reform in an attempt to craft a state that demonstrates respect for the liberal values of democracy, human rights and the rule of law. Like in Kosovo and East Timor, the intention was to reproduce a state typical of any Western-style liberal democracy.

However, there is a very significant difference between the liberal reconstruction of Iraq and the liberal reconstructions of Kosovo and East Timor. The difference is legal, rather than factual. Unlike Kosovo and East Timor, the liberal reconstruction of Iraq was not conducted under an exclusive UN Security Council mandate. Instead, those conducting the liberal reconstruction of Iraq were regarded as occupiers (as opposed to administrators like in Kosovo and East Timor) and so subject to the international law of belligerent occupation.[1]

The significance of this status lies in the fact that the law of occupation – codified principally in the Hague Regulations 1907 and the Fourth Geneva Convention 1949 – imposes a legal framework that is extremely

[1] This is in contradistinction to Kosovo and East Timor, where the international law of belligerent occupation had no application.

reluctant to allow an occupier to make alterations to the legal or political framework of an occupied territory. The law of occupation perceives the occupier to be only a temporary custodian that is required to maintain the status quo during the (limited) period between the end of military hostilities and the conclusion of a final peace treaty, when the defeated government will resume control. Thus, according to the law of occupation the occupant does not possess any general power to make permanent changes to the political or legal framework of the occupied territory. Such decisions are instead reserved for the displaced sovereign. In this sense, the law of occupation can be regarded as a product of the international society and an attempt to protect its core values of sovereign equality and non-intervention in domestic affairs. Consequently, because the law of occupation is so restrictive, many of the sweeping political and legal reforms imposed by the occupiers in Iraq must be regarded as unlawful. In short, the liberal reconstruction of a previously authoritarian state is inimical to the requirements of the law of occupation.

This being said, the occupying powers did suggest that other sources of authority existed that could justify the implementation of reforms that could not find their legal basis in the law of occupation. These include the contention that an Iraqi sovereign authority consented to the reforms introduced; that developments in international human rights law now enable (or even require) an occupier to pursue liberally orientated reforms; and that the Security Council authorised the occupiers to exceed the strictures of the law of occupation and pursue a programme of liberal reform.

I argue, however, that these alternative sources of legality cannot be regarded as providing a sound legal basis for the introduction of sweeping liberal reforms. Instead, it was the law of occupation that provided the yardstick against which to test the legality of the occupiers' activities. On this basis, many of the profound liberal changes introduced in Iraq were clearly unlawful. However, that the occupiers nevertheless aggressively pursued these liberal reforms regardless of the fact that their conduct clearly went beyond what was permitted by the law of occupation illustrates that for the international community it is liberal values that command normative supremacy; because of the close nexus between the respect for liberal values and the maintenance of international peace and security (the liberal peace thesis), the pursuit of liberal democracy by the international community justifies deviation from norms of international law that frustrate the expansion of the zone of liberal peace. In this sense, the occupation of Iraq therefore provides important insights into the international community's likely (or rather lack of) compliance with principles of international law that inhibit the promotion of liberal democratic standards.

With these issues in mind, this discussion will proceed as follows. In the next section I outline the nature and magnitude of the reforms that were undertaken in Iraq during the period of occupation. In Section 3 I examine the Hague Regulations and Fourth Geneva Convention so as to reveal the scope of reforms an occupier can introduce. Concluding that the law of occupation is very restrictive and only permits at most 'tinkering on the edges of societal reform',[2] in Section 4 I suggest that many of the reforms instituted by the Coalition Provisional Authoity cannot be justified by the law of occupation. To this end, my attention will turn to alternative sources of authority that have been proposed to justify the occupier's actions. In Section 5 I conclude by discussing the impact of the international community upon international law where provisions of international law do not allow for the dissemination of liberal values.

2. THE COALITION PROVISIONAL AUTHORITY AND THE LIBERAL RECONSTRUCTION OF IRAQ

By 1 May 2003 the Iraqi army had been substantially defeated and Saddam Hussein's government had relinquished control over the territory and population to coalition forces. Consequently, on 8 May 2003 the United States (US) and the United Kingdom (UK) informed the UN Security Council that they had established the Coalition Provisional Authority (CPA) to provide for the provisional administration of Iraq (the CPA was formally established on 21 April 2003).[3] On 16 May 2003 Paul Bremer, the Administrator of the CPA, promulgated the first CPA Regulation, which conferred on the CPA all the powers of temporary government to conduct the administration.[4] Indeed, it was determined that all of the CPA's future Regulations and Orders would 'take precedence over all other laws and publications to the extent such other laws are inconsistent'.[5]

Although the CPA only exercised these powers for just over 14 months (the CPA was dissolved on 28 June 2004),[6] during this period it exercised its governmental powers extensively, formulating a series of Orders and Regulations that radically altered the political, legal, economic and social landscape of Iraq. From the briefest examination of these instruments the intentions of the CPA become clear: to eliminate the Ba'ath regime whilst

[2] D Scheffer, 'Beyond Occupation Law' (2003) 97 *American Journal of International Law* 842, 851.

[3] Letter from the Permanent Representative of the United Kingdom and the United States to the United Nations, Addressed to the President of the Security Council, UN Doc S/2003/538 (8 May 2003).

[4] '[The CPA is] vested with all executive, legislative and judicial authority necessary to achieve its objectives': CPA/REG/2003/1 (16 May 2003).

[5] ibid.

[6] Although Roberts argues that the period of occupation may have in fact been longer on the basis that the occupiers remained physically present in Iraq and may have continued to exercise effective control over Iraqi territory: A Roberts, 'The End of Occupation: Iraq 2004' (2005) 54 *ICLQ* 27.

simultaneously establishing the necessary foundations so that Iraq could be transformed into a liberal state which demonstrates respect for human rights, the rule of law and democracy; '[t]he ultimate goal for Iraq is a durable peace for a unified and stable, democratic Iraq that is underpinned by new and protected freedoms and a growing market economy'.[7]

Elimination of the Ba'ath regime was an immediate concern. On the same day that the CPA announced its establishment and the remit of its powers it issued Order Number 1, which was entitled the 'De-Ba'athification of Iraq Society'.[8] This Order required that the Ba'ath Party be quickly 'disestablished', 'eliminating the party's structures and removing its leadership from positions of authority and responsibility in Iraqi society'.[9] All senior and junior affiliates of the party were removed and barred from future employment in the public sector.[10] This was later extended to cover all governmental entities that had been used by the Ba'ath party 'to oppress the Iraqi people and as institutions of torture, repression and corruption',[11] such as the Iraqi army.[12] This radical de-Ba'athification programme was considered necessary in order to illustrate to Ba'athist loyalists that such a form of governance was unacceptable and to reassure the Iraqi people that they could embrace liberal democracy without the threat of Ba'athist leaders returning to power.[13]

To fully complete this process of 'de-Bathification' it was also necessary for the CPA to undertake a thorough revision of the existing legislative framework, engineered by the Ba'ath regime to suppress political opponents and perpetuate religious and ethical divisions, and to repeal those laws which were contrary to fundamental human rights. In addition, the CPA also began enacting legislative reforms in order to meet obligations under international human rights law. The CPA created the Ministry of

[7] 'An Historic Review of the CPA Accomplishments 2003–2004', available at: pdf.usaid.gov/pdf_docs/PCAAB654.pdf. In fact, the CPA made these objectives quite clear in its first regulation: 'The CPA shall exercise powers of government temporarily in order to provide for the effective administration of Iraq during the period of transitional administration, to restore conditions of security and stability, to create conditions in which the Iraqi people can freely determine their own political future, including by advancing efforts to restore and establish national and local institutions for representative governance and facilitating economic recovery and sustainable reconstruction and development': ibid at section 1(1).

[8] CPA/ORD/2003/01 (16 May 2003).

[9] ibid.

[10] ibid.

[11] CPA/ORD/2003/02 (23 May 2003).

[12] The CPA established a 'new Iraqi army' in its place complete with a new system of ranks, command structures and civilian relations: CPA/ORD/2003/22 (8 August 2003). This new army was overseen by a new Ministry of Defence, established 21 March 2004: CPA/ORD/2004/67 (21 March 2004).

[13] Order Number 1 (2003) stated that the CPA would 'ensure that the representative government in Iraq is not threatened by Ba'athist elements returning to power and that those in positions of authority in the future are acceptable to the people of Iraq': s 1(1). In addition, all aspects of the party were removed from public life and all Ba'athist symbols were removed and banned from public display.

Human Rights on 19 February 2004 to coordinate and oversee this task of repeal and replace.[14] Furthermore, as the occupation came to an end (when full sovereign powers were transferred to the interim Iraqi administration), the CPA drafted an interim constitution (the Transitional Administrative Law) that sought to provide Iraqi citizens with a bill of rights, and which the interim administration was required to respect.[15] Equally importantly, the interim constitution guaranteed a qualified, independent and impartial judicial process (in both civil and criminal proceedings) to vindicate protected rights and render them effective, and to uphold the rule of law which the CPA had sought to establish.[16]

Significantly, the interim constitution also committed Iraq to a democratic future, requiring that the Iraqi administration hold free elections no later than 31 January 2005, where 'the system of government in Iraq shall be republican, federal, democratic, and pluralistic'.[17] Moreover, the interim constitution charged this new democratic government with the responsibility of crafting a 'permanent and legitimate constitution' so that Iraq could finally achieve 'full democracy'.[18]

In addition to these political and legislative adjustments, the CPA was required to introduce an economic structure orientated by capitalist theory and premised upon economic liberalism, where the pursuit of individual interest in a free market was considered to be an essential precondition for any durable liberal democracy.[19] The economic policy endorsed by the Ba'ath regime, in contrast, was 'avowedly socialist' and so 'redolent with social values',[20] prohibiting the foreign ownership of, or investment in, real property, imposing high levels of taxation (45 per cent), and reserving strong central government control over the regulation and organisation of the public sector. Thus, for Iraq to be transformed into a liberal democracy it was necessary to engage in a profound market-orientated economic adjustment, taking a 'leap into robust capitalism'.[21]

[14] CPA/ORD/2004/60 (19 February 2004).

[15] This included, inter alia, freedom of expression (Article 13(B)), freedom of peaceful assembly (Article 13(C)) and the freedom of thought, conscience and religious belief and practice (Article 13(F)).

[16] Article 15. The CPA had already established the new Central Criminal Court (to hear serious criminal cases) and the Iraqi Special Tribunal (to hear alleged crimes against humanity), complete with special procedures to ensure fairness of trial and guarantee adherence to the rule of law; see CPA/ORD/2003/13 (18 June 2003) and CPA/ORD/2003/48 (10 December 2003) respectively.

[17] Article 4 Transitional Administrative Law.

[18] ibid, preamble.

[19] Indeed, Administrator Bremer considered the reform of Iraq's 'closed, dead-end [economic] system' as the 'most immediate priority': Administrator Bremer, *Address at the World Economic Forum* (23 June 2003), transcript available at: reliefweb.int/report/iraq/chief-us-administrator-iraq-reviews-progress-plans-iraq-reconstruction.

[20] C McCarthy, 'The Paradox of the International Law of Military Occupation: Sovereignty and the Reformation of Iraq' (2005) 10 *Journal of Conflict and Security Law* 43, 52.

[21] Scheffer, 'Beyond Occupation Law' (n 2) at 849.

Indeed, the CPA acknowledged the need for a 'transition from a non-transparent centrally planned economy to a market economy characterised by a substantial economic growth through the establishment of a dynamic private sector'.[22] In this context, Order 39 provided for the foreign ownership of, and investment in, real property and for foreign investors to be subject to 'national treatment'.[23] Similarly, the CPA reduced taxation to 15 per cent[24] and introduced a comprehensive programme for privatisation,[25] allowing market economics to be responsible for the supply of public services. As McCarthy summarises,

> there is a marked difference between the structure of Iraq's economic system before and after the war. At a general level, the change is from a centrally controlled, protectionist socialist economic dispensation to a capitalist, privatised and free trade economic model. Indeed, two more diametrically opposed economic policies are hard to envisage.[26]

Evidently, the magnitude of the political, legal and economic reforms undertaken during the period of occupation can be hardly overstated. As Fox neatly puts it, the changes wrought by the CPA were so extensive 'that it is no exaggeration to describe the CPA as having engaged in a social engineering project in Iraq'.[27] Importantly, though, Security Council Resolution 1483 made it quite clear that the CPA was in fact an 'occupying authority' in Iraq and so subject to the law of occupation.[28] As I will now illustrate, the law of occupation is extremely reluctant to allow an external power to introduce changes to the political and legal framework of an occupied territory.

3. THE LAW OF OCCUPATION AS A PRODUCT OF THE INTERNATIONAL SOCIETY

3.1 Hague Regulations

Article 43 of the Hague Regulations is regarded as the 'gist of the law of occupation',[29] providing the occupying power with a 'mini-constitution'[30] of how to administer the territory.

[22] CPA/ORD/2003/39 (19 September 2003).
[23] ibid.
[24] CPA/ORD/2004/49 (19 February 2004).
[25] See generally House of Commons Research Paper, *Iraq – The Law of Occupation*, 03/51 (2 June 2003), available at: www.parliament.uk/briefing-papers/RP03-51.
[26] McCarthy, 'The Paradox of the International Law of Military Occupation' (n 20) at 54–55.
[27] G Fox, 'The Occupation of Iraq' (2005) 36 *Georgetown Journal of International Law* 195, 208.
[28] SC Res 1483 (22 May 2003).
[29] E Benvenisti, *The International Law of Belligerent Occupation* (Princeton NJ/Woodstock, Princeton University Press, 2004) 7.
[30] ibid at 9.

> The authority of the legitimate power having in fact passed into the hands of the occupant, the latter shall take all the measures in his power to restore and ensure, as far as possible, public order and [civil life], while respecting, unless absolutely prevented, the laws in force in the country.

Although Article 43 binds only those states that are signatories to the Hague Regulations, undoubtedly this provision is reflected in customary international law.[31] International law therefore imposes two obligations upon any state that exercises effective control over foreign territory:[32] 1) a positive obligation to restore and ensure, so far as is possible, public order and civil life in the occupied territory; and 2) a negative obligation that requires that whilst in pursuit of this objective the occupier must, unless absolutely prevented, respect the laws in force in the country.

The phrasing of Article 43 suggests that the occupier must only respect local legislation when acting to restore and ensure public order and civil life. However, this is an erroneous interpretation of Article 43. Instead, these two obligations are distinct. Rather than being read together, Article 43 should be instead regarded as providing a general rule concerning the permissible legislative powers of the occupying power.[33] Indeed, in the Brussels Declaration (the *travaux préparatoires* of the Hague Regulations) the obligation to restore and ensure public order and civil life was situated in a different article to the requirement to preserve local legislation. As Sassoli explains, '[t]his means that the obligation to respect local laws (and its exception) must be seen as a general principle'.[34] Importantly, in this chapter I am not concerned with whether or not the CPA discharged its obligation to restore and ensure public order and civil life. Instead, my concern is whether the legislative changes introduced by the CPA were lawful according to Article 43 of the Hague Regulations. This requires us to identify the circumstances in which Article 43 permits an occupying power to make alterations to the legislative framework prevailing in occupied territory.

Evidently, Article 43 establishes a presumption in favour of preserving the *status quo ante bellum*.[35] There is, however, an exception to this pre-

[31] *Trial of the Major War Criminals*, International Military Tribunal in Nuremburg, published in (1947) 41 *American Journal of International Law* 172, 248–49.

[32] Article 43 therefore applies only to territory over which effective control is exercised. In certain instances this may mean only part of a state. In Iraq, however, the CPA was regarded as exercising effective control over all of the territory of Iraq: see House of Commons Research Paper (n 25).

[33] 'The text of Article 43 seems to deal with the respect of local legislation by the occupying power only when the latter restores and ensures public order and civil life, but legislative history and current practice show that that article constitutes a general rule about the legislative powers of an occupying power': M Sassoli, 'Legislation and Maintenance of Public Order and Civil Life by Occupying Powers' (2005) 16 *European Journal of International Law* 661, 663.

[34] ibid at 663, fn 8.

[35] '[Article 43] views occupiers as trustees, preserving the status quo ante bellum': Fox, 'The Occupation of Iraq' (n 27) at 234.

sumption: where an occupying power is absolutely prevented from respecting the laws in force legislative changes can be made. Thus, it is the 'unless absolutely prevented' phrase that provides the yardstick to be used to judge the legality of the CPA's legislative activities. But this necessitates the question: in what circumstances will an occupier be 'absolutely prevented' from respecting the laws in force?

I suggest that our understanding of the exact limitations that this exception imposes benefits from an appreciation of the political philosophy that existed at the time of its creation. When the delegates met at the Hague Peace Conference the nature of international relations was undergoing a profound normative change. As I explained in chapter one, as a result of concerns for international peace and security, a transition was underway from an exclusionary European international society (where only so-called civilised states were considered sovereign equals) towards an inclusive international society, where all states *qua* states were regarded as sovereign equals;[36] at the end of the nineteenth century the first steps were being taken towards constructing a universal international society. The Hague Regulations are, I suggest, both indicative of this normative change and a product of it.[37] The Hague Regulations were created in a political atmosphere that was determined to protect the sovereign equality of all states.

The principle of sovereign equality has important implications for an occupying power. Inherent to the principle of sovereign equality is that when one sovereign state occupies another sovereign state, the occupying state only acquires temporary authority over that territory, not sovereign title. This is part of the international society's determination to prevent the capture of sovereign title through the use of force; 'the foundation upon which the entire law of occupation is based is the inalienability of sovereignty through the actual or threatened use of force'.[38] Thus, the occupier has only a de facto power; it is the displaced sovereign that possesses de

[36] 'The Hague Peace Conferences at the end of the 19th Century were the first major multilateral negotiations to include representatives from non-European and non-Western powers on an equal basis . . . As such, they represent an important evolutionary step from what had hitherto been known as the "public law of Europe" toward a more inclusive international law among formally equal sovereign states from every region of the world': B Brown, 'Intervention, Self-Determination, Democracy and the Residual Responsibilities of the Occupying Power in Iraq' (2004) 11 *University of California, Davis Journal of International Law and Policy* 23, 32.

[37] 'A leading feature of the Hague System was its approach toward universality. Whereas the first conference was attended by only twenty-six states and was predominantly European in composition, the second involved representatives of forty-four states, including the bulk of Latin American republics . . . This was a significant step toward broadening the focus of international diplomacy, toward escaping the increasingly unrealistic European-fixation, and toward defining more accurately the boundaries of the community of nations with whose problems statesmen had to deal': I Claude Jr, *Swords into Ploughshares: The Problems and Process of International Organization* (New York, Random House, 1971) 21.

[38] Benvenisti, *The International Law of Belligerent Occupation* (n 29) at 5.

jure authority to administer the territory and so retains reversionary ownership. All in all, the principle of sovereignty itself requires that any occupation must be transitory. As the occupant is not the de jure sovereign, he is merely a trustee who must preserve the territory until the de jure sovereign is returned to power to resume active control.[39] For this reason, unlike the displaced sovereign, the occupant has no interest in how the people are governed and certainly has no power to interfere in how their lives are regulated. An occupying power is therefore an 'inactive custodian',[40] a 'disinterested occupier'.[41] This is what Fox calls the 'conservationist principle'.[42]

However, this being said, it was always accepted that there was one legitimate area of concern for an occupying power: maintaining the security of the occupying forces during the period of occupation. The occupant can therefore make changes to the existing legislative framework where the security of the occupying forces necessitates such change. Consequently, the 'absolutely prevented' test of Article 43 has always been interpreted as military necessity: '[t]he supreme authority of the occupant is not sovereignty and, therefore, he has no right to make changes in institutions, laws or administration other than those which are demanded by military necessity'.[43] Thus the Hague Regulations, imbued with the desire to protect state sovereignty, only allow an occupying power to introduce reforms to the territory of an occupied state where military necessity demands. To put the matter differently, an occupying power will only be 'absolutely prevented' from respecting domestic legislation in the event of military necessity:

> [i]t was certainly the intention of those who framed the Hague Convention that the occupier's law-making powers could be exercised only where it was a matter of military necessity that they should and not merely where expedient to do so.[44]

[39] '[A]t the turn of the twentieth century the law of occupation functioned as a pact between heads of state, providing that if one leader was temporarily ousted, a stand-in would operate as trustee, handing the territory back to the rightful ruler once hostilities had ended': M Patterson, 'Who's Got the Title? or, The Remnants of Debellatio in Post-Invasion Iraq' (2006) 47 *Harvard International Law Journal* 467, 469.

[40] E Benvenisti, 'Water Conflicts During the Occupation of Iraq' (2003) 97 *American Journal of International Law* 860, 863.

[41] ibid.

[42] Fox 'The Occupation of Iraq' (n 27) at 295.

[43] The Judge Advocate General's School, *Law of Belligerent Occupation* (1944) 37. Consequently, '[t]he law of belligerent occupation is an attempt to substitute for chaos some kind of order, however harsh it may be': A McNair and A Watts, *The Legal Effects of War* (Cambridge, Cambridge University Press, 1966) 371.

[44] P Rowe, *Defence: The Legal Implications* (London, Brassey's *Defence* Publishers, 1987) 184. '[T]he interests of the occupant are paramount and . . . every act and measure undertaken by military government has to be judged by the yardstick of military necessity': H McCoubrey and ND White, *International Law and Armed Conflict* (Aldershot, Dartmouth 1992) 264.

Article 43 is therefore 'exceedingly restrictive'.[45] Certainly, its approach to legislative change lies very uncomfortably with the idea of an occupation being humanitarian rather than belligerent;[46] this being where a state does not occupy a territory in order to enhance its bargaining power when concluding a peace treaty, for example, but instead seeks to liberate a population from tyranny and suffering. Article 43 would strictly prohibit such humanitarian occupations. The law of occupation would prevent radical overhaul of a legislative framework that violates human rights and would certainly preclude the *introduction* of new laws designed to protect fundamental human rights. In light of this, the only conclusion is that those legislative changes introduced in Iraq that were designed to protect individual rights would be unlawful. Properly construed, Article 43 would only justify the repeal of existing Iraqi laws and the introduction of new laws that were strictly necessary to protect military forces operating within the occupied territory. This would include, for example, the CPA's introduction of legislation that prohibited the carrying of weapons and the suspension of certain liberties, such as the holding of public assemblies.[47]

This being said, there are those that have suggested alternative interpretations of Article 43, arguing that Article 43 is more permissive of legislative change. In particular, Western commentators have argued that Article 43 does not require an occupier 'to respect laws in force in the country to the extent of respecting laws which are contrary to natural justice';[48] or that Article 43 permits legislative changes where there is 'sufficient justification' to do so;[49] or where changes are considered 'reasonable';[50] or where the 'welfare' of the population demands alteration.[51] Notably, Dinstein has suggested a 'sincerity test', where legislative measures can be introduced providing the intended reforms operate in the occupying power's native territory; the test for legality is therefore 'whether or not the occupant is equally concerned about his own population'.[52] If this interpretation is correct, where 'the existence of a law

[45] Y Dinstein, 'Legislation under Article 43 of the Hague Regulations: Belligerent Occupation and Peacebuilding', Occasional Paper, Program on Humanitarian Policy and Conflict Research, Harvard University (Fall 2004) 4, available at: www.hpcrresearch.org/sites/default/files/publications/OccasionalPaper1.pdf.

[46] The phrase 'humanitarian occupation' was coined by Fox: G Fox, *Humanitarian Occupation* (Cambridge, Cambridge University Press, 2008).

[47] CPA/ORD/2003/19 (9 July 2003).

[48] R Jennings, 'Government in Commission' (1946) 23 *British Yearbook of International Law* 112, 112 at fn 1.

[49] E Feilchenfeld, *The International Economic Law of Belligerent Occupation* (Washington DC, Carnegie Endowment for International Peace, 1942) 89.

[50] M Greenspan, *The Modern Law of Land Warfare* (Berkeley CA, Stanford University Press, 1959) at 224 ('International law allows a reasonable latitude in such circumstances').

[51] H-P Gerson, 'War, Conquered Territory and Military Occupation in the Contemporary International Legal System' (1977) 18 *Harvard International Law Journal* 535, 535.

[52] Y Dinstein, 'The International Law of Belligerent Occupation and Human Rights' (1978) 8 *Israel Yearbook on Human Rights* 104, 113.

in the occupant's own country will generally serve as evidence of the occupant's lawfulness in introducing a similar law in the occupied territory',[53] it would clearly provide liberal-minded occupants with the necessary authority to reconstruct the existing legislative framework upon a liberal basis. In essence, it would allow for the reproduction of the legal framework that operates in the state of the occupying power. If correct, such an interpretation of Article 43 would render many of the CPA's liberal legislative reforms lawful.

However, whilst Article 43 'has never been literally interpreted',[54] such a pervasive interpretation is wholly inconsistent with the political spirit that engendered its creation and which indeed runs through the Hague Regulations.[55] It is therefore unsurprising that such a wide interpretation of Article 43 is predominantly located in Western academic material. Beyond this it is the 'military necessity' test that has received most support. For this reason, it is submitted that military necessity is the correct test for permissible legislative changes. In the words of Benvenisti, '[m]ilitary necessity was deemed . . . the sole relevant consideration that could "absolutely prevent" an occupant from maintaining the old order'.[56]

3.2 Fourth Geneva Convention

Article 64 of the Fourth Geneva Convention 1949 elaborates upon the instances in which an occupying power can introduce changes to the legislative framework of an occupied territory

> The penal laws of the occupied territory shall remain in force, with the exception that they may be repealed or suspended by the Occupying Power in cases where they constitute a threat to its security or an obstacle to the application of the present Convention . . .
>
> The Occupying Power may, however, subject the population of the occupied territory to provisions which are essential to enable the Occupying Power to fulfil its obligations under the present Convention, to maintain the orderly government of the territory, and to ensure the security of the occupying Power, of the members and property of the occupying forces or administration, and likewise of the establishments and lines of communication used by them.

It is first necessary to note that paragraph one refers to penal laws only. However, the second paragraph refers to 'provisions' without any quali-

[53] Benvenisti (n 29) at 15.

[54] Feilchenfeld, *The International Economic Law of Belligerent Occupation* (n 49) at 89, fn 102.

[55] Article 3 of the Brussels Declaration 1874, which represents Article 43's initial draft, also emphasises military necessity: '[The occupier can] modify, suspend or replace [the laws in force] where necessity obliges him to do so'.

[56] E Benvenisti, 'The Security Council and the Law of Occupation: Resolution 1483 on Iraq in Historical Perspective' (2004) 4, available at: www.lex.unict.it/stipil2008/documenti/benvenisti.pdf.

fication (and therefore presumably includes administrative laws and even constitutional norms). Indeed, the preparatory work for Article 64 illustrates that 'it is not a mere coincidence that the adjective "penal" is missing in the second paragraph'.[57] Article 64 can be therefore regarded as applying to all legislation.

Some suggest that Article 64 has significantly altered the circumstances in which an occupying power can introduce legislative reforms to an occupied territory. In particular, Benvenisti contends that Article 64 represents a 'departure' from the restrictiveness of Article 43 and has thereby introduced 'innovative elements' into the law of occupation,[58] signalling a more permissive attitude to legislative change. Benvenisti considers that Article 64 represents a fundamental change in focus of the law of occupation. Benvenisti suggests that whilst the Hague Regulations sought to protect the political interests of the displaced sovereign during the period of occupation, the Fourth Geneva Convention focuses upon the population and their protection whilst in the enemy's hands.[59] Specifically, he argues that the Convention provides a bill of rights for the occupied population: a set of internationally recognised guidelines that must be adhered to whilst administering an occupied territory. Thus, the Convention allows (or even mandates) the occupier to adjust legislation in order to ensure that the population is not exposed to discrimination on the grounds of 'race, religion or political opinion' (Article 27), physical or moral coercion (Article 31), collective punishments (Article 33), destruction of personal property (Article 53), or mass or individual forced transfers (Article 49). Existing legislation contrary to these rights must be removed. Indeed, where necessary legislation can be positively introduced in order to protect these rights (in relation to guaranteeing a fair trial, for example). For Benvenisti, therefore, the occupier 'is no longer the disinterested watch guard, but instead a very involved regulator and provider'; 'Article 64 retains little of Hague's Article 43's strong bias against modifying local law'.[60]

That this Convention requires an occupier to respect and protect these enumerated rights has introduced important elements into the law of occupation. Now, an occupier may legislate not only where necessary to protect his military personnel, but also in order to ensure that a certain minimum standard of humanitarian conditions is met. However, as Fox recognises, the rights protected by the Convention are quite narrow: the

[57] Benvenisti (n 29) at 101–3.

[58] ibid at 15.

[59] 'The more humanitarian character of this particular Geneva rule, as opposed to its Hague law predecessor, should be understood in the context of a gradual evolution from a 19th century law of armed conflict, focused on the rights and obligations of states, to a more people-based international humanitarian law in the mid-20th century': Brown, 'Intervention, Self-Determination, Democracy' (n 36) at 37.

[60] Benvenisti, 'The Security Council and the Law of Occupation' (n 56) at 12.

Convention seeks to avoid instances of 'egregious misconduct'.[61] The Convention certainly does not confer the power upon the occupant to make legislative reforms simply because it considers them normatively justifiable. Changes can be made only where it is 'essential to enable' these core human rights to be protected. Thus, rather than relaxing the restrictiveness of Article 43, Article 64 actually reinforces it, providing only an 'amplification'[62] of Article 43 where 'the framers of article 64 took it for granted that it had not exceeded the traditional scope of the occupation legislation'.[63] In this regard, Benvenisti concedes that 'its [Article 64] relevance was lost on international scholars, and article 43 continued to provide the framework for discussing the occupant's prescriptive powers'.[64] Except where changes are essential to protect the exhaustively delineated rights in the Fourth Convention, an occupant is only able to introduce legislative changes where they can be 'justified by the limited objectives of military necessity'.[65]

Thus far my analysis has concerned legislative reforms only. Can an occupant make reforms to the political and legal *institutions* of an occupied territory? The Hague Regulations are silent in relation to institutional change. Presumably, the rights protected by the Fourth Geneva Convention would require institutional as well as legislative changes if necessary to ensure the adequate protection of the guaranteed rights. Examples would include institutional changes to ensure due process in criminal proceedings and humane conditions for detainees. But these are exceptions; is there a general rule relating to the permissibility of institutional change?

Article 47 of the Fourth Geneva Convention does mention institutional changes. It explains that 'protected persons shall not be deprived of the benefits of the present convention by any change introduced, as a result of the occupation of a territory, into the institutions of government of the said territory'. However, this only provides that institutional changes cannot be made where they would deprive protected persons of the benefits conferred by the Fourth Geneva Convention.[66] Article 47 therefore

[61] Fox (n 27) at 243.

[62] R Yingling and R Ginnane, 'The Geneva Conventions of 1949' (1952) 46 *American Journal of International Law* 393, 422.

[63] G Schwarzenberger, *The Law of Armed Conflict* (London, Steven and Sons, 1968) 194. 'Article 64 may be seen as interpreting the expression "unless absolutely prevented" contained in the Hague Regulations': M Sassoli, 'Article 43 of the Hague Regulations and Peace Operations in the Twenty-First Century', Background Paper, International Humanitarian Law Research Initiative (June 2004) 7, available at: www.hpcrresearch.org/sites/default/files/publications/sassoli.pdf.

[64] Benvenisti (n 29) at 106.

[65] Fox (n 27) at 237.

[66] As the International Committee of the Red Cross (ICRC) suggests, '[t]he text is of an essentially humanitarian character; its object is to safeguard human beings and not to protect the political institutions and government machinery as such': ICRC, *1949 Conventions and Additional Protocols, and their Commentaries*, available at: www.icrc.org/IHL.NSF/COM/380-600054?OpenDocument.

provides no guidance as to whether an occupying power can radically transform the political and legal institutions in the occupied territory where such action does not adversely affect the benefits granted to the population by international humanitarian law. Consequently, providing that modifications to institutions do not adversely affect these protected rights, what restrictions are there upon an occupant that wishes to undertake institutional reform? Indeed, what if the occupier considers that institutional changes might be an improvement, where the installation of liberal institutions (for example) would bolster and further the humanitarian objectives of the Geneva Convention?[67] Would such changes be lawful?

Evidently, such an approach would be inimical to the 'conservationist principle which lies at the doctrinal core of occupation law':[68] namely, that the powers of the occupant to introduce changes must be heavily circumscribed because the legitimate authority to make such changes resides with the ousted sovereign.[69] Dinstein thus suggests that because 'there is a disquieting possibility that the structural innovations . . . may take root and have enduring consequences', the occupying power should be proscribed from 'interfering with fundamental institutions of government in the occupied territory'.[70]

Sassoli contends that institutional alterations should be determined against the 'absolutely prevented' test of Article 43 because political institutions are only one aspect of the laws in force of the country.[71] For Sassoli, an occupying authority can interfere in the institutional arrangements of the occupied territory only if demanded by *military necessity*. Unless the occupier can demonstrate military necessity, the occupant may not, for example, transform 'a democratic republic into an absolute monarchy . . . [or] change the regional or racial organizations of an occupied territory'.[72]

If the test for permissible institutional alterations is that of military necessity then it has been suggested that where the 'political system constitutes a

[67] As Picket explains, '[institutional changes] might conceivably be necessary and even an improvement': J Picket (ed), *Commentary, IV Geneva Convention Relative to the Protection of Civilian Persons in Times of War* (Geneva, International Committee of the Red Cross, 1958) 274.

[68] Fox (n 27) at 295.

[69] Dinstein explains that '[t]he structuring of the political institutions is conspicuously a matter that should be undertaken solely by the territorial sovereign': Dinstein, 'Legislation under Article 43 of the Hague Regulations' (n 45) at 10.

[70] ibid. McDougal and Feliciano offer a similar approach, suggesting that 'the occupant's competence to establish and operate processes of governmental administration in the territory occupied does not extend to the reconstruction of the fundamental institutions of the occupied territory': M McDougal and F Feliciano, *Law and Minimum World Public Order* (New Haven CT, Yale University Press, 1961) 767.

[71] Sassoli (n 33) at 671.

[72] Feilchenfeld (n 49) at 89–90. This general prohibition on the changes to the institutions of the occupied territory is called the Fauchille doctrine: P Fauchille, *Traite de droit International Public* (Paris, Rousseau, 1921) 228 ('Comme la situation est eminemment proviso ire, il ne doit pas bouleverser les institutions du pays').

permanent threat to the maintenance and safety of the military forces of the occupant . . . there is [an] "absolute necessity" to abolish it'.[73] For example, the Allied powers' de-Nazification of Germany at the end of the Second World War was justified on this basis. Eradication of all institutions of the Nazi regime was considered lawful on the basis that its continued existence represented a permanent threat to the security of the occupying Allied powers. For this reason, the occupying powers were 'absolutely prevented' from respecting the prevailing (albeit defeated) regime.

Factual parallels between Nazi Germany and Ba'athist Iraq immediately become apparent. Relations between the Ba'athist regime and the occupying forces were extremely antagonistic. Ba'athist loyalists refused to acknowledge the authority of the occupying powers and resisted the occupation violently. Given this security situation (arguably analogous to the security situation in Nazi Germany), can the de-Ba'athification of Iraq be justified upon the same legal basis: namely, that the prevailing yet defeated regime posed a constant and permanent threat to military security and therefore its removal was a military necessity and thus within the meaning of Article 43? In response, three important points need to be identified:

1. It is disputed whether or not this doctrine exists. This is because the viability of this doctrine is based exclusively on the German precedent. However, as I reveal below, a more convincing argument is that the Allied occupation of Germany was conducted under *debellatio*, not the law of occupation. The issue was not that the Nazi regime posed a permanent security threat to the Allied forces but that the regime had been totally defeated and effectively obliterated. It did not exist in any substantive form and so could not therefore pose any threat to the security of the military. Instead, Germany was in a condition of *debellatio*.
2. Even if we concede that this doctrine does exist, *debellatio* would only justify the removal of the regime that poses the threat. At best, this doctrine justifies the removal of the institutions that represent a threat to the security of the military. Thus, whilst undoubtedly the Ba'ath regime represented a security threat to the occupying forces, this could not justify the installation of a *new* political regime, irrespective of how normatively attractive that new regime is. This doctrine could not therefore provide the CPA with a source of authority for its liberal reconstruction of Iraqi infrastructure.
3. This doctrine is objectionable for good policy reasons. All occupiers are likely to have an uneasy relationship with any remaining governmental institutions during the period of occupation (it is, after all, termed a *belligerent* occupation). By their very nature, occupations engender an

[73] E Schwenk, 'Legislative Power of the Military Occupant under Article 43, Hague Regulations' (1945) 54 *Yale Law Journal* 393, 403.

antagonistic relationship. In practicality, this doctrine could be utilised by any occupier to circumvent the strictures of the law of occupation. Indeed, this doctrine could be exploited (where the threat posed by the existing regime is exaggerated or simply fabricated) to the extent that the law of occupation would cease to exist. State sovereignty would therefore be vulnerable and the population's existing way of life threatened.[74] To allow such a subjective exception would confer upon an occupant a 'license to transform . . . [whereby] the door would be wide open for abuse by aggressive and benevolent armies alike'.[75]

4. ALTERNATIVE SOURCES OF AUTHORITY

It would be a mistake to conclude that the Hague Regulations and Fourth Geneva Convention are so restrictive that they would render unlawful all of the legislative and institutional reforms undertaken by the CPA. Where reforms were made on the basis that they were demanded by military necessity or because they were necessary to secure protection of those rights outlined in the Geneva Convention, they would be lawful.

Whilst this is true, such was the magnitude of the CPA reforms it is quite apparent that many of the more radical changes introduced cannot be justified on the basis of the Hague Regulations or Fourth Geneva Convention. As Fox explains, the law of occupation 'would likely find most of the CPA's reforms invalid'.[76] This is particularly apposite in relation to the economic reforms undertaken by the CPA. It is very difficult to see how such reforms are connected to either military necessity or humanitarian concerns.

However, are there any other sources of authority that may render these changes lawful? Four possible alternative sources of authority for the liberal reforms present themselves. Each will be discussed in turn.

4.1 *Debellatio*

> [The] minimum content of any definition of *debellatio* is that one of the belligerent states has been defeated so totally that its adversary or adversaries are able to decide alone what the fate of the territory of that State and of the State authorities will be.[77]

[74] 'The law of occupation prohibits sweeping changes to the occupied state's structure for good reason. The law is designed to at least partially preserve the occupied state's status quo and with it the population's way of life': Patterson, 'Who's Got the Title?' (n 39) at 473.

[75] Scheffer (n 2) at 851.

[76] Fox (n 27) at 240.

[77] K-M Meyn, *Debellatio*, in R Benhardt (ed), *The Encyclopaedia of Public International Law* (Max Planck Institute, 1992) 969.

Debellatio therefore describes both a factual and legal state of affairs. Factually, it 'refers to a situation in which a party to a conflict has been totally defeated in war, its national institutions have disintegrated, and none of its allies continue militarily to challenge the enemy on its behalf'.[78] Legally, *debellatio* 'pass[es] sovereign title to the occupant in case of total defeat and disintegration of the governing regime'.[79] Thus, where there is *debellatio* there is no law of occupation; the strictures of the law of occupation are completely avoided. As Bhuta explains, '*occupatio bellica* develops a legal status defined in contraposition to debellatio'.[80] Instead, the conqueror will possess sovereignty over the territory and the population and be entitled to administer it as the de jure sovereign without any limitations.

The case of Nazi Germany is perhaps the most widely cited example of *debellatio*. The defeat of the Nazi Germany at the end of the Second World War was so complete that its 'sovereign identity' was wholly destroyed.[81] 'Germany was reduced to a condition of *debellatio*, in which all its state institutions and constitutive order were destroyed and its population exhausted and demoralized'.[82] Thus, sovereign power passed to the Allied forces who could then reconstruct Germany as they considered fit. Can this argument be made in relation to Iraq? Was there a complete destruction of the sovereign identity of the Ba'athist regime? If there was, then all the legislative and institutional changes undertaken by the CPA would be lawful as 'debellatio effectively wipes the legal slate clean'.[83] For all intents and purposes, the CPA would have been the sovereign authority in Iraq.

At first glance, there is a strong case for *debellatio* in Iraq. Incontrovertibly, Iraq had been totally defeated. All governmental institutions had disintegrated. Saddam Hussein and his senior officials had all fled office and had either been captured, were in exile or in hiding. Often governments that have been forced out of office still continue to issue decrees and proclamations, conferring the impression that they still consider themselves the legitimate ruler. In Iraq this did not happen. The Ba'ath government was silent, appearing emasculated. Moreover, civil society had broken down, with mass looting and violence being committed with impunity.[84]

However, there is a significant obstacle that would prevent the CPA from being able to rely upon the doctrine of *debellatio*. Importantly, in

[78] Benvenisti (n 29) at 92.

[79] Benvenisti (n 40) at 862.

[80] N Bhuta, 'The Antinomies of Transformative Occupation' (2005) 16 *European Journal of International Law* 721, 725.

[81] Patterson (n 39) at 477.

[82] Bhuta (n 80) at 734.

[83] Patterson (n 39) at 485.

[84] E Schmitt and D Sanger, 'Looting Disrupts Detailed US Plan to Restore Iraq', *New York Times* (19 May 2003), available at: www.nytimes.com/2003/05/19/world/aftereffects-reconstruction-policy-looting-disrupts-detailed-us-plan-restore.html?pagewanted=all&src=pm.

Resolution 1483 the Security Council described the CPA as an 'occupying authority'. As this resolution was adopted under Chapter VII of the UN Charter, this must be regarded as an authoritative determination of the CPA's legal status in Iraq. Indeed, to put the matter beyond any doubt the Council proceeded to demand that the CPA 'comply fully with their obligations under . . . the Geneva Conventions of 1949 and the Hague Regulations of 1907'. For this reason, whilst the doctrine of *debellatio* would have been extremely attractive for the CPA (as it would enable all the changes that they introduced to be legally justified), the CPA never once attempted to justify its actions on the basis of *debellatio*.[85] By virtue of Security Council Resolution 1483, *debellatio* cannot be regarded as a source of authority for the liberal transformation of Iraq.

4.2 IGC and Iraqi Consent

During the period of occupation the CPA established the Iraqi Governing Council (IGC) to facilitate the administration of Iraq. The objective of this Council was to allow the opinions and objections of the Iraqis to be voiced in relation to policies being proposed by the CPA.[86] This Council comprised 25 members, all of which were individually selected by the CPA and most of which had been in exile whilst Saddam Hussein was in power.

A possible source of authority for the reforms introduced by the CPA is that the IGC was able to provide consent to the reforms introduced by the CPA. The argument is that the IGC embodied the sovereignty of Iraq and so could authorise the introduction of any reforms that could not be justified by the military necessity test of the Hague Regulations and Fourth Geneva Convention.

Indeed, the CPA appears to rely on the IGC as a source of authority for many of its most drastic reforms. These have included Order 39, concerning foreign investment, and Order 40 that radically altered the structure of Iraqi banking law. Without any doubt, neither of these economic reforms could be justified under the law of occupation. Significantly, these Orders included statements such as '[h]aving worked closely with the Governing Council to ensure that economic change occurs in a manner acceptable to the people of Iraq' and '[a]cknowledging the Governing Council's desire to bring about significant change to the Iraqi economic system'[87] The implication is that the IGC possessed the power to consent to these reforms and the fact that they

[85] 'No Coalition member, in any event, argued that *debellatio* applied in Iraq': B McGurk, 'A Lawyer in Baghdad' (2004) 8 *The Green Bag* 51, 52. Brett McGurk was a member of the General Counsel to the CPA during the period of occupation.
[86] CPA/REG/2003/06 (13 July 2003).
[87] CPA/ORD/2003/39 (19 September 2003).

did rendered them lawful; in essence, that these orders received the imprimatur of the sovereign.

This argument, though, rests upon whether the IGC could actually be regarded as embodying the sovereignty of Iraq. If the IGC was sovereign then it could have perhaps possessed the capacity to authorise reforms. What would then be necessary is that we look to each reform undertaken by the CPA which cannot be justified on the basis of the Hague Regulations or Fourth Geneva Convention and determine whether the IGC provided its consent to it.

However, before such a question is addressed, it is first necessary to determine whether the IGC did actually embody the sovereignty of Iraq. This is important because historically occupying powers established indigenous governmental regimes and termed them sovereign. The occupying power then instigated many harsh reforms, although imputing responsibility for these reforms to the installed regime on the basis that it was the sovereign authority. In reality, though, such authorities were puppet regimes, exercising little control over the territory and thus could not be regarded as a sovereign authority. As von Glahn explains in the context of puppet regimes, '[t]he experience of both world wars clearly indicated the need of circumventing a variety of ingenious devices by which occupants avoided the observance of rules of international law'.[88]

Ostensibly, it would appear that the IGC was in fact a sovereign authority on the basis that the Security Council, acting under Chapter VII of the UN Charter, determined

> that the [I]GC and its ministers are the principal bodies of the Iraqi administration which, without prejudice to its further evolution, embodies the *sovereignty* of the state of Iraq during the transitional period until an internationally recognized, representative government is established and assumes the responsibilities of the Authority' (emphasis added).[89]

Moreover, Security Council Resolution 1511 '[a]ffirms that the administration of Iraq will be progressively undertaken by the evolving structures of the Iraqi interim administration'.[90] Such proclamations by the Security Council provide the basis for the argument that the IGC represented the sovereign authority in Iraq and thus possessed the legal capacity to consent to the extensive reforms introduced by the CPA.

However, that the Security Council regarded the IGC as a sovereign body was not consistently adopted. For example, in Resolution 1500 the Council

[88] G von Glahn, *The Occupation of Enemy Territory* (Minneapolis MN, University of Minnesota Press, 1957) 74.
[89] SC Res 1511 (16 October 2003).
[90] ibid at para 3.

> welcome[d] the establishment of the broadly representative Governing Council of Iraq on July 13 2003, *as an important step towards the formation* by the people of Iraq of an internationally recognized, representative government that *will* exercise the sovereignty of Iraq (emphasis added).[91]

The use of the future tense in this resolution suggests that the Security Council did not consider the IGC to be a sovereign authority, but merely a temporary body that was part of the process towards the creation of an Iraqi administration that was endowed with sovereign authority. Moreover, in Resolution 1511 the Security Council called for the CPA to 'return governing responsibilities and authorities to the people of Iraq as soon as practicable', which again indicates that the Security Council did not consider the IGC to possess sovereign powers at that time.[92]

The Security Council therefore provided conflicting opinions as to whether the IGC embodied the sovereignty of Iraq. I suggest that this ambiguity should be interpreted in favour of the argument that the IGC *did not* embody the sovereign of Iraq, not least because the practice of the CPA indicates that it did not itself regard the IGC as a sovereign authority. Instead, the CPA perceived the IGC as being subservient to it. For example, CPA Regulation 6 (which created the IGC) did not adjust its previous description of itself as being vested with all executive, legislative and judicial authority in Iraq. In fact, Regulation 6 only required the CPA to 'consult and coordinate' with the IGC. In this sense, it would appear that the CPA regarded the IGC as an advisory authority whose objections to CPA decisions could be ignored.[93] In this sense, the CPA wielded a veto power over the activities of the IGC. Indeed, there are several instances where the Administrator, Paul Bremer, threatened to withhold CPA support for IGC initiatives, a threat that was considered fatal to the proposal. 'In sum, the Governing Council appeared to play a purely advisory role'.[94] In light of this, it is very difficult to sustain the argument that the IGC was a sovereign authority during the period of occupation. To this end, the IGC was incapable of providing consent to (and therefore authorising) CPA reforms which could not be justified under the law of occupation.

[91] SC Res 1500 (14 August 2003).

[92] Indeed, statements made in the Security Council also indicate that the IGC did not embody the sovereignty of Iraq. The Chinese representative on the Security Council, for example, explained that during the period of occupation the primary goal in Iraq was the 'restoration' of its sovereignty. Such statements were typical: UN Doc S/PV.4844 (16 October 2003).

[93] Debating Resolution 1500, which welcomed the creation of the IGC, the Mexican Ambassador explained that 'welcome does not constitute legal recognition. Nor should it be interpreted as endorsement. It is not, because the Governing Council is still under the authority of the occupying powers': UN Doc S/PV.4808 (14 August 2003) 5.

[94] Fox (n 27) at 210.

4.3 International Human Rights Law

It is firmly established in international law that where a state exercises effective control over the territory of another state its obligations under international human rights law (conventional or customary) continue to apply.[95] As occupying powers are in effective control of territory, international human rights law binds an occupying power vis-à-vis the local population; an occupying power must protect the internationally recognised human rights of those individuals in territory under its effective control.

This being said, there are those that argue that because an occupation occurs in the context of an armed conflict, as *lex specialis* international humanitarian law provides for automatic derogation from international human rights law, which therefore ceases to apply.[96] However, in the words of Sassoli, 'UN practice and judicial decisions clearly indicate that International Human Rights Law binds an occupying power with respect to the population of an occupied territory'.[97] Sure, in occupied territory provisions of international humanitarian law will apply as *lex specialis* to the *specific* issues they regulate (provisions relating to the security of the occupying power, for example), and this will mean that in these circumstances an occupying power is relieved from its obligation to protect certain internationally recognised human rights (such as the right to freely assemble in public places). But the point is that in relation to issues that international humanitarian law is of no concern, such as the freedom of the press or the right to social security, the protections afforded by international human rights law will continue to apply.

The consequence is that there are instances where an occupier will be legally entitled (or rather required) to make changes to an occupied territory in order to comply with international human rights standards.[98] Of course, this would include the repeal of rights-offensive legislation. But more importantly it would also include the introduction of new legisla-

[95] *Al-Skeini and others v United Kingdom*, Application no 55721/07 (2011) 53 EHRR 18. See generally M Milanovic, *Extraterritorial Application of Human Rights Treaties: Law, Principles, and Policy* (Oxford, Oxford University Press, 2011)

[96] Israel maintains this position. See A Roberts, 'Prolonged Military Occupations: the Israeli-Occupied Territories since 1967' (1990) 84 *American Journal of International Law* 44, 71-72.

[97] Sassoli (n 63) at 13.

[98] As Sassoli explains, 'certain other changes may be necessary to respect international human rights law': M Sassoli, 'Occupation and Peacebuilding, Background Paper, International Humanitarian Law Research Initiative' (November 2003) 4, available at: ihl.ihlresearch.org/_data/n_0002/resources/live/briefing3294.pdf. Note that this is not a discretionary power; international human rights law requires that the occupant protect these rights.

tion in order to protect internationally recognised human rights.[99] For example, in Iraq the CPA introduced legislation to ensure due process in criminal proceedings, to prohibit discrimination by public officials and to enhance the supervision of the judiciary.[100] Indeed, it may be necessary to remove old and establish new institutions in order to guarantee these protected rights.[101] Examples include the creation of the Central Criminal Court, the Special Tribunal to try former regime members and the Human Rights Ministry. As Sassoli explains, 'one may even go so far as to allow the occupying power to replace abolished rules and institutions when genuinely necessary to protect international human rights standards'.[102]

The relationship between international human rights and the law of occupation should be cast in terms of the 'absolutely prevented' test contained within Article 43 of the Hague Regulations; the occupant will be considered 'absolutely prevented' from respecting local laws and institutions where they are contrary to international human rights law.[103] Clearly, developments in international human rights law have expanded the area in which the occupying power will be regarded as absolutely prevented from respecting the prevailing legislative framework and institutional infrastructure of the occupied territory. In particular, the rights protected by international human rights law go well beyond those protected by international humanitarian law (specifically the Fourth Geneva Convention) and so will permit (or necessitate) greater changes to an occupied territory that has a history of human rights abuses (such as Iraq).

[99] cf Fox (n 27) at 210 ('commentators who argue for a human rights exception to the conservationist principle do so in order to allow for the repeal of offensive laws. None speaks of replacement legislation').

[100] CPA/MEM/03 (18 June 2003), CPA/ORD/07 (9 June 2003) and CPA/ORD15 (23 June 2010) respectively.

[101] For example, Article 2 of the International Covenant on Civil and Political Rights (1966) requires parties to the Covenant to take effective steps to guarantee protected rights. The Human Rights Committee's General Comment on Article 2 explains that 'article 2 of the Covenant generally leaves it to the States parties concerned to choose their method of implementation in their territories within the framework set out in that article. It recognizes, in particular, that the implementation does not depend solely on constitutional or legislative enactments, which in themselves are often not *per se* sufficient. The Committee considers it necessary to draw the attention of the States parties to the fact that the obligation under the Covenant is not confined to the respect of human rights, but that States parties have also undertaken to ensure the enjoyment of these rights to all individuals under their jurisdiction. This aspect calls for specific activities by the States parties to enable individuals to enjoy their rights': Human Rights Committee, General Comment Number 3: Implementation at the National Level (Article 2) (1981) para 1.

[102] Sassoli, 'Occupation and Peacebuilding' (n 98) at 4. Indeed, Sassoli further suggests that where an ousted regime has previously subjected the people to treatment contrary to human rights law 'an occupying power may even by recognised to exercise (provisionally) the latitude granted to States on how they implement the prescriptions of international human rights law': ibid at 5.

[103] R Buchan, 'The International Community and the Occupation of Iraq' (2008) 12 *Journal of Conflict and Security Law* 37.

However, this being said, it must be remembered that the emergence of international human rights law does not provide an occupying power with carte blanche to make all the changes that it considers normatively desirable. This is particularly salient in relation to liberal states that become occupying powers and wish to introduce legislative and institutional reforms in order to realise the liberal ideal. The limitations to permissible reforms are to be found in the prevailing standards that bind the occupying powers under international human rights law. The consequence is that many changes that are necessary to transform a state into a liberal democracy cannot be justified on the basis of developments in international human rights law. Thus, whilst international human rights law has certainly reduced the degree of deference that an occupier owes to the deposed regime, quite demonstrably it would not permit the liberal reconstruction of a formerly non-liberal state.

4.4 Security Council Resolution 1483

The final possible source of authority for CPA reforms that cannot be justified by the Hague Regulations, the Fourth Geneva Convention or developments in international human rights law is Security Council authorisation. Specifically, that the Security Council authorised the CPA to deviate from the requirements of international law and instead promote liberal democratic standards in Iraq:

> [t]he only possible justification under international law for an occupying power to introduce such changes [liberal democratic reforms] would be to have such changes prescribed, or at least explicitly authorised, by a UN Security Council resolution;[104]

> [i]t is only with the authorization and support of the United Nations that the occupying powers can legitimately claim the time and international support needed to sustain any realistic hope of achieving the democratization of Iraq.[105]

Indeed, the CPA sought to justify its liberal reconstruction on the basis that it had been authorised by the Security Council. Under Article 103 UN Charter (which provides that states' obligations under the UN Charter prevail over other treaty obligations) the Security Council can 'carve out'[106] those restrictive parts of the law of occupation and confer powers on the occupying power that would permit more extensive reforms. The CPA insists that this was the approach adopted by the Security Council;

[104] Sassoli (n 98) at 5.
[105] Brown (n 36) at 45.
[106] T Grant, 'Iraq How to Reconcile Conflicting Obligations of Occupation and Reform' (2003) American Society of International Law Insight, available at: www.asil.org/insigh107a1.cfm.

that the transformation of the Iraqi political, legal and economic system (and thus deviation from the law of occupation) was authorised by the UN Security Council, thus providing it with the necessary authority to implement liberal democratic reforms which could not find their legal basis elsewhere.[107] For example, in relation to the economic reforms undertaken, described by McCarthy 'as inimical to the concept of a socialist system mandated by the [Ba'ath] Iraqi constitution and run counter to some of the most basic provisions of Iraq's constitutional law and Commercial Code',[108] the British government explained that 'SC [Security Council] resolution 1483 provides a sound legal basis for the CPA investment Orders'.[109] As Zwanenburg observes, '[t]his strongly suggests that in their own opinion these actions and positions went beyond the limits of the law of occupation', but that the CPA 'explicitly or implicitly relied on Security Council authorisation and not on the law of occupation to justify their actions'.[110]

This notwithstanding, it is also true that paragraph 5 of Resolution 1483 also demanded that the CPA, as an 'occupying power', 'comply fully with [its] obligations under . . . the Geneva Conventions of 1949 and the Hague Regulations of 1907'. This determination comes immediately after the requirement that the CPA promote the welfare of the Iraqi people and assist them in creating a representative government in Iraq.[111] The consequence is that Resolution 1483 becomes 'rather puzzling . . . looking in two alternative directions simultaneously',[112] where the extent of the powers conferred upon the occupants is 'difficult to reconcile'.[113] On the one hand to promote liberal reforms yet on the other to adhere to international

[107] See Resolution 1483 which required the CPA 'to promote the welfare of the Iraqi people through the effective administration of the territory, including in particular working towards the restoration of conditions of security and stability and the creation of conditions in which the Iraqi people can freely determine their own political future'. Moreover, Resolution 1500 encouraged the CPA to begin constructing a new political and economic order, including the establishment of 'national institutions of representative government', the promotion of 'economic reconstruction and the conditions for sustainable development' and the promotion of 'legal and judicial reform'.

[108] McCarthy (n 20) at 53.

[109] HC Deb 20 November C. 1304W. Indeed, see the House of Common Research paper which explains that 'the purpose of obtaining a mandate in the form of a Security Council resolution was to evade the legal difficulties if the occupying power sought to move beyond the limited rights conferred by the Hague Regulations and Geneva Convention IX to vary existing arrangements': House of Commons Research Paper (n 25) at 25.

[110] M Zwanenburg, 'Existentialism in Iraq: Security Council Resolution 1483 and the Law of Occupation' (December 2004) 86 *International Review of the Red Cross* 745, 747.

[111] '[The Security Council] calls upon the Authority [CPA] . . . to promote the welfare of the Iraqi people through the effective administration of the territory, including in particular working towards the restoration of conditions of security and stability and the creation of conditions in which the Iraqi people can freely determine their own political future': SC Res 1483 (22 May 2003) para 4.

[112] McCarthy (n 20) at 68.

[113] Zwanenburg, 'Existentialism in Iraq' (n 110) at 766.

obligations that would clearly prevent liberal reforms. Quite clearly, in light of this ambiguity Security Council Resolution 1483 cannot be regarded as providing a clear and unequivocal basis for the extensive liberal reforms pursued in Iraq.[114]

5. CONCLUSION

In this chapter I have argued that the occupation of Iraq provides a good example of the determination of the international community to promote liberal democratic standards to a post-conflict society. Iraq is a very interesting example because the liberal reconstruction was not authorised by the UN under its mandatory Chapter VII powers. Rather, the CPA was an occupying power that was subject to the law of occupation. As I have revealed, the law of occupation is a product of the international society and thus seeks to protect the political and legal framework of the occupied state. In short, the occupier 'is not entitled to enact comprehensive changes to the political, legislative, administrative, and social structures in the occupied territory'.[115]

Although developments in international humanitarian law (principally the Fourth Geneva Convention) and international human rights law have expanded the circumstances in which an occupying power can make changes to the occupied territory, these developments would still not permit many of the more fundamental political, economic and legal reforms introduced by the CPA. No doubt this is why the CPA suggested that the Security Council had authorised departure from the strictures of its international legal obligations under Article 103 of the UN Charter. Although provisions of Security Council Resolution 1483 indicate that the Council did provide the CPA with authority to pursue liberal reforms in Iraq, this authority is far from unequivocal as subsequent paragraphs explicitly demanded adherence to the restrictive provisions of the law of occupation. For these reasons, it seems clear to the present author that it is the law of occupation, and in particular the test of military necessity, that should be used to judge the legality of the reforms introduced by the CPA. As I have argued in this chapter, this test would prohibit many of the institutional and legislative reforms implemented by the CPA.

Notwithstanding that the CPA went beyond what was permitted under international law, what is interesting is that the CPA nevertheless aggres-

[114] cf Bhuta who explains that 'Resolution 1483 . . . [is] sufficiently ambiguous to permit a colourable claim of legitimation – if not legalization – of the idea that the occupying power is authorized, in the interests of the population, to exceed its order-preserving functions and embark on a project of state-building': Bhuta (n 80) at 735.

[115] WH von Heinegg, 'The Rule of Law and Post-Conflict Situations: Factors in War to Peace Transitions' (2004) 27 *Harvard Journal of Law and Public Policy* 843, 862.

sively pursued these sweeping liberal reforms. I have argued that for the international community the authority to introduce these liberal reforms was derived from the belief that the promotion of liberal democracy in Iraq would further the maintenance of international peace and security.[116] Thus, for the international community the close nexus between liberalism and international peace justified departure from established international legal principles (the law of occupation in this instance) on the basis that they frustrated the protection and promotion of liberal values.

[116] The so-called liberal peace thesis; see chapter 3 of this volume.

Conclusion

THE OBJECTIVE OF this book has been to propose an explanatory framework that enables a better understanding of the changes that have occurred to the political and legal structure of the world order since the end of the Cold War and the tensions that are currently being experienced within it. My intention has been to explain the normative conduct of the principal actors within the world order rather than to make any normative judgements about the desirability of their behaviour. I have sought to achieve this by deploying the concepts of the international society and the international community. Indeed, it is upon these concepts that this entire explanatory framework has been built. To this end, much attention has been devoted to elaborating upon the modus operandi of these two associations. To briefly recapitulate, I have deployed the concept of the international society in order to describe an association of states that emerged in the years following the end of the Second World War. This international society is the product of an explicit recognition by states that they possess a common interest in maintaining their sovereignty (and therefore international peace and security more generally). Pursuant to this common interest, states formulated an international legal framework that prohibits intervention in the domestic affairs of other states. Thus, all entities that qualify as a state under international law are cast as legal equals regardless of their political constitution. This is an international society that is therefore universal in scope and which is constituted by the principle of the sovereign equality of its members. Importantly, the international society sought to formally institutionalise its association by creating the United Nations (UN). International peace and security is to be maintained within this association by the creation of universally applicable legal rules and the establishment of an international organisation that is designed to enhance compliance with these rules and, where they are violated, undertake enforcement.

With the end of the Cold War, however, I have argued that within this politically pluralist international society an international community of liberal states has formed that is bound together by a mutual respect for liberal democracy.[1] The defining feature of the international community is

[1] By defending the ontological existence of the international community I have therefore sought to challenge the likes of Philip Allot who argue that 'the use of the term [international community] by politicians, diplomats, journalists, and academic specialists is tending to establish within general consciousness a fictitious conceptual entity with the effects and characteristics which surpass the practical purposes of those who make use of it': P Allot,

its tendency to consider only liberal states to be legitimate equals. Perhaps more importantly, this international community has demonstrated a tendency to consider only liberal states to be *sovereign* equals. As I have revealed, non-liberal states have been consistently dismissed as illegitimate and stripped of their previously held sovereign rights. Thus, liberal states now largely reject the legal framework endorsed by the international society. Although technically the international society remains universal in scope (on the basis that membership of this society is conferred on all states *qua* states), in reality the international society only comprises non-liberal states, as it is only non-liberal states that advocate its defining norm of sovereign equality. Indeed, motivated by the theory that international peace and security can be only maintained in a world composed exclusively of liberal states (known as the liberal peace thesis), the international community has been prepared to intervene in the otherwise sovereign affairs of non-liberal states in order to promote respect for liberal democracy. Consequently, it is the interface between the international society and the international community (or rather the international community's desire to transplant its liberal values into the international society) that can account for contemporary violations to international peace and security.

Significantly, this change to the political configuration of the world order has resulted in substantial revision to the existing international legal framework. Whereas historically the international society had formulated international legal norms with the explicit objective of protecting and promoting state sovereignty, with the growing influence of the international community within the world order international law is now being re-interpreted (or adapted) in order to prevent non-liberal states from egregiously violating fundamental human rights. Moreover, the international community has sought to develop new legal rules in order to protect and promote liberal values. In this sense international law has become a tool of the international community, which is being utilised to further its campaign for liberal development. Indeed, such is the international community's determination to expand its zone of liberal peace that it has instituted a form of global governance. In particular, I have argued that the international community has attempted to locate this governance within the UN Security Council. Of course, as an institution of the international society when the UN was devised it was envisaged that the Security Council would only use its mandatory enforcement powers to protect state sovereignty and thus ensure the wider objective of maintaining international peace and security. As I have suggested in chapter four, at least during the Cold War this is how the Security Council interpreted its mandatory powers under Chapter VII of the UN Charter. With the end of the Cold War,

'The True Function of Law in the International Community' (1998) 5 *Journal of Global Legal Studies* 391, 411.

however, the Security Council has demonstrated a clear willingness to engage Chapter VII in order to promote liberal values on the basis that it will contribute to the maintenance of international peace and security. Thus, I have argued that the international community has sought to locate its governance within the Security Council; and the extent to which the Security Council has articulated an inextricable nexus between liberal democracy and the maintenance of international peace and security is attributable to the growing influence of the international community and the dominance of its ideas, values and objectives within the world order.

This book has also examined the various mechanisms that the international community employs in order to promote respect for its liberal values. In particular, I have focused upon post-conflict reconstruction in the post-Cold War era and suggested that this phenomenon can be regarded as an important and prevalent part of the international community's campaign for liberal development. During the Cold War the international society created the doctrine of peacekeeping in order to prevent conflict between (and eventually within) states so as to protect the legal edifice of statehood and thus maintain the universal application of the covenant to non-intervention. In the post-Cold War era, however, the international community has appropriated peacekeeping and developed it into a mechanism that enables post-conflict societies to be reconstructed upon a liberal basis. In adopting the language of the UN, I characterised this new type of peacekeeping as *peacebuilding*. Kosovo and East Timor have been offered as examples of peacebuilding par excellence. In these instances, the determination of the international community (acting through the UN) to reconstruct these territories upon a liberal basis is clearly visible. Consequently, the creation and implementation of peacebuilding operations can be perceived as a tool of the international community and an attempt to defend and expand its zone of liberal peace.

In chapter seven I examined the international community's presence in Iraq in 2003. The international community's involvement in post-conflict Iraq is interesting because, unlike in Kosovo and East Timor, the liberal reconstruction was not authorised by the UN under Chapter VII. Rather, in seeking to reconstruct Iraq upon a liberal basis the Coalition Provisional Authority (CPA) (comprising members of the international community) was required to adhere to the law of occupation. The CPA was thus an occupying power. As I have illustrated, the law of occupation can be regarded as a product of the international society and its attempt to protect state sovereignty by preventing an external power from intervening in the domestic political affairs of another state. The law of occupation would have therefore prevented the CPA from pursuing its extensive programme of liberal reforms in Iraq. Indeed, the law of occupation would have required the CPA to preserve the *status quo ante bellum*. This notwithstanding, the CPA aggressively pursued a liberal reconstruction. This is significant because it demonstrates that for the international community it is the promotion of liberal values that commands normative supremacy; specifically, because of the close relationship between liberal democracy and international peace, for the international community the pursuit of liberal democracy is justified regardless of the fact that it deviates from established principles of international law.

It should be noted that post-conflict reconstruction is only one (albeit important) mechanism that the international community employs in order to promulgate respect for its liberal values. Other mechanisms have been touched upon in this book, such as restricting membership of international organisations to liberal states only or, in extremis, using military force to (re)install democracy or protect fundamental human rights. The use of development aid and the deployment of sanctions by both individual liberal states and liberal international organisations represent other mechanisms that are utilised by the international community in order to promote respect for liberal democracy. Space, however, has precluded a detailed assessment of these mechanisms, although they are clearly in need of further research. Additionally, the relationship between the UN's specialised agencies (such as the International Monetary Fund, the World Bank and the International Labour Organization) and the international community would also form an interesting research agenda, as these organisations have in recent years clearly moved towards an approach that regards liberal democracy as the only form of legitimate political governance.[2] In the context of the international community and its determination to expand its zone of liberal peace, the contribution of these specialised agencies to the promotion of liberal values would allow an interesting extension to the thesis that I have elaborated in this book. Indeed, the doctrine of the international community will not be fully theorised until these mechanisms are subject to further research.

As a concluding point, however, it is important to appreciate that although the theoretical framework that I have developed is explanatory in nature it nevertheless yields an important prescriptive function. However grandiose the claim maybe, if the *telos* of the international community is to achieve a perpetual peace by constructing a world composed exclusively of liberal states then it is highly probable that international relations and international law will continue to develop consistently with the desires of the international community. Indeed, as more states undergo liberal revolution[3] the international community will become an even more

[2] In relation to the World Bank, for example, see generally D Gillies, 'Human Rights, Democracy and Good Governance: Stretching the World Bank's Policy Frontiers' in J Gresgaber and B Gunter (eds), *The World Bank: Lending on a Global Scale* (London, Pluto, 1996).

[3] And d'Aspremont explains that there is an 'irresistible march' towards liberal democracy: J d'Aspremont, 'Post-Conflict Administration as Democracy-Building Instrument' (2008) 9 *Chicago Journal of International Law* 1, 15.

powerful actor in the world order. The consequence is that non-liberal states will become increasingly marginalised and subject to significant pressure to reform. Where they are unwilling to undergo voluntary reform, the international community will encourage if not compel liberal reformation (see the assistance given to pro-democracy forces in the context of the Arab Spring). In this sense, the explanatory framework that I have constructed can be also used as a model or blueprint to predict future developments to the political and legal structure of the world order.

Bibliography

BOOKS

Ackerman, B, *We the People: Foundations* (Cambridge, MA, Belknap Press of Harvard University, 1991).

Aksu, E, *The United Nations, Intra-State Peacekeeping and Normative Change* (Manchester, Manchester University Press, 2003).

Anderson, J, Ikenberry, GJ, and Risse, T, (eds), *The End of the West? Crisis and Change in the Atlantic Order* (Ithaca NY, Cornell University Press, 2008).

Aust, A, *Modern Treaty Law and Practice* (Cambridge, Cambridge University Press, 2007).

Barber, B, *Fear's Empire: War, Terrorism and Democracy* (New York, WW Norton & Company, 2003).

Beiner, R, *What's the Matter with Liberalism?* (Berkeley CA, University of California Press, 1992).

Bellamy, A, Williams, P, and Griffin, S, *Understanding Peacekeeping* (Oxford, Polity Press, 2003).

Bentwich, N, and Martin, A, *A Commentary of the Charter of the United Nations* (London, Routledge & Kegan Paul, 1950).

Benvenisti, E, *The International Law of Belligerent Occupation* (Princeton NJ/ Woodstock, Princeton University Press, 2004).

Bobbit, P, *The Shield of Achilles: War, Peace and the Course of History* (London, Allen Lane, 2002).

Bond, J, *Peacetime Foreign Data Manipulation as One Aspect of Offensive Information Warfare: Questions of Legality under the United Nations Charter Article 2(4)* (US Dept of Commerce, National Technical Information Service, 1996).

Bowett, D, *United Nations Forces* (London, David Davies Memorial Institute, 1964).

Brownlie, I, *Principles of Public International Law*, 7th edn (Oxford, Oxford University Press, 2008).

Bull, H, *The Anarchical Society: A Study of Order in World Politics* (Basingstoke, Palgrave, 2002).

Carr, EH, *The Twenty Years' Crisis, 1919–1939: An Introduction to the Study of International Relations* (London, Papermac, 1995).

Cassese, A, *International Law in a Divided World* (Oxford, Clarendon Press, 1986).

Chayes, A, and Chayes, A, *The New Sovereignty: Compliance with International Regulatory Agreements* (Cambridge MA/London, Harvard University Press, 1995).

Chesterman, S, *Just War or Just Peace?: Humanitarian Intervention and International Law* (Oxford, Oxford University Press, 1999).

—— *You, The People: The United Nations, Transitional Administration and State-Building* (Oxford, Oxford University Press, 2004).

Clark, I, *Legitimacy in International Society* (Oxford, Oxford University Press, 2005).

Claude Jnr, I, *Swords into Ploughshares: The Problems and Process of International Organization* (New York, Random House, 1971).

Crawford, J, *The Creation of States in International Law* (Oxford, Clarendon Press, 2006).

Cronin, B, *Community under Anarchy: Transnational Identity and the Evolution of Cooperation* (New York, Columbia University Press, *1999*).

d'Aspremont, J, *L'État Non Démocratique en Droit International. Étude Critique du Droit International Positif et de Law Pratique Contemporaine* (Paris, Pedone, 2008).

Dayal, R, *Mission for Hammarskjöld: The Congo Crisis* (Princeton NJ, Princeton University Press, 1976).

Diamond, L, Linz, J, and Lipset, S, *Politics in Developing Countries: Contemporary Experiences with Democracy* (Boulder CO, Lynne Rienner, 1995).

Dinstein, Y, *War, Aggression and Self-Defence* (Cambridge, Cambridge University Press, 2010).

Diehl, P, *International Peacekeeping* (Baltimore MD, Johns Hopkins University Press, 1994).

Donnelly, J, *Universal Human Rights in Theory and Practice* (Ithaca NY/London, Cornell University Press, 2003).

Duxbury, A, *The Participation of States in International Organisations: The Role of Human Rights and Democracy* (Cambridge, Cambridge University Press, 2011).

Elster, J, *The Cement of Society: A Study of Social Order* (Cambridge, Cambridge University Press, 1989).

Falk, R, *On Humane Governance: Towards a New Global Politics* (*Pennsylvania PA,* Pennsylvania State University Press, 1995).

Fauchille, P, *Traite de Droit International Public* (Rousseau, Paris, 1921).

Feilchenfeld, E, *The International Economic Law of Belligerent Occupation* (Washington DC, Carnegie Endowment for International Peace, 1942).

Fox, G, *Humanitarian Occupation* (Cambridge, Cambridge University Press, 2008).

Franck, T, *Nation against Nation* (New York, Oxford University Press, 1985).

——*Fairness in International Law and Institutions* (Oxford, Clarendon Press, 1998).

——*Recourse to Force: State Acts against Threats and Armed Attacks* (Cambridge, Cambridge University Press, 2002).

Frederking, B, *The United States and the Security Council: Collective Security since the Cold War* (London and New York, Routledge, 2007).

Friedmann, W, *The Changing Structure Of International Law* (London, Stevens & Sons, 1964).

Glahn, G von, *The Occupation of Enemy Territory* (Minneapolis MN, University of Minnesota Press, 1957).

Gong, G, *The Standard of 'Civilization' in International Society* (Oxford, Clarendon Press, 1984).

Goodrich, L and Hambro, E, *Charter of the United Nations: Commentary and Documents* (New York, Columbia University Press, 1969).

Gordon, J, *The United Nations in the Congo: A Quest for Peace* (New York, Carnegie Endowment for International *Peace,* 1962).

Grant, T, *Admission to the United Nations: Charter Article 4 and the Rise of Universal Organization* (Leiden, Martinus Nijhoff, 2009).

Greenspan, M, *The Modern Law of Land Warfare* (Berkeley CA, Stanford University Press, 1959).

Haas, R, *Intervention: The Use of American Military Force in the Post-Cold War World* (Washington DC, Brookings Institution Press, 1999).

Hardt, M and Negri, A, *Empire* (Cambridge MA, Harvard University Press, 2000).

Held, D, *Models of Democracy* (Cambridge, Polity Press, 2006).

Henkin, L, *How Nations Behave* (Cambridge, Polity Press, 1979).

Higgins, R, *United Nations Peacekeeping, 1946–1967: Documents and Commentary* (London, Oxford University Press, 1969).

Hobbes, T, *Leviathan* (Peterborough, Ont, Broadview Press, 2002).

Hobsbawm, E, *Age of Extremes: The History of the Short Twentieth Century 1914–91* (London, Abacus, 1995).

Hollis, M and Smith, S, *Understanding and Explaining International Relations* (Oxford, Clarendon Press, 1991).

Huntington, S, *The Clash of Civilizations and the Remaking of World Order* (London, Touchstone, 1998).

Ignatieff, M, *Empire Lite: Nation-Building in Bosnia, Kosovo and Afghanistan* (London, Vintage, 2003).

Jackson, R, *The Global Covenant: Human Conduct in a World of States* (Oxford, Oxford University Press, 2000)

Jennings, R and Watts, A (eds), *Oppenheim's International Law*, 9th edn (Oxford, Oxford University Press, 2008).

Kant, I, 'Perpetual Peace' (translation by H Reiss), *Kant's Political Writings* (Cambridge, Cambridge University Press, 1991).

Kelsen, H, *The Law of the United Nations* (New York: Frederick A Praeger, 1964).

Kennedy, P, *The Parliament of Man: The United Nations and the Quest for World Government* (London, Allen Lane, 2006).

Knutsen, TL, *A History of International Relations Theory* (Manchester, Manchester University Press, 1997).

Kooijmans, P, *Internationaal Publiekrecht in Vogelvucht* (Deventer, Kluwer, 2000).

Korhonen, O, Gras, J and Creutz, K, *International Post-Conflict Situations: New Challenges for Co-Operative Governance* (Helsinki, Ius Gentium Association, 2006).

Koskenniemi, M, *The Gentle Civilizer of Nations: The Rise and Fall of International Law* (Cambridge, Cambridge University Press, 2002).

Kouchner, B, *Les Guerriers de la Paix* (Paris, Grasset, 2004).

Lefever, E, *Crisis in the Congo: A United Nations Force in Action* (Washington DC, Brookings Institution, 1965).

Legler, T, Lean, S and Doniface, D (eds), *Promoting Democracy in the Americas* (Baltimore MD, The Johns Hopkins University Press, 2007).

Litwak, R, *Rogue States and US Foreign Policy: Containment after the Cold War* (Baltimore MD, The Johns Hopkins University Press, 2000).

Lorimer, J, *Institutes of International Law: A Treatise of the Jural Relations of Separate Political Communities* (Edinburgh/London, W Blackwood & Sons, 1883).

MacFarlane, S, *Intervention in Contemporary World Politics* (Oxford, Oxford University Press, 2002).

MacFarlane, S and Khong, YF, *Human Security and the UN: A Critical History* (Bloomington, Indiana Press, 2006).

Malone, D, *The International Struggle over Iraq: Politics in the United Nations Security Council 1980–2005* (New York, Oxford University Press, 2006).
Martin, I, *Self-Determination in East Timor: the United Nations and International Intervention* (Boulder CO, Lynne Rienner Publishers, 2001).
McCoubrey, H and White, ND, *The Blue Helmets: Legal Regulation of United Nations Military Operations* (Aldershot, Dartmouth, 1991).
——*International Law and Armed Conflict* (Aldershot, Dartmouth, 1992).
McDougal, M and Feliciano, F, *Law and Minimum World Public Order* (New Haven CT, Yale University Press, 1961).
McGoldrick, D, *From '9-11' to the Iraq War 2003: International Law in an Age of Complexity* (Oxford, Hart Publishing, 2004).
McNair, A, and Watts, A, *The Legal Effects of War* (Cambridge, Cambridge University Press, 1966).
Meron, T, *The Humanization of International Law* (The Hague, Martinus Nijhoff, 2006).
Milanovic, M, *Extraterritorial Applications of Human Rights Treaties: Law, Principles, and Policy* (Oxford, Oxford University Press, 2011).
Morgenthau, HJ, *Politics among Nations: The Struggle for Power and Peace* (New York, McGraw-Hill, 1985).
Müllerson, R, *Ordering Anarchy: International Law in International Society* (The Hague, Martinus Nijhoff, 2000).
Murphy, R, *UN Peacekeeping in Lebanon, Somalia and Kosovo: Legal and Operational Issues in Practice* (Cambridge, Cambridge University Press, 2007).
Oppenheim, L, *International Law, Vol I* (London, Longmans Green & Co, 1920–1921)
Österdahl, I, *Threat to the Peace and the Interpretation by the Security Council of Article 39* (Stockholm, Iustus Forlag, 1998).
Pelt, A, *Libyan Independence and the United Nations: A Case of Planned Decolonization* (New Haven CT, Yale University Press, 1970).
Perreau-Saussine, A and Murphy, JB (eds), *The Nature of Customary International Law: Legal, Historical and Philosophical Perspectives* (Cambridge, Cambridge University Press, 2007).
Ponzio, R, *Democratic Peacebuilding: Aiding Afghanistan and other Fragile States* (Oxford/New York, Oxford University Press, 2011).
Ratner, S, *The New UN Peacekeeping: Building Peace in Lands of Conflict after the Cold War* (Basingstoke, Macmillan, 1995).
Rham-Azimi, N de, *The United Nations Transitional Authority in Cambodia (UNTAC): Debriefing and Lessons: Report and Recommendations of the International Conference* (Singapore, Institute of Policy Studies, 1994).
Rikhye, I, *The Theory and Practice of Peacekeeping* (London, C Hurst & Co, 1984).
Roth, B, *Governmental Illegitimacy in International Law* (Oxford, Clarendon Press, 1999).
Rowe, P, *Defence: The Legal Implications* (London, Brassey's *Defence* Publishers, 1987).
Russett, B, *Controlling the Sword: the Democratic Governance of National Security* (Cambridge MA, Harvard University Press, 1990).
——*Grasping the Democratic Peace* (Princeton NJ, Princeton University Press, 1993).
Sadeniemi, P, *Principles of Legitimacy and International Relations* (Helsingfors, Helsingfors Universitet, 1995).

Sands, P and Klein, P, *Bowett's Law of International Institutions* (London, Sweet & Maxwell, 2001).
Schwarzenberger, G, *The League of Nations and World Order* (London, Constable & Co Ltd, 1936).
——*The Law of Armed Conflict* (London, Steven and Sons, 1968).
Shaw, M, *Politics and Globalization: Knowledge, Ethics and Agency* (London/New York, Taylor and Francis, 1999).
Simma, B, *The Charter of the United Nations: A Commentary* (Oxford, Oxford University Press, 2002).
Simpson, G, *Great Powers and Outlaw States: Unequal Sovereigns in the International Legal Order* (Cambridge, Cambridge University Press, 2004).
Stahn, C, *The Law and Practice of International Territorial Administration: Versailles to Iraq and Beyond* (Cambridge, Cambridge University Press, 2008).
Stothard, P, *Thirty Days: Tony Blair and the Test of History* (New York, Harper Collins, 2003).
Sutterlin, J, *The UN and the Maintenance of International Security* (Westport CT, Praeger, 2003).
Taylor, J, *East Timor: The Price of Freedom* (New York, Zed Books Ltd, 1999).
Tanzi, V, Chu, K and Gupta, S (eds), *Economic Policy and Equity* (Washington DC, International Monetary Fund, 1999).
Teson, F, *Humanitarian Intervention: An Inquiry into Law and Morality* (Irvington-On-Hudson NY, Transnational, 1997).
Tönnies, F, *Community and Association* (East Lansing MI, Michigan State University Press, 1957).
Tsagourias, N, *Jurisprudence of International Law: The Humanitarian Dimension* (Manchester, Manchester University of Press, 2000).
Tsagourias, N and White, ND, *Collective Security: Law, Theory and Practice* (Cambridge, Cambridge University Press, 2013).
Tunkin, G, *Law and Force in the International System* (Moscow, Progress Publishers, 1985).
Urquhart, B, *Hammarskjöld* (New York, WW Norton, 1994).
Visscher, C de, *Theories et Realites en Droit International Publique* (Paris, Pedone, 1970).
Waltz, K, *Theory of International Politics* (London, McGraw-Hill, 1979).
Watson, J, *Theory and Reality in the International Protection of Human Rights* (Ardsley NY, Transnational Publishers, 1999).
Weissman, S, *American Foreign Policy in the Congo 1960–1964* (London, Cornell University Press, 1974).
Wendt, A, *A Social Theory of International Politics* (Cambridge, Cambridge University Press, 1999).
Westlake, J, *Collected Papers on International Law*, Oppenheim, L (ed), (Cambridge, Cambridge University Press, 1914).
White, ND, *Toward International Justice: The United Nations System* (Boulder CO, Lynne Rienner, 2002).
Wight, W, *Systems of States* (Leicester, Leicester University Press, 1977).
Zwanenburg, M, *Accountability of Peace Support Operations* (Leiden/Boston MA, Martinus Nijhoff, 2005).

CHAPTERS FROM EDITED COLLECTIONS

Abi-Saab, G, 'United Nations Peacekeeping Old and New: An Overview of the Issues' in Warner, D (ed), *New Dimensions of Peacekeeping* (Dordrecht, Martinus Nijhoff, 1995).

Alvarez, J, 'Constitutional Interpretation in International Organisations' in Coicaud, J-M and Heiskinman, V (eds), *The Legitimacy of International Organizations* (Tokyo, United Nations University Press, 2001).

Brown, C, '"Really Existing Liberalism", Peaceful Democracies and International Order' in Fawn, R and Larkins, J (eds), *International Society after the Cold War: Anarchy and Order Reconsidered* (Basingstoke, Macmillan/New York, St Martin's Press, 1996).

Brownlie, I, 'Humanitarian Intervention' in Moore, J (ed), *Law and Civil War in the Modern World* (Baltimore MD, The Johns Hopkins University Press, 1974).

Brus, M, 'Bridging the Gap between State Sovereignty and International Governance: The Authority of Law' in Kreijin, G (ed), *State, Sovereignty and International Governance* (Oxford, Oxford University Press, 2002).

Bull, H and Watson, A, 'Introduction' in Bull, H and Watson, A (eds), *Expansion of International Society* (Oxford, ClarendonPress, 1989).

Cassese, A, 'Powers and Duties of an Occupant in Relation to Land and Natural Resources' in Playfair, E (ed), *International Law and the Administration of Occupied Territories* (Oxford, Clarendon Press, 1992).

Chesterman, S, 'Building Democracy through Benevolent Autocracy: Consultation and Accountability in UN Transitional Administrations' in Newman, E and Rich, R (eds), *The UN Role in Promoting Democracy: Between Ideals and Reality* (New York, United Nations University Press, 2004).

Cremona, M, 'Variable Geometry and Setting Membership Conditionalities: A Viable Strategy?' in Clapham, C, Mills, G, Morner, A and Sidiropolous, E (eds), *Regional Integration in Southern Africa: Comparative International Perspectives* (Johannesburg, South African Institute of South African Affairs, 2001).

Devereux, A, 'Searching for Clarity: a Case Study of UNTAET's application of International Human Rights Norms' in White, ND and Klassen, D (eds), *The UN, Human Rights and Post-Conflict Situations* (Manchester, Manchester University Press, 2005).

Durch, W, 'Introduction' in Durch, W (ed), *The Evolution of Peacekeeping* (New York, St Martin's Press, 1993).

Farer, T, 'The Promotion of Democracy: International Law and Norms' in Newman, E and Rich, R (eds), *The UN Role in Promoting Democracy: Between Ideals and Reality* (New York, United Nations University Press, 2004).

Franck, T, 'The Security Council and "Threats to the Peace": Some Remarks on Remarkable Recent Developments' in Depuy, R-J (ed), *Peace Keeping and Peace Building: The Development of the Role of the Security Council* (Leiden, Martinus Nijhoff, 1993).

——'Legitimacy and the Democratic Entitlement' in Fox, G and Roth, B (eds), *Democratic Governance in International Law* (Cambridge, Cambridge University Press, 2000).

Franck, T and Carey, J, 'The Role of the United Nations in the Congo – a Retrospective Perspective' in Tondel Jr, J (ed), *The Legal Aspects of the United Nations Action in the Congo* (1963).

Gillies, D, 'Human Rights, Democracy and Good Governance: Stretching the World Bank's Policy Frontiers' in Gresgaber, J and Gunter, B (eds), *The World Bank: Lending on a Global Scale* (London, Pluto, 1996).

Goodson, L, 'The Lessons of National-Building in Afghanistan' in Fukuyama, F (ed), *Nation-Building: Beyond Afghanistan and Iraq* (Baltimore MD, The Johns Hopkins University Press, 2006).

Gray, C, 'The Use of Force and the International Legal Order' in Evans, M (ed), *International Law* (Oxford, Oxford University Press, 2010).

Hohe, T, 'Delivering Feudal Democracy in East Timor' in Newman, E and Rich, R (eds), *The UN Role in Promoting Democracy: Between Ideals and Reality* (New York, United Nations University Press, 2010).

Hysa, Y, 'Kosovo: A Permanent International Protectorate?' in Newman, E and Rich, R (eds), *The UN Role in Promoting Democracy: Between Ideals and Reality* (New York, United Nations University Press, 2004).

Ingram, S, 'Mission Implementation: Developing Institutional Capacities' in Azimi, N and Ling, C (eds), *The United Nations Transition Administration in East Timor (UNTAET): Debriefing and Lessons–Report of the 2002 Tokyo Conference* (Leiden, Martinus Nijhoff, 2003).

Jennings, R, 'Broader Perspectives in International Law' in Anghie, A and Sturgess, G (eds), *Legal Visions of the 21st Century: Essays in Honour of Judge Christopher Weeramantry* (The Hague, Kluwer Law International, 1998).

Kumar, K, 'Post-Conflict Elections and International Assistance' in Kumar, K (ed), *Post-Conflict Elections, Democratization and International Assistance* (Boulder CO, Lynne Rienner, 1998).

Lee, M, 'North Korea and the Western Notion of Human Rights' in Hsiung, J (ed), *Human Rights in East Asia: A Cultural Perspective* (New York, Paragon House Publishers, 1985).

Levy, J, 'Domestic Politics and War' in Rotberg, R and Rabb, T (ed), *The Origin and Prevention of Major Wars* (Cambridge, Cambridge University Press, 1989).

McCorquodale, R, 'International Community and State Sovereignty: An Uneasy Symbiotic Relationship' in Warbrick, C and Tierney, S (eds), *Towards an International Legal Community?* (London, British Institute of International and Comparative Law, 2006).

McGoldrick, D, 'The Principle of Non-Intervention: Human Rights' in Lowe, L and Warbrick, C (eds), *The United Nations and the Principles of International Law: Essays in Memory of Michael Akehurst* (New York, Routledge, 1994).

Oppenheim, L (ed), *The Collected Papers of John Westlake on Public International Law* (Cambridge, Cambridge University Press, 1914).

Owen, J, 'How Liberalism Produces Peace' in Brown, M, Lynn-Jones, S and Miller, S (eds), *Debating the Democratic Peace* (Cambridge MA/London, MIT Press, 1996).

——'Perceptions and the Limits of the Liberal Peace: Mexican-American and Spanish-American Wars' in Elman, M (ed), *Paths to Peace: Is Democracy the Answer?* (Cambridge MA/London, MIT Press, 1997).

Paulus, A, 'The Influence of the United States on the Concept of the International Community' in Byers, M and Nolte, G (eds), *United States Hegemony and the Foundations of International Law* (Cambridge, Cambridge University Press, 2003).
Randelzhofer, A, 'Article 2(4)' in Simma, B (ed), *The Charter of the United Nations: A Commentary* (Oxford, Oxford University Press, 2002).
Rikhye, I, 'Peacekeeping and Peacemaking' in Wiseman, H (ed), *Peacekeeping: Appraisals and Proposals* (New York, Pergamon, 1983).
Robinson, F, 'Globalising Liberalism? Morality and Legitimacy in a Liberal Global Order' in Shaw, M (ed), *Politics and Globalization: Knowledge, Ethics and Agency* (London, Routledge, 1999).
Roling, B, 'The Ban on the Use of Force and the U.N. Charter' in Cassese, A (ed), *The Current Legal Regulation of the Use of Force* (The Hague, Martinus Nijhoff, 1986).
Russet, B, 'Why Democratic Peace?' Brown, M, Lynn-Jones, S and Miller, S (eds), *Debating the Democratic Peace* (Cambridge MA / London, MIT Press, 1996).
——'The Fact of Democratic Peace' in Brown, M, Lynn-Jones, S and Miller, S (eds), *Debating the Democratic Peace* (Cambridge MA / London, MIT Press, 1996).
Saikal, A, 'The United Nations and Democratization in Afghanistan' in Newman, E and Rich, R (eds), *The UN Role in Promoting Democracy: Between Ideals and Reality* (New York, United Nations University Press, 2004).
Sens, A, 'From Peacekeeping to Peacebuilding: The United Nations and the Challenge of Intrastate War' in Price, R and Zacher, M (eds), *The United Nations and Global Security* (2004).
Tsagourias, N, 'The Will of the International Community as a Normative Source of International Law' in Dekker, I and Werner, W (eds), *Governance and International Legal Theory* (Leiden, Martinus Nijhoff, 2004).
Wallenstein, P and Johansson, P, 'Security Council Decisions in Perspective' in Malone, D (ed), *The UN Security Council: From the Cold War to the 21st Century* (Boulder CO, Lynne Rienner, 2004).
Whitehead, L, 'Democratization with the Benefit of Hindsight' in Newman, E and Rich, R (eds), *The UN Role in Promoting Democracy: Between Ideals and Reality* (New York, United Nations University Press, 2004).

ARTICLES

Afsah, E and Guhr, A, 'Afghanistan: Building a State to Keep the Peace' (2005) 9 *Max Planck Yearbook of United Nations Law* 373.
Alder, E, 'Imagined (Security) Communities: Cognitive Regions in International Relations' (1997) 26 *Millennium Journal of International Studies* 249.
Alexander, K, 'Ignoring the Lessons of the Past: The Crisis in Darfur and the Case for Humanitarian Intervention' (2005) 15 *Journal of Transnational Law and Policy* 1.
Allot, P, 'The True Function of Law in the International Community' (1998) 5 *Journal of Global Legal Studies* 391.
Axelrod, R, 'An Evolutionary Approach to Norms' (1986) 80 *American Political Science Review* 1097.
Bain, W, 'The Political Theory of Trusteeship and the Twilight of International Equality' (2003) 17 *International Relations* 59.

Barnes, S, 'The Contribution of Democracy to Rebuilding Post Conflict Societies' (2001) 95 *American Journal of International Law* 86.
Bayefsky, A, 'Cultural Sovereignty, Relativism, and International Human Rights: New Excuses for Old Strategies' (1996) 9 *Ratio Juris* 42.
Beauvais, J, 'Benevolent Despotism: A Critique of U.N. State-Building in East Timor' (2000) 33 *New York University Journal of International Law and Politics* 1101.
Benvenisti, E, 'Water Conflicts During the Occupation of Iraq' (2003) 97 *American Journal of International Law* 860.
Benzing, M, 'Midwifing a New State: The United Nations in East Timor' (2005) 9 *Max Planck Yearbook of United Nations Law* 295.
Bhuta, N, 'The Antinomies of Transformative Occupation' (2005) 16 *European Journal of International Law* 721.
Bodansky, D, 'The Legitimacy of International Governance: A Coming Challenge for International Environmental Law?' (1999) 93 *American Journal of International Law* 596.
Boutros-Ghali, B, 'Democracy: A Newly Recognised Imperative' (1995) 1 *Global Governance* 3.
Brand, M, 'Institution-Building and Human Rights Protection in Kosovo in the Light of UNMIK Legislation' (2001) 70 *Nordic Journal of International Law* 461, 479.
Brandtner, B and Rosas, A, 'Human Rights and the External Relations of the European Community: An Analysis of Doctrine and Practice' (1998) 9 *European Journal of International Law* 468.
Brown, B, 'Intervention, Self-Determination, Democracy and the Residual Responsibilities of the Occupying Power in Iraq' (2004) 11 *University of California, Davis Journal of International Law and Policy* 23.
Buchan, R, 'The International Community and the Occupation of Iraq' (2008) 12 *Journal of Conflict and Security Law* 37.
——'A Clash of Normativities: International Society and International Community' (2008) 10 *International Community Law Review* 3.
Burchill, R, 'The Promotion and Protection of Democracy by Regional Organizations in Europe: The Case of Austria' (2001) 7 *European Public Law* 79.
Burke-White, W, 'Human Rights and National Security: The Strategic Correlation' (2004) 17 *Harvard Human Rights Journal* 249.
Burley (Slaughter), A-M, 'Toward and Age of Liberal Nations' (1992) 33 *Harvard International Law Journal* 393
Buzan, B, 'From International System to International Society; Structural Realism and Regime Theory meet the English School' (1993) 47 *International Organization* 327.
Buzan, B and Gonzalez-Pelaez, A, 'International Community after Iraq' (2005) 81 *International Affairs* 31.
Caprioli, M and Trumbore, P, 'Identifying "Rogue" States and Testing their Interstate Conflict Behaviour' (2003) 9 *European Journal of International Relations* 377.
Cerna, C, 'The Case of Haiti before the OAS' (1992) *American Society of International Law Proclamation* 378.
——'Universal Democracy: An International Legal Right or the Pipe Dream of the West?' (1995) 27 *New York University Journal of Law and Politics* 289.

Chan, S, 'In Search of Democratic Peace: Problems and Promise' (1997) 41 *Mershon International Studies Review* 59.
Cogen, M and de Brabandere, E, 'Democratic Governance and Post-Conflict Reconstruction' (2007) 20 *Leiden Journal of International Law* 669.
Cox, M, 'Beyond the West? Terror in Transatlantica' (2005) 11 *European Journal of International Relations* 203.
d'Aspremont, J, 'Legitimacy of Governments in the Age of Democracy' (2006) 38 *New York University Journal of International Law and Politics* 877.
——'Post-Conflict Administrations as Democracy-Building Instruments' (2008) 9 *Chicago Journal of International Law* 1.
——'The Rise and Fall of Democracy Governance in International Law: A Reply to Susan Marks' (2011) 22 *European Journal of International Law* 549.
Daalder, I and Lindsay, J, 'Democracies of the World, Unite' (March/April 2007) *The American Interest* 5.
Dinstein, Y, 'The International Law of Belligerent Occupation and Human Rights' (1978) 8 *Israel Yearbook on Human Rights* 104.
Dixon, W, 'Democracy and the Peaceful Settlement of International Conflict' (1994) 88 *American Political Science Review* 14.
Dobriansky, P, 'The Core of US Foreign Policy' (2003) 82 *Foreign Affairs* 141.
Donald, D, 'Neutral is Not Impartial: The Confusing Legacy of Traditional Peace Operations Thinking' (2003) 29 *Armed Forces and Society* 415.
Donnelly, J, 'Human Rights: a New Standard of Civilization?' (1998) 74 *International Affairs* 1.
Donoho, L, 'Evolution or Expediency: The United Nations Response to the Disruption of Democracy' (1996) 29 *Cornell International Law Journal* 329.
Downs, G and Jones, M, 'Reputation, Compliance and International Law' (2002) 31 *Journal of Legal Studies* 95.
Doyle, M, 'Kant, Liberal Legacies, and Foreign Affairs: Part I' (1983) 12 *Philosophy and Public Affairs* 205.
——'Kant, Liberal Legacies, and Foreign Affairs: Part II' (1983) 12 *Philosophy and Public Affairs* 323.
——'Liberalism and World Politics' (1986) 80 *American Political Science Review* 1151.
Dupuy, P-M, 'The Place and Role of Unilateralism in International Law' (2004) 11 *European Journal of International Law* 19.
Eldar, O, 'Vote-trading in International Institutions' (2008) 19 *European Journal of International Law* 3.
Evans, G, 'From Humanitarian Intervention to the Responsibility to Protect' (2006) 24 *Wisconsin International Law Journal* 704.
Fassbender, B, 'The United Nations Charter as Constitution of the International Community' (1998) 36 *Columbia Journal of Transnational Law* 529.
Fellmeth, A, 'Feminism and International Law: Theory, Methodology and Substantive Reform' (2000) 2 *Human Rights Quarterly* 658.
Fidler, D, 'Caught between Traditions: The Security Council in Philosophical Conundrum' (1995–96) 17 *Michigan Journal of International Law* 411.
——'A Kinder, Gentler System of Capitulation? International Law, Structural Adjustment Policies, and the Standard of Liberal, Globalised Civilisation' (2000) 35 *Texas Journal of International Law* 389.

Finnemore, M and Sikkink, K, 'International Norm Dynamics and Political Change' (1998) 52 *International Organization* 887.
Fox, G, 'The Right to Political Participation in International Law' (1992) 17 *Yale Journal of International Law* 539.
——'The Occupation of Iraq' (2005) 36 *Georgetown Journal of International Law* 19.
Franck, T, 'Who Killed Article 2(4)?' (1970) 64 *American Journal of International Law* 809.
——'The Emerging Right to Democratic Governance' (1994) 86 *American Journal of International Law* 46.
——'Are Human Rights Universal?' (2001) 80 *Foreign Affairs* 191.
——'What Happens Now? The United Nations after Iraq' (2003) 97 *American Journal of International Law* 607.
Friedrich, J, 'UNMIK in Kosovo: Struggling with Uncertainty' (2005) 9 *Max Planck Yearbook of United Nations Law* 227.
Fukuyama, F, 'The End of History' (1989) 16 *National Interest* 3.
Gagnon, M, 'Peace Forces and the Veto: The Relevance of Consent' (1967) 21 *International Organization* 812.
Galtung, J, 'Peace: Negative and Positive' (1964) 1 *Journal of Peace Research* 1.
Gersham, C, 'Democracy as Policy Goal and Universal Value' (2005) 6 *The Whitehead Journal of Diplomacy and International Relations* 19.
Glennon, M, 'Sovereignty and Community After Haiti: Rethinking the Collective Use of Force' (1995) 89 *American Journal of International Law* 70.
——'Why the Security Council Failed' (2003) 82 *Foreign Affairs* 16.
Gerson, H-P, 'War, Conquered Territory and Military Occupation in the Contemporary International Legal System' (1977) 18 *Harvard International Law Journal* 535.
Golub, S, 'Make Justice the Organizing Principle of the Rule of Law Field' (2009) 1 *Hague Journal on the Rule of Law* 61.
Goodhand, J, 'From War Economy to Peace Economy? Reconstruction and State Building in Afghanistan' (2004) 58 *Journal of International Affairs* 155.
Goodson, L, 'Bullets, Ballots, and Poppies in Afghanistan' (2005) 16 *Journal of Democracy* 24.
Gordon, R, 'United Nations Intervention in Internal Conflicts: Iraq, Somalia, and Beyond' (1993–94) 15 *Michigan Journal of International Law* 519.
Goulding, M, 'The Evolution of United Nations Peacekeeping' (1993) 69 *International Affairs* 451.
Grant, T, 'A League of their Own: The Rationale for an International Alliance of Democracies' (2009) 41 *George Washington International Law Review* 243.
Griffin, M, 'Accrediting Democracies: Does the Credentials Committee of the United Nations Promote Democracy through its Accreditation Process and Should It?' (1999) 32 *New York University Journal of International Law and Politics* 725.
Happold, M, 'Fourteen Against One: The EU member States' Response to the Freedom Party Participation in the Austrian Government' (2000) 49 *International Comparative Law Quarterly* 953.
Hayes, J, 'Identity and Securitization in the Democratic Peace: The United States and the Divergence of Response to India and Iran's Nuclear Programs' (2009) 53 *International Studies Quarterly* 977.

Heinegg, HW von, 'The Rule of Law and Post-Conflict Situations: Factors in War to Peace Transitions' (2004) 27 *Harvard Journal of Law and Public Policy* 843.

Henkin, L, 'The Reports of the Death of Article 2(4) are Greatly Exaggerated' (1971) 65 *American Journal of International Law* 544.

——'Kosovo and the Law of "Humanitarian Intervention"' (1999) 93 *American Journal of International Law* 824.

——'That "S" Word: Sovereignty, And Globalization, and Human Rights, Et Cetera' (1999) 68 *Fordham Law Review* 1.

Jubilut, L, 'Has the "Responsibility to Protect" Been a Real Change in Humanitarian Intervention: An Analysis From the Crisis in Libya' (2012) 14 *International Community Law Review* 309.

Koh, H, 'On American Exceptionalism' (2002–03) 55 *Stanford Law Review* 1479.

Hohe, T, 'The Clash of Paradigms: International Administration and Local Political Legitimacy in East Timor' (2002) 24 *Contemporary Southeast Asia* 569.

Ikenberry, J, 'The End of the Neo-Conservative Moment' (2004) 46 *Survival* 7.

Jamnejad, M and Wood, M, 'The Principle of Non-Intervention' (2009) 22 *Leiden Journal of International Law* 345.

Jennings, R, 'Government in Commission' (1946) 23 *British Yearbook of International Law* 112.

Jouannet, E, 'What is the use of International Law? International Law as a 21st Century Guardian of Welfare' (2007) 28 *Michigan Journal of International Law* 815.

Kagan, R, 'America's Crisis of Legitimacy' (2004) 83 *Foreign Affairs* 83.

Kahl, C, 'Constructing a Separate Peace: Constructivism, Collective Liberal Identity, and Democratic Peace' (1999) 8 *Security Studies* 94.

Keohane, R and Martin, L, 'The Promise of Internationalist Theory' (1995) 20 *International Security* 20.

Kingsbury, B, 'Sovereignty and Inequality' (1998) 9 *European Journal of International Law* 599.

Kirgis, F, 'The Security Council's First 50 Years' (1995) 89 *American Journal of International Law* 506.

Komano, K, 'The Role of Elections in the Peace-Building and Reconstruction of Afghanistan' (2005) 12 *Asia-Pacific Review* 1.

Koskemniemi, M, 'Legal Cosmopolitanism: Tom Franck's Messianic World' (2003) 35 *NYU Journal of International Law and Policy* 417.

Kouchner, B, 'The Challenge of Rebuilding Kosovo' (1999) 3 *NATO Review* 1.

Kristof, N, 'The Problem of Memory' (1998) 77 *Foreign Affairs* 37.

Layne, C, 'Kant or Cant: The Myth of the Democratic Peace' (1994) 19 *International Security* 5.

Leffler, M, '9/11 and the Past and Future American Foreign Policy' (2003) 79 *International Affairs* 1054.

Leininger, J, 'Democracy and UN Peace-keeping-Conflict Resolution through State-Building and Democracy Promotion in Haiti' (2006) 10 *Max Planck Yearbook of United Nations Law* 465.

Lindsay, J, 'The Case for a Concert of Democracies' (2009) 23 *Ethics and International Affairs* 5.

Luban, D, 'Just War and Human Rights' (1980) 9 *Philosophy and Public Affairs* 160.

Malone, D, 'The Security Council in the Post-Cold War Era: A Study in the Creative Interpretation of the UN Charter' (2003) 35 *New York Journal of International Law and Politics* 487.

Marks, S, 'What has Become of the Emerging Right to Democratic Governance?' (2011) 22 *European Journal of International Law* 507.

Marsden, P, 'Afghanistan: the Reconstruction Process' (2003) 79 *International Affairs* 91.

Mazarr, M, 'George W. Bush, Idealist' (2003) 79 *International Affairs* 503.

McCarthy, C, 'The Paradox of the International Law of Military Occupation: Sovereignty and the Reformation of Iraq' (2005) 10 *Journal of Conflict and Security Law* 43.

McGurk, B, 'A Lawyer in Baghdad' (2004) 8 *The Green Bag* 51.

McNerney, M, 'Stabilization and Reconstruction in Afghanistan: Are PRTs a Model or a Muddle? (2005–06) *Parameters, US Army War College Quarterly* 32.

Mégret, F, 'The Politics of International Criminal Justice' (2002) 13 *European Journal of International Law* 1261.

Moravcsik, A, 'Taking Preferences Seriously: A Liberal Theory of International Politics' (1997) 51 *International Organization* 513.

Mullerson, R, 'NATO Enlargement and the NATO-Russian Founding Act: The Interplay of Law and Politics' (1998) 47 *International and Comparative Law Quarterly* 174.

Murphy, S, 'The Security Council, Legitimacy and the Concept of Collective Security after the Cold War' (1994) 32 *Columbia Journal of Transnational Law* 201.

Murphy, S, 'Democratic Legitimacy and the Recognition of States and Governments' (1999) 48 *International and Comparative Law Quarterly* 545.

O'Connell, M, 'Regulating the Use of Force in the 21st Century: The Continuing Importance of State Autonomy' (1998) 36 *Columbia Journal of Transnational Law* 473.

Onuf, N, 'The Constitution of International Society' (1994) 5 *European Journal of International Law* 1.

Opie, R, 'International Human Rights Promotion and Protection' (2002) 7 *International Peacekeeping* 100.

Owen, J, 'How Liberalism Produces Democratic Peace' (1994) 19 *International Security* 87.

Patrick, S, 'Don't Fence Me In: The Perils of Going it Alone' (2001) 18 *World Policy Journal* 2.

Patterson, M, 'Who's Got the Title? or, The Remnants of Debellatio in Post-Invasion Iraq' (2006) 47 *Harvard International Law Journal* 467.

Puchala, D, 'World Hegemony and the United Nations' (2005) 7 *International Studies Review* 571.

Ramirez, F, Soysal, Y and Shanahan, S, 'The Changing Logic of Political Citizenship: Cross-National Acquisition of Women's Suffrage Rights, 1890 to 1990' (1997) 62 *American Sociological Review* 735.

Raymond, G, 'Democracies, Disputes, and Third Party Intermediaries' (1994) 38 *Journal of Conflict Resolution* 24.

Redmond, T, 'The Rules, And How they Were Broken: The Changing Face of State Sovereignty' (2002) 10 *Irish Student Law Review* 50.

Reisman, MW, 'Sovereignty and Human Rights in Contemporary International Law' (1990) 84 *American Journal of International Law* 866.

Reus-Smit, C, 'The Strange Death of Liberal International Theory' (2001) 12 *European Journal of International Law* 573.

Rich, R, 'Bringing Democracy into International Law' (2001) 12 *Journal of Democracy* 20.

Richmond, O, 'UN Peace Operations and the Dilemmas of the Peacebuilding Consensus' (2004) 11 *International Peacekeeping* 83.

Richmond, O and Franks, J, 'Liberal Peacebuilding in Timor Leste: The Emperor's New Clothes' (2008) 15 *International Peacekeeping* 187.

Risse-Kappen, T, 'Democratic Peace – Warlike Democracies? A Social Constructivist Interpretation of the Liberal Argument' (1995) 1 *European Journal of International Relations* 491.

Roberts, A, 'Prolonged Military Occupations: the Israeli-Occupied Territories since 1967' (1990) 84 *American Journal of International Law* 44.

——'NATO's "Humanitarian War" over Kosovo' (1999) 41 *Survival* 102.

——'The End of Occupation: Iraq 2004' (2005) 54 *International and Comparative Law Quarterly* 27.

Root, E, 'The Effect of Democracy on International Law' (1917) 11 *American Society of International Law Proclamation* 10.

Roscini, M, 'World Wide Warfare – Jus ad bellum and the Use of Force' (2010) 14 *Max Planck Yearbook of United Nations Law* 85.

Rubin, B and Hamidzada, H, 'From Bonn to London: Governance Challenges and the Future of Statebuilding in Afghanistan' (2007) 14 *International Peacekeeping* 8.

Sassoli, M, 'Legislation and Maintenance of Public Order and Civil Life by Occupying Powers' (2005) 16 *European Journal of International Law* 661.

Scheffer, D, 'Beyond Occupation Law' (2003) 97 *American Journal of International Law* 842.

Schwenk, E, 'Legislative Power of the Military Occupant under Article 43, Hague Regulations' (1945) 54 *Yale Law Journal* 393.

Simes, D, 'America's Imperial Dilemma' (2003) 82 *Foreign Affairs* 94.

Simma, B, 'NATO, the UN and the Use of Force: Legal Aspects' (1999) 10 *European Journal of International Law* 1.

Simma, B and Paulus, A, 'The "International Community": Facing the Challenge of Globalization' (1998) 9 *European Journal of International Law* 266,

Simpson, G, 'Two Liberalisms' (2001) 12 *European Journal of International Law* 537.

Slaughter, A-M, 'International Law and International Relations Theory: A Dual Agenda' (1993) 87 *American Journal of International Law* 205.

——'International Law in a World of Liberal States' (1995) 6 *European Journal of International Law* 503.

——'A Liberal Theory of International Law' (2000) *American Society of International Law Proclamation* 240.

Small, M and Singer, D, 'The War-Proneness of Democratic Regimes' (1976) 1 *Jerusalem Journal of International Relations* 50.

Sohn, L, 'Expulsion and Forced Withdrawal from an International Organisation' (1964) 77 *Harvard Law Review* 1381.

Spiro, D, 'The Insignificance of the Democratic Peace' (1994) 19 *International Security* 50.
Stahn, C, 'The United Nations Transitional Administration in Kosovo and East Timor: A First Analysis' (2001) 5 *Max Planck Yearbook of United Nations Law* 105.
——'Institutionalising Brahimi's "Light Footprint": A Comment on the Role and Mandate of the Peacebuilding Commission' (2005) 2 *International Organization Law Review* 403.
——'Responsibility to Protect: Political Rhetoric or Emerging Legal Norm?' (2007) 101 *American Journal of International Law* 99.
Strohmeyer, H, 'Building a new Judiciary for East Timor: Challenges of a Fledgling Nation' (2001) 11 *Criminal Law Forum* 259.
——'Making Multilateral Interventions Work: The UN and the Creation of Transitional Justice Systems in Kosovo and East Timor' (2001) 25 *Fletcher Forum of World Affairs* 107.
Tadjbakhsh, S and Schoiswohl, M, 'Playing with Fire? The International Community's Democratization Experiment in Afghanistan' (2008) 15 *International Peacekeeping* 252.
Talbott, S, 'Democracy and the National Interest' (1996) 75 *Foreign Affairs* 47.
Tansey, O, 'The Concept and Practice of Democratic Regime-Building' (2007) 14 *International Peacekeeping* 633.
Taylor, P, 'The United Nations in the 1990s: Proactive Cosmopolitanism and the Issue of Sovereignty' (1999) 47 *Political Studies* 538.
Thier, A and Chopra, J, 'The Road Ahead: Political and Institutional Reconstruction in Afghanistan (2002) 23 *Third World Quarterly* 893.
Tomuschat, C, 'Obligations Arising for States Without or Against their Will' (1993-IV) *Recuiels Des Cours* 195.
Traub, J, 'Inventing East Timor' (2000) 79 *Foreign Affairs* 74.
Travis, H, 'Freedom or Theocracy?: Constitutionalism in Afghanistan and Iraq' (2005) 3 *Northwestern University Journal of International Human Rights* 1.
Tsagourias, N, 'The Shifting Laws on the Use of Force and the Trivialization of the UN Collective Security System: The Need to Reconstitute It' (2003) XXXIV *Netherlands Yearbook of International Law* 55.
——'Consent, Neutrality/Impartiality and the Use of Force in Peacekeeping: Their Constitutional Dimension' (2006) 11 *Journal of Conflict and Security Law* 465.
Voeten, E, 'Outside Operations and the Logic of Security Council Action' (2001) 95 *American Political Science Review* 845.
Vohra, S, 'Impartiality in UN Peacekeeping' (1996) 9 *Leiden Journal of International Law* 63.
Waltz, K, 'The Emerging Structure of International Politics' (1993) 18 *International Security* 44.
Wendt, A, 'Anarchy is What States Make of It: a Social Construction of Power Politics' (1992) 46 *International Organization* 391.
——'Constructing International Politics' (1995) 20 *International Security* 71.
Weston, B, 'Security Council Resolution 678 and Persian Gulf Decision Making: Precarious Legitimacy' (1991) *American Journal of International Law* 516.

Wet, E de, 'The Direct Administration of Territories by the United Nations and its Member States in the Post-Cold War Era: Legal Bases and the Implications for National Law' (2004) 8 *Max Planck Yearbook of United Nations Law* 291.
Wheatley, S, 'Democracy in International Law: A European Perspective' (2002) 51 *International and Comparative Law Quarterly* 225.
White, ND, 'UN Peacekeeping-Development or Destruction?' (1994) 12 *International Relations* 129.
——'Empowering Peace Operations to Protect Civilians: Form over Substance' (2009) 13 *International Peacekeeping* 327.
Wilde, R, 'From Danzig to East Timor and Beyond: The Role of the United Nations Missions in Kosovo and East Timor' (2001) 95 *American Journal of International Law* 46.
Williams, P and Pecci, F, 'Earned Sovereignty: Bridging the Gap between Sovereignty and Self-Determination' (2004) 39 *Stanford Journal of International Law* 347.
Yamashita, H, 'Reading "Threats to International Peace and Security"' 1946–2005' (2007) 18 *Diplomacy and Statecraft* 551.
Yingling, R and Ginnane, R, 'The Geneva Conventions of 1949' (1952) 46 *American Journal of International Law* 393.
Zakaria, F, 'The Rise of Illiberal Democracies' (1997) 76 *Foreign Affairs* 22.
Zwanenburg, M, 'Existentialism in Iraq: Security Council Resolution 1483 and the Law of Occupation' (December 2004) 86 *International Review of the Red Cross* 745.

Index

www.ingramcontent.com/pod-product-compliance
Ingram Content Group UK Ltd.
Pitfield, Milton Keynes, MK11 3LW, UK
UKHW020804290926
15470UKWH00003B/951

9 781849 46244